AESTHETICS, FORM AND EMOTION

AESTHETICS
FORM AND EMOTION

David Pole

edited by
George Roberts

ST. MARTIN'S PRESS   NEW YORK

All rights reserved. For information, write:
St. Martin's Press, Inc., 175 Fifth Avenue, New York, NY 10010
Printed in Great Britain
First published in the United States of America in 1983

ISBN 0–312–00845–7

Library of Congress Cataloging in Publication Data
Pole, David.
  Aesthetics, form and emotion.

  1. Aesthetics—Addresses, essays, lectures. I. Title.
BH39.P62 1983   700'.1   82–25010
ISBN 0–312–00845–7

Acknowledgments

The chapters in this book first appeared as follows, and thanks are due to the editors and publishers involved for permission to include them. 1: in *Philosophy*, vol. 30, 1955. 2: in *Proceedings of the Aristotelian Society*, supp. vol. 31, 1957. 3: in *Philosophy*, vol. 37, 1962. 4: in *British Journal of Aesthetics*, vol. 3, 1963. 5: in *British Journal of Aesthetics*, vol. 9, 1969. 6: in *Proceedings of the Aristotelian Society*, 1971–2. 7: in *Value and Valuation—essays in honour of R. S. Hartman*, ed. J. W. Davies. 8: in *Philosophy and the Arts*, Royal Institute of Philosophy vol. 6, 1973. 9: in *British Journal of Aesthetics*, winter 1974. 10: in *Mind*, July 1976. 11: in *British Journal of Aesthetics*, summer 1976. 12: in *Philosophy*, vol. 51, 1976. 13: as 'Literature as prophecy: Sartre's *Nausea*' in *Philosophy and Literature*, vol. 5, 1981 (first presented at a conference at Warwick University in 1974). 14: previously unpublished. The publishers are grateful to J. O. Urmson and W. H. Righter for permission to reprint copyright material on pp. 13–26 and 207–16.

700.1
P763

Printed in Great Britain
by Ebenezer Baylis & Son Limited
The Trinity Press, Worcester and London

Contents

Foreword

David Pole doubted the value of his own work, and was always anxious to recognise and draw attention to the achievements of others. Yet in many areas his writings have proved to be of leading importance, and to have conveyed a vision that is central and original. This is particularly true of aesthetics, a subject that had suffered much from the philistinism of post-war analytical philosophy, and which Pole, along with a few others of his generation, wished to see restored to its rightful place as one of the main areas of philosophical enquiry. Throughout the decade leading to his tragic death in 1977 Pole devoted his creative powers to aesthetics, and the present volume contains those of his papers which he set aside as being, in his view, worthy of republication. They show that the seriousness, circumspection and learning which characterised all his work were here employed to their best advantage. Pole brought to the subject of aesthetics a wide-ranging philosophical competence, together with a deep love of literature and architecture, two arts which exemplify, more vividly perhaps than any others, the varied problems posed by aesthetic interest, and the immense difficulties that impede the philosopher's search for a unified theory of its nature. Pole's knowledge of these arts lent fertility to his philosophical perceptions, and led him to explore problems that many of his contemporaries overlooked to their cost. No student of aesthetics should neglect these papers, which seem to me to contain important insights, springing from an informed and original intelligence.

It should be recognised just how badly aesthetics had fared during the post-war period in Britain and America. When it was not regarded merely as an unimportant appendage to ethics (a further and minor example of that 'evaluative' use of language which modern philosophy has devoted itself to denigrating), it was considered to be a field of disconnected 'puzzles', to be solved by extending analytical techniques from more central areas of philosophy. Two such puzzles — 'What is art?', and 'What is the criterion of identity of the work of art?' — are discussed by Pole and, rightly I believe, dismissed as intellectual diversions. Readers of analytical aesthetics must often have thought that the subject is nothing more than an elaborate philosophical response to modernism, an attempt to answer the question 'Is this, or is it not, art?', when faced with the dull jokes of Dada, or the more serious confidence tricks that have sustained the art market in America. All such verbal questions are without significance until the purpose of classification is explored. The same is true, as Pole points out in the first two papers here reprinted, of such terms as 'aesthetic', 'aesthetic attitude', and 'aesthetic experience'. The analytical method, which may well deliver a consistent and defensible account of 'what we would say' tends, in this area, to ignore the point of saying it. Yet there are real questions, concerning the nature and value of those things that have been called art, and those experiences that have been called aesthetic, which are left untouched by the technicalities that philosophers have brought to bear on them. In particular, we seem to believe that works of art and our responses to them have moral significance and value, and that aesthetic experience is integral to our nature as rational beings. There is, in short, a vast reservoir of significance contained in aesthetic experience, which seems to remain untapped by the normal philosophical classifications that are brought to bear on it. It is in analysing this significance, and the problems concerning art, morality and human nature which it uniquely illustrates, that David Pole excelled.

There is one element of Pole's complex outlook that served, I believe, to distinguish his philosophy, both in its perspective and in its results, from those of many of his contemporaries. This was his wide knowledge and appreciation of the achievements of modern literary criticism, particularly of those schools, centred on Richards and Leavis in England, and on Brooks and Winters in America, which have done so much to impress upon students of English literature the immovable human centrality of their subject. Pole was one of the few philosophers to recognise that the work of these critics, and of their nineteenth-century predecessors, has irreversibly changed, not only our present understanding of literature, but also our understanding of the philosophical questions to which the study of literature gives rise. While one may not agree with all of Pole's observations, in the essays on Morality and the Assessment of Literature, on Leavis, and on the criticism of Milton, one cannot fail to take note of the new philosophical perspective that is evinced in them.

Pole also brought fresh insights to the study of the abstract arts. His love of architecture led him to recognise that this art too, despite its seeming remoteness from the moral preoccupations of poetry and drama, is steeped in moral significance, and makes demands on our attention that cannot be summarised in the idea of form alone. Form is, indeed, one of the major architectural virtues; but what makes form significant? To answer that question is, as Pole demonstrates, to show the relation of our experience of buildings to our perception of people, and to show the deep relation between our responses to architectural form and to human physiognomy. He argues that the formal features of architecture are on a par with the 'tertiary qualities' that comprise expressiveness, and that our appreciation of both involves an inevitable extension of concepts that derive their significance from inter-personal understanding. The position at which Pole hints, in the essays on the Excellence of Form and on Expressiveness, is one which I believe to be of fundamental importance, not only to aesthetics, but to philosophy as a whole. It is part of Pole's achievement to have indicated the centrality not only of the questions which immediately concerned him, but also of the subject which he sought to revive.

An idea of Pole's range of interests can be derived from his intriguing discussion of disgust, in which he points out that there is always an element of self-identification in the reaction of disgust, and that it is this which explains the peculiar place of disgust in our outlook both on the animate and on the inanimate world. Here as elsewhere Pole's knowledge of and respect for Freudian psychoanalysis entered into fruitful relation with his philosophy. Pole was more than ordinarily open to such intellectual influences, and attempted to incorporate them into a unified philosophical outlook. He came, in the end, to distrust psychoanalysis, both for its fraudulent practices, and for the ease with which it lends itself to destructive interpretations of human experience. But at the higher levels, he believed, Freudian theory had become an indispensable instrument of human understanding; it was at that higher level that he wished his own psychoanalytic observations to be situated, and it was there that he sought for the intellectual redemption of the shabby practices which he had so much reason to deplore. The final vision presented by these papers is of psychoanalysis as one integral part of a cultivated modern outlook, comparable and complementary to the criticism and philosophy that have arisen alongside it, and indispensable to the understanding of the aesthetic experiences which order and enrich our lives.

June 1982   Roger Scruton

1

Varieties of Aesthetic Experience

The traditional business of aestheticians has been to supply an answer to the question, 'What is art?' A single question is put, and apparently it is assumed—though recently the assumption has been fairly widely challenged—that there is a single answer to be supplied; that there is one definition or one essence of art from which all its properties can be shown to derive. However the problem is also quite frequently reformulated: some theorists prefer to ask, 'What is aesthetic experience?' Here we find a second assumption: it seems to be taken for granted that it is appropriate to put either one question or the other, but not both; aesthetic experience having been characterised, art can be defined in terms of it, or vice versa. And it is assumed here, as before, that there is one essential answer to give. It is supposed, that is to say, that all aesthetic experience—the experience of reading *War and Peace* or Herrick's two lines *Of Julia, Weeping*, the experience of looking at York Minster or the pattern on the carpet, if by good fortune the carpet is well designed—has some one distinguishing characteristic in all instances, in virtue of which alone they are to be called aesthetic.

As far as I know, no evidence has ever been advanced in favour of the first, initially unplausible thesis, and the most that has been urged on its behalf is the somewhat inconclusive appeal to language—the usage of the single word 'art'. Perhaps if one tinkered with the notion of 'contemplation' or of non-utility, one might find a definition, at least a negative definition, which would make some show of justifying this general usage, and, at a stretch, cover all the varieties; but after all the Oxford Dictionary gives at least half a dozen separate headings for 'art', which are little more than historically related. 'Work of art' and 'artistic' have a good deal in common with 'ornament' and 'ornamental', yet no one supposes that all ornaments share some vastly significant characteristic. If we were to hunt down the characteristic shared by all works of art I fear that it would prove philosophically disappointing.

Now, if this first assumption—the single essence of all art—is given up, it appears that the second is also undermined. It becomes possible to hold that there are occasions on which it is appropriate to talk of aesthetic experience, and others on which it is appropriate to talk of works of art. We are no longer committed to one or the other formulation throughout. It is notable that though philosophers often ask the question, 'What is science?' or again, 'What is mathematics?' they hardly ever ask, 'What is scientific experience?' Presumably scientists have a great variety of different experiences, none of a kind that is theirs exclusively. But what of art? A novel reader too, has many experiences: he is absorbed, excited, impressed; he follows with interest the analysis of character and the unfolding of situation; but there is nothing here that might not in principle be got from a work of history or biography or even a government white paper. To a large part of what we value in art the language of 'experience' seems to have no special appropriateness; and yet it can scarcely be for nothing that it has been so widely invoked.

Here we could easily involve ourselves in large questions. It is possible that anything we ever wish to say could, in principle, be said in terms of experience: phenomenalism might be regarded as the assertion of such a claim. I wish, if I can, to confine myself to more limited issues; I am concerned with the contexts in which such talk seems to have a special applicability. And this is when we wish to concentrate on the seeing or hearing of something—the moment of doing so—rather than the thing seen or heard; we talk of experience when we want to specify something distinctive about our seeing or hearing of things, which we cannot attribute to the things themselves—and also, of course, about our feelings concerning them. Art, like first love, opium and the immediate prospect of death, is usually classed under this head. These things, death, opium and art, are among those that connoisseurs of experience characteristically interest themselves in: first love is generally beyond their power.

Here there are certain fine distinctions that must be noticed: to call a thing an experience is often only to say that we enjoyed or hated it very much. Seeing St Paul's for the first time will very likely be an experience in a way that simply seeing St Paul's, however appreciatively, is not. But simply seeing St Paul's is still very different from seeing St Pancras, supposing that before St Pancras—I mean the station, not the church, though that might also serve—we enjoy no aesthetic experience. It is also different from seeing an object which we are interested to see for other, non-aesthetic reasons: a very old model typewriter for example. One might find looking at the typewriter the more enjoyable experience—when we are comparing them we say 'experience'; but one is not on that account the more inclined to discuss the merits of typewriters in terms of experience. It is the intimate way in which the seeing is bound up with the feeling, and with certain attitudes of the spectator, that inclines us to use this language of art. And since there has been in some recent writing a tendency to dismiss 'aesthetic experience' as a theorist's myth, and in nearly all traditional writing, as I hinted before, a tendency to claim for it far more than it will bear, there is at present, perhaps, some occasion for a fair re-examination of the facts. The features that have been said to characterise aesthetic experience are, I believe, really to be found; but it is necessary to consider them open-mindedly, as they are, to accept them in all their variousness, without preconceptions, and so determine what may fairly be claimed for them and what may not.

But, now, what is the right way to go about such an enquiry? Nowadays one can hardly get a question asked in philosophy, but one finds oneself confronted with a counter-demand: what sort of question is one asking? Is it empirical: does it merely concern matters of psychological fact? If so, a way must be found of testing it, and that is a matter for the scientists. Well, we wish to test certain hypotheses about people's aesthetic experiences. How is it to be done? A hard problem: but psychologists, who may be regarded as specialists in the field, once hit on the device of asking them; to which end they gathered them in psychological laboratories and confronted them with questionnaires. Clearly if the questions had not been put in psychological laboratories, the answers would not have been scientific. Often the answers of the best subjects confirmed those views of aesthetic experience that the questions were designed to test. The rest of us, who are not scientists, must make do with the vast bulk of published testimony of critics, artists and writers concerning their various experiences in face of works of art; and, reduced to the last extremity, we may even reflect upon our own.

Aesthetic experience has often been said to be characterised by a peculiar detachment; it requires a disengaged, purely contemplative attitude: or again it is said to consist in the simple consciousness of the material before us. Both views are concerned with the aesthetic as a mode of experiencing other things—all varieties of material being brought under this presentation. Let me begin with the identification of art with consciousness.

I wish to ask first, in accordance with the aim I indicated, what someone would make of this suggestion, who took it at its face-value, unsophisticatedly; who attached it not to any high philosophical masts and mooring, but to ordinary language and ordinary situations. Certainly in the ordinary sense the present writer at the present moment would properly be said to be conscious—and, he hopes, most of his readers at the moment of reading. Yet neither he nor they are enjoying any aesthetic experience. I suppose such consciousness is as dim as twilight compared to that of the artist in creation; and this would become apparent if the comparison could be made. We must then ask whether aesthetic experience is to be associated not merely with consciousness, but with a heightened state of consciousness in the reader or spectator. Perhaps it may be often; I am sure not always; nor exclusively. A heightened state of consciousness, if the terms are to be understood as they normally are, can also be induced by certain drugs; Charlotte Brontë describes in *Villette*, I am told very accurately, the effects of an opiate, and Aldous Huxley has recently been indulging in drug-induced orgies of heightened consciousness. A somewhat similar condition is sometimes brought on by working alone, concentratedly, late into the night: one rises at last from one's books with the feeling that all the world of ordinary objects has acquired, as it were, a new edge, a new depth of quality or vividness.

I shall be told, very likely, that I am entirely missing the point of the theory. It may be: I shall return to it. Meanwhile I am concerned to consider the heightening of consciousness as a fairly familiar psychological phenomenon, and to ask about its connection with art. After all, we understand the meaning of the words; we acknowledge the plausibility of the thesis only because we understand them; we can hardly ignore the other contexts in which they would normally be used.

Now I believe that our appreciation of much art is associated with a mental state somewhat resembling those I have mentioned; and it has been plausibly suggested that the function of metre in poetry is, among other things, to induce a partly trance-like condition in which the attention is at once heightened and concentrated. There are obvious analogies in the other arts. But this at once suggests further considerations. A heightening of consciousness, in the present sense, means too a heightening of receptivity, of responsiveness to impressions of all sorts. This receptivity can be turned to good or bad account. The question is what sort of wares the artist has to offer—having got his audience into a state in which he is ready to receive them. Our account suggests, in brief, that this feature of aesthetic experience, where it occurs, is less to be valued in itself than as a condition of our appreciation of other things. It is, on the other hand, the idealist aesthetician's contention that consciousness and its objects, the state of mind and the 'contents' of the state of mind, are essentially bound up together. If so 'consciousness' must mean much more than I have been so far attributing to it. What more, I shall presently ask.

But before doing so, let me recall the other account of aesthetic experience that I have mentioned—as an attitude of mind marked by a peculiar detachment. This, I believe, also occurs. The object is, in some way, distanced in contemplation; by dint of the aesthetic attitude, it is said, we *see* things, that otherwise we merely respond to or classify. Our common lives are immersed in the practical. Roger Fry[1] speaks of the effect of looking at a street, with people passing, as reflected in a mirror in a shop window: with a sort of click, our vision changes; the frame serves to isolate and the glass plane to distance the scene that previously was amorphic and all around us. It becomes in a rudimentary way a work of art.

Now the exponents of the two theories I have mentioned will have little truck with each other; they regard their views as widely divergent. Yet it would seem that the states of heightened consciousness that I have spoken of, are also states in which objects are distanced, or seen with detachment, in the way Fry describes. One might, I suppose, experience one without the other; yet in turning from the street itself to the mirror, we surely experience, even if only very slightly, a heightening of our awareness of the visual qualities of things; and it is hard to distinguish the distancing from the heightening.

I have said that this condition is associated with the appreciation of many works of art, but not exclusively with works of art. We must add that it is associated with some kinds of art more than others; with poetry rather than with prose, and, perhaps, with the theatre rather than the art gallery.

So far I have been considering a concept of consciousness that might be put on a scale, leading from unconsciousness, as in sleep, to half-consciousness, as in the moment of waking, to normal consciousness, as, probably, the reader's at the moment of reading, to heightened consciousness, as in some of the unusual states I have mentioned. Now I wish to come on to consider something more, and perhaps radically different, that the word might be used to signify. To be conscious of one's experience, it might be said, is to know what one is experiencing—which might be called the subsumption of the experience under a concept. To feel say, bitterness tinged with contempt, is different from both feeling and knowing that one is feeling 'bitterness tinged with contempt'—and different in various obscure ways. One set of differences concerns our feelings and behaviour in other contexts: a man who knows what he is feeling can tell us if we ask him; can, with better prospects of success, seek to diagnose its cause, make allowance for it, if allowance is required, in assessing the things or people it is directed on. But this is not all that is involved: to know what one's feeling is also, or may also be, to experience a subjective difference, as it were, in the feeling itself. One might know it and yet do nothing and say nothing—either silently or aloud: as one might meet the Ancient

[1] *Vision and Design* (Design, 1928; Phoenix ed.), pp. 19–20.

Mariner in a dream, and know him for the Ancient Mariner in the way
one does in dreams, and yet say nothing. One knows that one feels
bitterness; there is both feeling and knowing, two things; but the contents of consciousness—to use rather inappropriate language—do not
stand side by side and retain their edges—if they ever have any edges;
they qualify and modify one another. Once one has said, 'This is
bitterness', one's state of consciousness is no longer precisely what it
was.

This, I maintain, occurs; yet in this sense consciousness, knowing
what one feels, cannot, certainly, be the prerogative of art appre-
ciators: it is, perhaps, the normal condition of certain excessively intro-
spective people. But to say that it is to be found elsewhere need not be,
save by perverse theory, to deny that it is to be found here; that it is an
element, perhaps among others, that we rightly value in our response
to art. Works especially of literature are sometimes criticised for falling
short in this respect: a character, it is said, or a situation, has been
created in accordance with a concept, so that the concept and the
character fall apart. But art, we are told, demands their integration. In
art we are not given abstract precepts or principles, not generalisations
as material for theory; we are given ideas, so to speak, in the concrete,
embodied in situations, situations felt and thought at once.

Here we must distinguish between a momentary or brief mental
state, such as I have given examples of, and the sort of knowing-cum-
feeling that we would associate with a whole novel or drama; the going
into a human situation at length, the feeling the full significance, the
impact, of each moment, by virtue of the felt impact of the whole. And
here it is natural to mention the critical methods and criteria of F. R.
Leavis; for Leavis evaluates works of literature much in these terms. He has
waged a lifelong war with the antithesis of 'ethical' and 'aesthetic'. Art
does not inculcate moral lessons; but it is valuable, and only valuable,
because it deals significantly with human experience; because it makes
us both feel and understand it, where the understanding is inseparable
from the feeling. The difference is in the kind of attitudes a piece of
writing demands: the difference between stock and stereotyped
responses, glib emotional reassurances and, in general, crude and un-
differentiating states of mind and feeling, as against subtle and stable
ones. I suspect that for Leavis, as for Socrates—or perhaps, as for
Spinoza rather than as for Socrates—virtue *is* knowledge in the end;
that he supposes that an adequate awareness in such cases brings with
it right attitudes necessarily. At least, without entering into these issues
here, we may agree that it goes a long way. It is the fullness of such
awareness of things, the full realisation, in Leavis's favourite word, of a
character or state of affairs, that is valuable in both ways at once.

And here, so it seems to me, though I believe it has never been remarked on, Leavis's critical canons reveal an unexpected resemblance to the aesthetic theory of Collingwood. Collingwood maintains that art is consciousness; that the falsification of experience—as he calls it, the corruption of consciousness—that occurs when from fear or shame or prejudice we disown or crush parts of our own being, drive back our own internal monsters to their den, is at once the negation of art and the disease of which society is sick. Our normal waking state, presumably, is little more than a kind of half-consciousness, and only in the creation or recreation of genuine art do we see things as they are, and to the full: and yet art is nothing more than merely awareness.

The language of the Cambridge school in criticism, of attitudes and the integration of attitudes, is different, but visibly related—for all Collingwood's denunciation of I. A. Richards. There is the same social orientation, the same seriousness; there is the same emphasis on moral integrity, on the facing, not shirking, of facts and problems—for this is what the 'maturity' of attitudes seems to come to. And lastly, the end of the process, realisation, the seeing of a situation to the full—but no more than this, simply the fullest possible feeling and seeing—seems to be not much removed from that raising into consciousness of a total, integrated experience, that for Collingwood is the real work of art. We may remark, too, in passing, that in each case the formal or unitary aspect of works of art receives little attention;[2] but there seems to be in each case the silent implication that really to cognise, to apprehend any body of material, is at the same time to relate its elements internally, to organise and unify it. But this I shall not pursue.

We now have before us accounts of two things that might be meant by 'consciousness'. Collingwood's theory, I suggest, gains in plausibility because when he speaks of consciousness, one part of what he is doing is to give a description, and so far an accurate description, of this characteristic of many great works of literature, this fuller realisation of a complex human situation. But if so, there are certain points that we must take note of: in the first place consciousness in the one sense has little connection with the other—save in as much as it might serve as a condition of our more adequate response. Secondly, though these things that make Leavis's theme are highly important in literature, and important sometimes in painting and sculpture, it is hard to see that they can have much to do, say, with ceramics. Here, within a limited field, we have given a concrete and significant interpretation to this concept of consciousness; but once we set it up as the one essence of art, or stretch it to cover all the seeming exceptions,

[2] This is not true of the earlier version of Collingwood's theory, as expounded in *Speculum Mentis* (Oxford, 1924); there formal problems are taken very seriously.

then, almost inevitably, in proportion as it becomes comprehensive it becomes vacuous.

There is a further qualification to make, and more important for our present purposes, if we are to relate Leavis's findings to the theory of art as consciousness. I should assert confidently (what Collingwood might, of course, have denied), that this kind of presentation, the conjunction of feeling with insight and subtlety, are things that we rightly value in works of art. The question for us is in what sense such appreciation can be called an 'experience'; what is the experience of reading *Vanity Fair* for example? The reader's case here may seem to be much the same as that of the scientist or the historian that I spoke of before: we have, in reading it, a great variety of experiences, more or less protracted and changing—I do not know the *principium individuationis* of experiences—perhaps more or less widely scattered in time. We read on from day to day. And when we come, finally, to the last sentence of all—when we are told to shut up the boxes and the puppets for our play is played out—we may look back, closing the volume in our hands, in a momentary mental perspective, over all the feelings we have passed through and all the scenes we have surveyed. It is a moment of synoptic vision, perhaps; but it is not identical with our 'experience of *Vanity Fair*'. Idealist philosophers for whom time, and hence temporal sequence are unreal, are more fortunately placed; for them a work of art may be comprised in a single unitary intuition. For the rest of us its value is not to be concentrated into any one moment, but belongs to many, though each interpenetrating, so to speak, and taking its significance from all the others.

There is no one experience, but perhaps there are many experiences. There is a kind of cognition that we sometimes distinguish, in our ordinary vocabulary, as 'understanding' or 'insight', rather than 'knowledge'. Or ought we to say that it is another dimension of knowledge? To know theories, to be master of abstract problems, even to understand people in the abstract, is, if you will, to cognise propositions or to be able to manipulate verbal forms; but this something more—something that psychoanalysts, among other people, are concerned with—involves the reintegration of such abstractions with experience.

I am aware that this is loose and unsatisfactory talk; but it is still, perhaps, better than none—which is the way these problems are usually disposed of. If this concrete knowing is possible, it is a great feature of our appreciation of works of art, and one thing that we value them for. It does not belong, as I have said, exclusively to art; it is to be hoped that we achieve it, at least in some measure, in all our human dealings. We must not on that account brand it as non-aesthetic and rule it out of the discussion. The point is worth making in passing: there are many other 'non-aesthetic' tastes, social curiosities and intellectual interests, embellishments rather than distractions, that fiction, for instance, satisfies. There is not, as far as I can see, any sense in which the satisfaction one gets from the penetrating analysis of character can as such be significantly said to be aesthetic; but this does not seem to me a good reason for denying it where it is to be found. It subserves the ends of an aesthetic whole, we shall be told. It may; and we may also value it for itself.

This however is incidental; our problem concerns the propriety in this context of the terminology of 'aesthetic experience'. And I have suggested that though there is no one experience which we can call 'the experience of' such and such a work, in the case of literary works, yet there are many experiences, in the detail of critical discussion the term is unavoidable. The language of literary criticism seems always to fall half way between subject and object. The best criticism, certainly, is that which fixes itself most tenaciously on the qualities that are actually in the work of art; we are not concerned with the critic's personal pangs or ecstasies: and the best writing is in general that in which the feeling clings closest to what one wants to call the words themselves; it is such writing as does not invite a loose emotional response, or call up feelings that might attach themselves indifferently to any number of objects.

This tendency in second-rate writing and criticism is another thing that may make one suspicious of the language of 'experience' in aesthetics. But consider the way even good critics naturally talk: suppose that our attention is drawn to a certain intimacy of tone in a writer's style—in a serious context it might convey a peculiar earnestness—or, to take a concrete case, suppose that we are made to hear more clearly that high note of ringing heroism, a faintly overstrained, overconscious grandeur, very significant in its setting, in the poetic utterance of Othello: we should say that if a reader or listener could not feel these things, he would not be able to appreciate the work properly; and it is as natural to say 'feel' as to say 'see'; and feeling can only be an experience. Literary criticism deals largely in adjectives; its language can never be the language of scientific textbooks.

This blurring the edges of our categories is, of course, not rare or strange; we are familiar with the coldness that we see in the ice, with the visible menace of overhanging rocks; and Wittgenstein says that when we see one thing *as* another, a shape as a picture, say, we 'see it in accordance with an interpretation'. It is in this context that it is natural to talk in terms of experience—which is not to deny that that kind of feeling knowledge we call 'insight', and this kind of visual sensibility that seems to usurp the province of touch, reveal qualities that

are really qualities of their objects. There is nothing to prevent our saying that visual depth is really a quality of the picture surface. We find
things out in different ways, and in more ways as our sensibility extends: and it is no part of my present purpose, as I said at the start, to
lay down an ontology that shall allocate things and qualities exclusively
to either the mental or the material world; I leave open the possibility
of a wholly phenomenalist language.

But the point here is this: certain things that are involved often and
intimately in the appreciation of art, this attitude of detachment, this
heightening of consciousness and this intensification of feeling, cannot
only be talked of in terms of experience—and we do so without pre-
judging other issues. But scientists and mathematicians differ in this,
that for the most part they can make their evaluations of the matter
before them, without the need of a capacity for special experiences: the
experience of seeing a necessary connection is not remarkable *in kind*.
The same is true of some art, but perhaps not most.

We have seen, then, the sort of situation that one would describe as a
'heightening of consciousness' in the ordinary and unsophisticated
sense; and what more might also be meant by saying that we were conscious of what we were experiencing. There is one other variety of
aesthetic experience which cannot be omitted in this context. It too
might be called the realisation, or heightened consciousness of a feeling
or a situation—perhaps it is only the extreme cases of the tendency I
have spoken of. This concerns less the apprehension of a complex of
characters and actions; it is rather the realisation, the making vivid to
the utmost, of a single moment of experience. I find it difficult to
express what I mean, and I shall try to do so with the help of an
example. I take it from the film *Limelight* which I expect most of my
readers will be familiar with. It will be recalled, then, how Chaplin, in
the character of a great clown fallen in old age upon evil days, after an
attempted come-back at which his audience walks out on him, returning—pushing his way past one or two other performers indifferently
preoccupied—to the dressing-room, sits down and, wiping the grease-
paint from his face, confronts himself in the mirror. For a moment
despair becomes tangible. We realise: we are made to see. A glimpse of
wan and hollow-looking features draws on itself, momentarily, all the
meaning of utter and ultimate failure.

I am in some doubt what to say of this sort of presentation. It is, at
first glance, the kind of thing for which the theory of art as the communication of emotions seems designed. But it fails: for if what we had
here were merely pain felt by us as the character is supposed to feel it,
as it might occur in the ordinary course of lives, we should not value it
as we do. Wherein then, is it different? In several ways: for one thing

we are sitting in an auditorium watching a film; we know, of course, that we are spectators at make-believe happenings, and that there is nothing we can appropriately do; hence we are the freer to watch. Similarly one's own suffering, T. S. Eliot says, 'is covered by the currents of action',

But the agony of others remains an experience . . .

In somewhat the same way this experience is presented to us; and however inappropriate the verb 'to know' may demonstrably be, regard being paid to the logical category of its usual predicates, it is natural to express a situation for which ordinary language has made no provision, by saying that with regard to this moment's experience, we do something more than feel.

We must remark, as of all the previous experiences we have noticed, that such an experience as this too, may quite possibly occur in a non-aesthetic situation; but the setting of such a moment in the course of a drama, a setting, that is, that points for us its meaning, and our own partial detachment as lookers-on who have merely suspended voluntarily their disbelief, greatly conduces to its bringing to birth. Were one to witness such a scene in reality, the suffering of a friend or an acquaintance, one would feel more, I expect, but see less. And here it is natural to recall the notion of the aesthetic attitude as involving a peculiar detachment, a disengagement from the practical. There is at least an analogy—probably not more—between the present case and Roger Fry's illustration mentioned above. To say we are detached is partly to say simply that we do not respond to the situation before us, and do not feel the need to respond, with practical actions; but such responses being excluded, whether by an effort of abstraction or the knowledge that they would be out of place, we can, as we could not before, simply dwell in the experience—as we often do, of course, in sensory pleasures. Addicts of melodrama also love to dwell in the experience: or, as the popular idiom has it, to wallow in it. But I have already sought to bring out what is peculiar to a moment such as I described, a moment of tragic insight. It is that—that it is a moment of insight; the feeling is there, but it is not merely feeling, it is made significant, revealed or understood.

This too, then, is a kind of aesthetic experience, and the last variety I wish to consider. I fear my discussion will seem both disjointed and inconclusive. Inconclusive it necessarily is; my aim has been no more than to run over—but more open-mindedly, more empirically and humbly than has sometimes been common— and briefly to distinguish and characterise the various distinctive experiences, where we are inclined to talk of 'experience', that are associated with the appreciation of art. Especially, I am concerned with their variousness, and the folly of a monopolistic view on the part of aestheticians as to the things we are to permit ourselves to value as aesthetic.

Whether what I have said will be held to belong to philosophy or psychology I do not know, and am not, really, deeply concerned. If to philosophy, then philosophy must be held to embrace whatever is to be settled by argument rather than experiment—which might not, perhaps, be a bad definition; if to psychology, it must be a kind of psychology that any man with a mind tolerably equipped, any man with experience and words, can do for himself.

2

What Makes a Situation Aesthetic?

(i) J. O. Urmson

Philosophers have hoed over the plot of aesthetics often enough, but the plants that they have raised thereby are pitifully weak and straggling objects. The time has therefore not yet come for tidying up some corner of the plot; it needs digging over afresh in the hope that some sturdier and more durable produce may arise, even if its health be rather rude. I therefore make no excuse for reopening what seems to me to be the central problem of aesthetics: I hope that by a somewhat new approach I may succeed in making a contribution, if but a small one, towards its solution.

We may refer to a person as, in a given situation, getting an aesthetic thrill or aesthetic satisfaction from something, or of his finding something aesthetically tolerable, or aesthetically dissatisfying, or even aesthetically hateful. In a suitable context the adjective 'aesthetic' and the adverb 'aesthetically' may well be superfluous, but it is sometimes necessary to introduce one of these words in order to make it clear that when we refer, say, to a person's satisfaction we are not thinking of moral satisfaction, economic satisfaction, personal satisfaction, intellectual satisfaction, or any satisfaction other than aesthetic satisfaction. If we merely know that someone gained satisfaction from a play we do not know for sure that we are in the aesthetic field. Thus a play may give me moral satisfaction because I think it likely to have improving effects on the audience; economic satisfaction because it is playing to full houses and I am financing it; personal satisfaction because I wrote it and it is highly praised by the critics; intellectual satisfaction because it solves a number of difficult technical problems of the theatre very cleverly. But the question will still be open whether I found the play aesthetically satisfying. Though these various types of satisfaction are not mutually exclusive, it is clear that when we call a satisfaction aesthetic the purpose must be to mark it off from the other types.

The philosophical task to be tackled in this paper is therefore this: to make explicit what it is that distinguishes aesthetic thrills, satisfactions, toleration, disgust, etc., from thrills, satisfactions, etc., that would properly be called moral, intellectual, economic, etc. I put the question in this form because I think that it is tempting to consider the aesthetic as an isolated matter and within the field of the aesthetic to concentrate unduly upon the most sublime and intense of our experiences; but I am convinced that it is important to ensure that our account of the aesthetic should be as applicable to toleration as to our most significant experiences and should make it clear that in characterising a reaction or a judgment as aesthetic the point is to distinguish it from other reactions and judgments that are moral, economic, and so on. Only thus can we hope to bring out the full forces of the term 'aesthetic'.

This is not intended to be a problem especially about the appreciation of works of art. No doubt many of our most intense aesthetic satisfactions are derived from plays, poems, musical works, pictures and other works of art. But to me it seems obvious that we also derive aesthetic satisfaction from artefacts that are not primarily works of art, from scenery, from natural objects and even from formal logic; it is at least reasonable also to allow an aesthetic satisfaction to the connoisseur of wines and to the gourmet. I shall therefore assume that there is no special set of objects which are the sole and proper objects of aesthetic reactions and judgments, and which are never the objects of an economic, intellectual, moral, religious or personal reaction or judgment. We may judge a power-station aesthetically and find economic satisfaction in a work of art that we own. We may take it, then, that we are not exclusively concerned with the philosophy of art, and that whatever the criteria of the aesthetic may be they cannot be found by trying to delimit a special class of objects.

If the aesthetic cannot be identified by its being directed to a special class of objects, it might be more plausibly suggested that the criteria of the aesthetic are to be sought by looking for some special features of objects which are attended to when our reaction or judgment is aesthetic; beauty and ugliness have often been adduced as the features in question. Alternatively it has often been suggested that aesthetic reactions and judgments contain or refer to some unique constituent of the emotions of the observer, either a special 'aesthetic emotion' or an 'aesthetic tinge' of some other emotion. I think that most commonly theories elicited by our problem have been variations on one or other of these two themes, a variation on the first theme being called an objectivist theory and a variation on the second being called subjectivist. I propose to give some reasons in this paper for finding both these theories unsatisfactory as answers to our problem, even if neither is wholly false as a mere assertion; in their place, I shall suggest that the correct answer is to be given in terms of the explanation of the reaction or the grounds of the judgment. I shall make some tentative remarks about what sort of grounds for a judgment make that judgment aesthetic, but cannot even begin the systematic treatment of the subject.

Let us revert to an illustration already casually used, and suppose that we observe a man in the audience at a play who is obviously beaming with delight and satisfaction. If I now maintain that his delight is purely economic, what have I to do in order to establish this contention? If the question at issue were whether he was delighted or merely contented it would no doubt be necessary to ascertain fairly accurately his emotional state; but if it be agreed that he is delighted and the only issue is whether his delight is properly to be called economic, it is surely clear that phenomenological study of his emotions is not necessary. If, however, we find him to be the impresario, and he agrees that the complete explanation of his delight is that there is a full house and the reaction of the audience indicates a long run, what more could possibly be needed to justify us in describing his delight as economic? It seems hard to dispute that in the case of economic delight, satisfaction, disappointment and the like the criterion of the reaction's being economic lies in the nature of the explanation of that reaction. Similarly it would be beyond dispute that a man's delight was wholly personal if it were conceded that its explanation was entirely the fact that his daughter was acquitting herself well in her first part as a leading lady; again his delight will be moral if wholly explained by the belief that the play will have a good effect on the conduct of the audience. It would, I suggest, be very surprising if the way of establishing that delight, satisfaction and other reactions were aesthetic turned out to be quite different from the way in which we establish them to be moral, personal, economic, intellectual, etc. Nor would it be surprising merely as a novelty; it would be logically disturbing to find that one had suddenly to depart from a single *fundamentum divisionis*, which had sufficed for all the other types, when one came to the aesthetic.

We must now note a further point about the logical relation between the concepts of the moral, the aesthetic, the economic, the intellectual, and the personal, as applied to reactions, both because it is of some logical interest and because a misunderstanding of it has led to some silly theories. *Triangular, square* and *pentagonal,* as applied to surfaces, are clearly species of a single genus and as such are mutually exclusive; there is a single *fundamentum divisionis* which is the number of sides that the rectilinear surface has. The same applies, *mutatis mutandis,* to *bachelor, married* and *widowed* as applied to men. On the other hand *triangular, red* and *large* are three logically unconnected predicates of surfaces, and *bachelor, bald* and *wealthy* are similarly unconnected predicates of men. What then are we to say about the predicates *moral, economic* and *aesthetic* as applied to, say, satisfactions? Clearly they are not technically species of a genus for they are not mutually exclusive as are species of a single genus; I may be simultaneously satisfied by a single object aesthetically, morally and economically, just as well as a man may be simultaneously bald, wealthy and a widower. But on the other hand to ask whether a satisfaction is moral or aesthetic makes as good sense as to ask whether a surface is square or triangular, whereas only in a very odd context can one ask whether a man is bald or a widower; furthermore, if a satisfaction is wholly moral it is not at all aesthetic, whereas being wholly bald does not prevent a man from being a widower. Thus moral, aesthetic and economic satisfactions seem neither to be logically disconnected nor to be true species of a genus.

Aesthetic and moral satisfactions thus seem to be related as are business and sporting associates. A man may be both a business and a sporting associate, yet the point of calling a man a business associate is to distinguish his status from that of a sporting or other type of associate, as it does not distinguish him from, say, an associate first met at Yarmouth. In the same way, to call a satisfaction aesthetic has the point of distinguishing its status from that of being a moral or economic satisfaction, though a satisfaction may be both aesthetic and moral. It surely follows that the criteria for a reaction's being aesthetic cannot be wholly unrelated to the criteria for its being moral or economic—they must be connected in such a way that we can see how being wholly one excludes being also another and yet how a single reaction can be both moral and aesthetic.

If we find the criterion for distinguishing aesthetic from kindred reactions in the nature of the explanation of the reaction we can readily account for this logical situation. To say that a satisfaction is wholly aesthetic, for example, will be to say that the explanation or grounds of the satisfaction are wholly of one sort, which will necessitate that the satisfaction cannot rest also on moral grounds; on the other hand there is clearly nothing to prevent our satisfaction from being multiply-grounded and thus simultaneously aesthetic and moral, aesthetic and economic, and so on.

But if we were to accept different kinds of criteria of the aesthetic, the moral and the economic we should be in difficulties here. Thus if a philosopher were to hold (and some apparently do) that a moral judgment is one that asserts an object to have a certain character and an aesthetic judgment to be one that announces or expresses the special emotional state of the speaker he would be maintaining views which, however plausible when consistently adhered to in isolation, are poor bed-fellows. For one would expect a wholly moral judgment interpreted as ascribing a moral character, to deny implicitly the presence of a special aesthetic or special economic character; similarly a wholly aesthetic judgment, interpreted as expressing a special aesthetic emotion, should deny implicitly the presence of a special moral or economic emotion. Consistency is required here.

So much for the logical point of being clear on the relation between the aesthetic, the moral, the economic etc. Unclarity on the point can lead to other less philosophical confusions. Thus the belief that moral considerations are relevant to a thing's aesthetic rank seems to stem from an awareness that appreciation may be simultaneously based on aesthetic and moral considerations coupled with a blindness to the fact that to call an appreciation aesthetic has as part of its point the effect of ruling out the moral as irrelevant. At the opposite extreme those who rage at any moral comment on a work of art are so conscious that the moral is irrelevant to the aesthetic that they suppose some error in allowing one's general satisfaction to have both a moral and an aesthetic component.

I have illustrated sufficiently the dangers of considering aesthetic reactions and judgments in abstraction from moral, economic and other kindred reactions and judgments. Similarly we must not concentrate on aesthetic delight and neglect other aesthetic reactions. The view that delight is aesthetic when that emotion has some special aesthetic tinge is not unplausible in isolation; we can no doubt bring aesthetic disgust under the same theory easily enough. But what if I am asked for an aesthetic judgment on what seems to me a very ordinary building and I reply truthfully that I find it merely tolerable? Am I reporting an emotion of toleration which has an aesthetic tinge, or perhaps an absolute tinge with no emotion to be tinged? But if I be taken to report merely the absence of any emotion or tinge by what criterion can we say that I am making an aesthetic judgment at all? It is surely important that we should be able to distinguish an aesthetic judgment of toleration from merely refraining from any aesthetic judgment at all; to regard a thing with mere aesthetic toleration is quite different from not considering it in an aesthetic light at all.

Thus the view that what distinguishes the aesthetic reaction and judgment is the presence of a special emotion or a special emotional tinge has already proved unsatisfactory on two counts. First, we have seen that we require a similar type of criterion of the aesthetic, the moral, the intellectual and the economic reaction, whereas the emotional criterion is very unplausible in some of these cases. Secondly, we have seen that however plausible with regard to strong emotional reactions, the emotional view is most unplausible when we consider such cool aesthetic reactions as that of bare toleration. Even if these difficulties were overcome, it is perhaps worth noticing that on this view a single reaction which involved, say, simultaneous economic, moral, aesthetic and intellectual satisfaction might well be required to involve an emotion having a quite kaleidoscopic variety of tinges.

But apart from these more logical points it is surely clear that when we experience emotions that we should wish to call aesthetic they are often very different from each other. Thus Tovey[1] speaks of a theme 'which gives Mozart's most inimitable sense of physical well-being' precisely because most of even the most delightful musical themes are so different in emotional effect. Or again, is it so clear that aesthetic emotions are different in mind from others? Tovey, we have seen, compares a Mozart theme to a quite non-aesthetic delight, and Housman can be adduced as a still more striking, since unwilling, witness. Enumerating three types of 'symptoms' of poetical delight in his lecture, *The Name and Nature of Poetry*, he says: 'One of these symptoms was described in connexion with another object by Eliphaz the Temanite: "A spirit passed before my face; the hair of my flesh stood up;"' another he describes by using Keat's words about his feelings for Fanny Brawne, "everything that reminds me of her goes through me like a spear"; the third, he says, 'consists in a constriction of the throat and a precipitation of water to my eyes', an experience which is surely common to many emotional situations, and not confined to the aesthetic.

The objection to the view that what distinguishes the aesthetic judgment or reaction from others is that it alone involves the recognition or awareness of beauty and ugliness, if offered as a solution to our problem, is rather different. As a minor objection it is worth pointing out that we should hesitate to call many things for which we have a great aesthetic admiration 'beautiful', that 'beautiful' is a relatively specialised word of aesthetic appraisal, though this will inevitably elicit the answer that here 'beauty' is being used with a wider meaning than is currently assigned to it. But granted that 'beauty' and 'ugliness' are being used with a wide enough significance, the trouble with this answer to our problem is not that it is false but that it is futile. Of course if I admire a thing aesthetically I must be aware of its beauty, or of its charm, or of its prettiness or some other 'aesthetic characteristic'; this is true in the same way as it is platitudinously true that moral admiration must involve awareness of a thing's moral goodness or rectitude or of some other 'moral characteristic'. But the trouble is that we have no independent way of telling whether we are aware of beauty or ugliness on the one hand or rightness or wrongness on the other; to know this we must know whether our admiration is aesthetic or moral,

[1] *Essays in Musical Analysis* (London, 1935), vol. 1, p. 200.

or, more accurately, to try to discover whether our admiration is aesthetic or moral and to try to discover whether we are aware of beauty or rightness are not two distinct enquiries but a single enquiry described in two ways neither of which is more luminous than the other. To identify the aesthetic judgment by the aesthetic characters of which it involves awareness is therefore not helpful.

Let me now set out more generally and completely the view that I wish to urge. The terms 'good', 'bad' and 'indifferent' are, I take it, among the widest terms of appraisal that we possess, and we do appraise things on the basis of criteria, criteria to be formulated in terms of the 'natural' features of the things appraised. But usually we wish at any time to appraise a thing only from a restricted point of view. We may, for instance, wish to appraise a career from the restricted point of view of its worth as a means to earning a livelihood; to do so we restrict our attention to a special set of the criteria of a good career, all others being for the purpose irrelevant. I wish to suggest that the moral, the aesthetic, the economic, the intellectual, the religious and other special appraisals should all be understood as being appraisals distinguished by their concentration on some special sub-set of criteria of value. To say that something is good as a means is not to say that it is good in some special sense distinct from that of 'good as an end' but to appraise it from a special point of view; similarly to judge a thing aesthetically good or first-rate is not to call it good in a sense different from that in which we call a thing morally good, but to judge it in the light of a different sub-set of criteria. We may if we wish choose to invent a special meaning for 'beautiful' in which it becomes shorthand for 'good from the aesthetic point of view', but that is only a dubious convenience of no theoretical significance. The central task of the philosopher of aesthetics is, I take it, to clarify the principles on which we select the special set of criteria of value that are properly to be counted as relevant to aesthetic judgment or appraisal. We may recognise an aesthetic reaction by its being due to features of the thing contemplated that are relevant criteria of the aesthetic judgment, and the aesthetic judgment is one founded on a special sub-set of the criteria of value of a certain sort of thing.

It may justly be said that so far I have done little more than to assert this view dogmatically, though I should wish to claim that I have given it some a priori probability by showing that it is a view which will enable us to deal with some of the difficulties that other views cannot surmount. Certainly I have as yet done nothing to indicate on what principles the criteria of value relevant to the aesthetic judgment are selected.

This lacuna can only be properly filled by field-work, and then only filled completely by a full-scale work on aesthetics. By doing field-work I mean studying examples of people actually trying to decide whether a certain judgment is or is not aesthetic and observing how they most convincingly argue the matter. Unfortunately to do this on an elaborate scale in one paper of a symposium is hardly possible; I can but ask you to believe that this paper has been written only after a considerable amount of such work, and produce one or two examples of it to show more clearly what I have in mind.

In his more philosophical moments A. E. Housman tried to account for the peculiar nature of the aesthetic in terms of emotional, and even physical, reactions; but here is an example of what he has to say at a more literary and less philosophical level:

> Again, there existed in the last century a great body of Words- worthians, as they were called. It is now much smaller; but true appre- ciation of Wordsworth's poetry has not diminished in proportion: I suspect that it has much increased. The Wordsworthians, as Matthew Arnold told them, were apt to praise their poet for the wrong things. They were most attracted by what may be called his philosophy; they accepted his belief in the morality of the universe and the tendency of events to good; they were even willing to entertain his conception of nature as a living and sentient and benignant being; a conception as purely mythological as the Dryads and the Naiads. To that thrilling utterance which pierces the heart and brings tears to the eyes of thousands who care nothing for his opinions and beliefs they were not noticeably sensitive; and however justly they admired the depth of his insight into human nature and the nobility of his moral ideas, these things, with which his poetry was in close and harmonious alliance, are distinct from poetry itself.[2]

It does not matter whether we agree with Housman about Words- worth; but I do hope that all will agree that this is the right sort of way to set about showing that an appreciation is not aesthetic. Clearly Housman does not deny that what the nineteenth century admired in Wordsworth was admirable; but he says that if your admiration of Wordsworth is based on certain grounds (the philosophical truth and moral loftiness of the content of the poetry) it is not aesthetic admira- tion, whereas if it is based on what Housman calls the 'thrilling utter- ance', by which the surrounding paragraphs abundantly show him to mean the sound, rhythm and imagery of the words used, then it is aesthetic admiration. Whether Housman is right about Wordsworth or not, whether he has selected the most important criteria of poetical

[2] A. E. Housman, 'The Name and Nature of Poetry', in J. Carter (ed.), *Selected Prose*, Cambridge 1961.

merit or not, this is the type of argument to be expected in a competent discussion; but to have argued the case by adducing the claim that Wordsworthians tended to concentrate rather on traits other than beauty would in fact have been to have restated the case rather than to have argued it. Moreover, if some Wordsworthian had maintained that Wordsworth's pantheism did bring tears to his eyes it would clearly have made no difference to the argument; it is concentration on the utterance, rather than having tears in your eyes, that makes you truly appreciative of the poetry.

Housman's *The Name and Nature of Poetry* is a mine of similar examples. Though he says in a theoretical moment: 'I am convinced that most readers, when they think that they are admiring poetry, are deceived by inability to analyse their sensations, and that they are really admiring, not the poetry of the passage before them, but something else in it, which they like better than poetry', in fact all the concrete examples are in accordance with my theory and not his own. Thus the later seventeenth-century writers are said by Housman to have but rarely true poetic merit not on the basis of any analysis of sensations but because, for example, they aimed to startle by novelty and amuse by ingenuity whereas their verse is inharmonious.

If, then, Houseman's practice is sound it vindicates my view and stultifies his; nor is the obvious fact that we would not rate highly poetry that did not move us, relevant to the question how we are to distinguish a high aesthetic rating from another type of high rating. If field-work and reflection in general vindicate my contention as do these examples from Housman I cannot see what else can be relevant; but I freely own that it is the cumulative weight of a large collection of examples from a variety of fields that is necessary, and these I have not supplied; nor could we ever attain a strict proof.

But all this being granted we are still only on the periphery of our subject and the most difficult question remains to be dealt with. It is comparatively easy to see that there must be general principles of selection of evaluation criteria which determine whether our evaluation is to be counted as aesthetic, moral, intellectual or of some other kind; nor is it at all difficult to give examples of what anyone, who is prepared to accept this way of looking at the matter, can easily recognise as being a criterion falling under one or another principle. It would be a very odd person who denied that the sound of the words of a poem was one of the criteria of the aesthetic merit of a poem, or who maintained that being scientifically accurate and up to date was another; similarly it is clear that the honesty of a policy is a criterion of its moral goodness whereas, even if honesty is the best policy, honesty is not a direct criterion of economic merit. But it is by no means so easy to formulate these as general principles.

This difficulty is by no means peculiar to aesthetics. Part of the general view of which the aesthetic doctrine given here is a fragment is that what determines whether a judgment is moral is what reasons are relevant to it; but everyone knows the difficulty of answering the question what makes a judgment a moral judgment. (In my terminology Kant's answer would be that the reasons must refer to the rationality or otherwise of consistently acting in a certain way.) Certainly it would be over-optimistic to expect to find very precise principles; probably there will be some overlap of criteria between the various spheres of evaluation in anybody's practice; certainly there are some overt borderline disputes whether this or that criterion is relevant to, say, aesthetic evaluation.

I think, however, that there is one peculiar difficulty in trying to find the principle, however vague, that determines what sort of reasons are relevant to a judgment if it is to be counted as aesthetic. When we think of giving reasons for an aesthetic judgment we tend at once to call to mind what we would give as reasons for our appreciation of some very complex works of art; rightly considering, for example, that the plays of Shakespeare are things intended especially for consideration from the aesthetic point of view (I believe that a work of art can most usefully be considered as an artefact primarily intended for aesthetic consideration), we tend to think that we can most usefully tackle our problem by examining what would be relevant to an appreciation of, say, *Hamlet*, merely leaving aside obvious irrelevancies like cost of production. But this is most unfortunate, because, dealing with things intended primarily for aesthetic appreciation, we are inclined to treat as relevant to aesthetic appreciation very much more than we would in the case of things not so officially dedicated to aesthetic purposes; for practical purposes it would be pedantic to do otherwise. Moreover it is obviously very difficult to get straight our grounds for appreciating anything so complex. I am inclined to think that if *Hamlet* were rewritten to give the essential plot and characterisation in the jargon of the professional psychologist there could still be a lot to admire that we at present mention in our aesthetic appreciations, but we would no longer regard it as aesthetic appreciation but rather as intellectual appreciation of psychological penetration and the like.

For these and other reasons, it seems to me hopeless to start an enquiry into the nature of aesthetic grounds by concentrating our attention on great and complex works of art. Among the other reasons is that in evaluating great works of art the reasons proximately given will almost inevitably already be at a high level of generality and themselves evaluative—we will refer to masterly style, subtle characterisation, inevitability of the action and so on. If we are to have any hope of success we must first set our sights less high and commence with the simplest cases of aesthetic appreciation; in this paper, at least, I shall try to look no further.

If we examine, then, some very simple cases of aesthetic evaluation it seems to me that the grounds given are frequently the way the object appraised looks (shape and colour), the way it sounds, smells, tastes or feels. I may value a rose bush because it is hardy, prolific, disease-resistant and the like, but if I value the rose aesthetically the most obvious relevant grounds will be the way it looks, both in colour and in shape, and the way it smells; the same grounds may be a basis for aesthetic dislike. Though I might, for example, attempt to describe the shape to make you understand what I see in it these grounds seem to me to be really basic; if I admire a rose because of its scent and you then ask me why I admire its scent I should not in a normal context know what you want. These grounds are also those that we should expect to be basic in aesthetics from an etymological point of view, and while one can prove nothing philosophically from etymologies, etymological support is not to be despised. Things, then, may have sensible qualities which affect us favourably or unfavourably with no ulterior grounds. Surely there is no need to illustrate further these most simple cases of aesthetic evaluation.

But there are some slightly more sophisticated cases which need closer inspection. I have in mind occasions when we admire a building not only for its colour and shape but because it looks strong or spacious, or admire a horse because it looks swift as well as for its gleaming coat. These looks are not sensible qualities in the simple way in which colour and shape are. It is clear that in this sort of context to look strong or spacious or swift is not to seem very likely to be strong or spacious or swift. I might condemn a building for looking top-heavy when I knew very well that it was built on principles and with materials which ensured effectively that it would not be top-heavy. It is no doubt a plausible speculation that if a building looks top-heavy in the sense relevant to aesthetics it would probably seem really to be top-heavy to the untutored eye; but if an architect, who knows technically that a building is not top-heavy, judges it to look top-heavy when he considers it aesthetically he is no way estimating the chances of its being blown over.

We are now considering the facts which, exclusively emphasised, lead to the functional view of aesthetics. The element of truth in that view I take to be that if a thing looks to have a characteristic which is a desirable one from another point of view, its looking so is a proper ground of aesthetic appreciation. What makes the appreciation aesthetic is that it is concerned with a thing's looking somehow without concern for whether it really is like that; beauty we may say, to emphasise the point, is not even skin-deep.

We have, then, isolated two types of aesthetic criteria, both of which are cases of looking (sounding etc.) somehow; in the simpler type it is the sensible qualities, in the narrowest sense, that are relevant; in the slightly more complex type it is looking to possess some quality which is non-aesthetically desirable that matters. We like our motor-cars in attractive tones and we like them to look fast (which does not involve peering under the bonnet); we like, perhaps, the timbre of a bird's note and we like it also for its cheerful or nobly mournful character, but would not be pleased if it sounded irritable or querulous; the smell of a flower may be seductive in itself but it will be still better if it is, say, a clean smell. Both these elementary types of criteria go hand in hand and are constantly employed.

The most obvious criticism of these suggestions is not that they are wrong but that they are incapable of extension to the more complicated situations in which we appraise a work of art. I cannot try now to deal with this sort of objection in any full way. But I should like to make two small points. First, I would repeat my suggestion that we are inclined to allow in non-aesthetic criteria 'by courtesy' when we are evaluating a work of art, so that we may even include intellectual merit. Secondly, the fact that such things as intellectual understanding are essential to an aesthetic appreciation of a work of art does not in itself establish the criticism. If for example we enjoy listening to a fugue it is likely that a part of our appreciation will be intellectual; no doubt intellectual understanding of what is going on is also necessary to aesthetic appreciation; but the fact that I cannot enjoy the sound of a theme being continually employed, sometimes inverted or in augmentation or in diminution, unless I have the theoretical training to recognise this, does not prevent my aesthetic appreciation from being of the sound. I am still appreciating the way a thing sounds or looks even when my intellect must be employed if I am to be aware of the fact that the thing does look or sound this way.

There remain many difficulties; above all the notion of 'looking in a certain way', especially in such cases as when we say something looks strong or swift, needs more elaboration. But to carry out this task is beyond the scope of this paper. Apart from a short appendix, I shall now close with a brief summary, a summary of a paper which is intended to do no more than to distinguish the aesthetic judgment and reaction from others and perhaps to indicate the best way in which to proceed to the further problems of the philosophy of aesthetics.

Summary
1. The problem raised is how an aesthetic judgment, reaction or evaluation is to be distinguished from others.
2. We should expect to find a criterion which allows us to distinguish the aesthetic, the moral, the economic, the intellectual and other evaluations by a single *fundamentum divisionis*.
3. All evaluations are made on the basis of criteria for the merit of the kind of thing in question.
4. An aesthetic evaluation is one which is made on the basis of a selection from the total body of relevant criteria of merit.
5. In at least the simpler cases of aesthetic evaluation the relevant criteria appear to be those which are concerned with the way the object in question looks or presents itself to the other senses.
6. It is impossible to distinguish the aesthetic by a special object, by a special characteristic attended to, or by a special emotion.

Appendix
It may appear to some that too little importance has been accorded to the emotions in this paper. To avoid misunderstanding I will mention one or two ways in which I recognise the importance of considering the emotions in aesthetics.

First, I recognise that we would be very little interested in the aesthetic aspect of things but for their emotional effect upon us.

Secondly, I acknowledge that if we experience an emotional thrill when we look at a picture or hear a piece of music we do not normally have to examine our grounds and reasons to know that we are reacting aesthetically in a favourable way. But I do want to maintain that it is the nature of the grounds that makes our appreciation aesthetic and that if on an examination of our grounds we find, as sometimes happens, that our reasons are appropriate rather to moral evaluation or are erotic, or what you will, we will, if we are honest, recognise that our reaction was not after all aesthetic. Of course we have trained ourselves to a great extent to approach pictures and music from the aesthetic angle so that we shall not in general be mistaken if we rely on an unanalysed impression.

Thirdly, there are a great number of terms that we use in aesthetic evaluation—*pleasant, moving, pretty, beautiful, impressive, admirable* and *exciting* among others. I do not know what makes one more appropriate than another in a given context; partly, perhaps, they are more or less laudatory, or are based on a still more restricted selection of criteria than a mere judgment of goodness or badness; but I suspect that the choice of word is at least in part determined by the precise character of the emotion experienced.

For these and other reasons I do not wish to belittle the importance of the emotions in the philosophy of aesthetics; but I do wish to deny most emphatically that the aesthetic field can be distinguished from others by an attempt to analyse the emotions involved therein: and that is all that the thesis of this paper requires.

(ii) David Pole

J. O. Urmson proposes a fresh start in aesthetics. He offers to show us the subject in a new light, shifting it in its logical setting; it is to be brought into line with its neighbours. The reorganisation he achieves is certainly striking in its simplicity and breadth. The terms, 'good', 'bad' and 'indifferent', he says, are the widest terms of appraisal we possess; and we appraise things, reacting to them favourably or unfavourably, under various aspects; we attend to different sets of criteria. Hence it is the set of criteria we appeal to, not the emotions which as spectators we may feel, that serve to make a situation aesthetic. I do not accept this account, but its attraction is very clear; it seems that we need only turn a single key and half a dozen doors fly open at once. The placing of moral and intellectual evaluation on a level is an important consequence; Urmson has in fact maintained elsewhere that 'valid' itself is (indeed even etymologically) a value-word. Granted the general doctrine, that seems to me the only consistent view. But I welcome it, too, for another and less amiable reason: I anticipate that it will be found unpalatable, and I hope that the currently popular view of morals will lose some of its appeal when once these consequences are clearly seen to follow.

Here, however, it is in its application to aesthetics that I am to criticise the new approach. I shall seek first to raise objections to Urmson's general method or treatment: for he brings new logical tackle to the job. I hope to show in the concrete that the real nature of an aesthetic situation still slips through his net, subtle as it is. And I shall indicate an alternative solution. I do not promise to bring the great fish to land; but it would be something to locate the shoals where it lurks.

Urmson makes it his starting point to consider 'the point of calling a reaction aesthetic'; the point, he finds, is to distinguish it from other kinds, such as those I have mentioned. From this he deduces that these reactions must at least be of the same genus; and, more especially, that the *differentia* of an aesthetic reaction cannot be the occurrence of some special sort of emotion unless that of moral and intellectual reactions is so too. Where we can ask whether S is a P or a Q, P's and Q's must in some sense be on a level: the criteria for identifying an instance of the one cannot be wholly unrelated to the criteria for identifying an instance of the other. Now a good a priori argument like this one, once we are fairly mounted on it, will carry us a long way; but it too often rides at a gallop over matters of fact. The point of calling a reaction aesthetic, let me repeat, is, according to Urmson, to distinguish it from others, intellectual or moral reactions; or, he later adds, erotic ones. Aesthetic reactions, he holds, do not—any more than intellectual reactions—necessarily involve emotions of any special sort. But erotic reactions plainly do. That is one way in which they are identified. And it is plainly sensible to ask whether someone's reaction to a particular person or picture was chiefly an aesthetic or an erotic one. Urmson speaks of the impossibility of our using two sets of criteria that are wholly unrelated: but when will they be 'wholly unrelated'? Certainly it is clear that the mentioning of two states of affairs in the same disjunctive clause does not entail that the occurrence of the one is verifiable in the same ways as that of the other. I may ask, for example, whether on some occasion a man (or a woman) acted from deliberate malice or unconscious jealousy, or from both. The case is parallel to Urmson's in that the disjuncts do not exclude each other. Now the first is known to the agent directly, by introspection, and to other people by his report if he confesses to it; the second is knowable in neither of these ways.

I confess that I should be better pleased to be able to give an adequate general account of these logical matters, rather than to make do with a few counter-examples. But space forbids, and I am, besides, far from clear in my own mind. But I am thus far satisfied—that Urmson's a priori argument cannot be accepted just as it stands and made to bear the weight which he puts on it.

He proposes, however, to reinforce the a priori approach with what he calls field-work: namely, the study of the sorts of considerations actually adduced when the aesthetic claims of particular reactions are in dispute. He goes on to quote the work of one critic and to indicate that he has others in the dossier. This is a programme, it seems to me, which no one could sensibly object to; but, of course, our findings will not do our work for us. They will certainly call for interpretation. (Urmson seems to write as if the example he gives speaks unequivocally for itself, leaving room for no interpretation but his own; indeed I suspect that he hardly thinks of what he says of it *as* an interpretation.) But that is not all; if we are to study the work of criticism, we should study it critically. The critics are not infrequently wrong; and they disagree sharply among themselves not only about particular works of art but, in general, about the right way of conducting their own craft. Sometimes they reinforce bad criticism with bad aesthetics; but it is truer to say that the distinction is constantly breaking down. Questions are constantly raised as to what things are aesthetically relevant. Kenneth Clark in his masterly work *The Nude*[3] has maintained the view that a right reaction to Botticelli's *Venus* will involve erotic elements, which his reviewer in the *Times Literary Supplement*[4] called in question; and behind this difference there lay differences, which were also touched on, as to the general criteria for judging visual art.

It is a current dogma—I call it so, for I know of no reason to support it, repeatedly as it is asserted—that philosophers of art, morals and the like, though they sit like Homeric gods, above the battle, unlike Homeric gods, are forbidden to intervene. If the ruling in general is arbitrary, the present state of criticism makes obedience to it here virtually impossible. If the critics are engaged in sorting out their own standards, we can hardly study them without joining in; nor does Urmson succeed in doing so, it seems to me, however austere his intentions.

In general we are not to pretend to be more blind and helpless than we are. In the very emphasis on the notion of field-work—of going further afield to find our evidence, of studying what other people have said—I suspect that I find a hint of this (as it seems to me) mistaken humility. In this subject one can do one's field-work at home; or at least a fair part of it. It may be that aestheticians in the past have studied the critics too little, being content, and supposing it sufficient, to reflect on their own experience. But after all it remains true that certain philosophers of art have known aesthetic experience: and there is no need here for a self-denying ordinance. We find that Urmson's own paradigm of an aesthetic reaction is a reaction simply to colour and sounds; and there seems to be little room for an appeal to the writings of critics here. He himself, indeed, reaches the eminently traditional conclusion, which Kant reached in his own critical way, that aesthetic pleasure is pleasure in the purely formal qualities of objects; for though Urmson may bring a new hoe, here and there it turns up an old root.

I turn next to consider the difference between aesthetic reactions and others, especially intellectual and moral ones: I hope to show that Urmson's account fails to do it adequate justice. The real difference has still to be brought out. Just as historians may write the history of the same period under different aspects, its religious or political or social history, so too one might speak of the moral history, or the aesthetic or intellectual history of an individual. It seems to me plain that his aesthetic history will be primarily a history of experiences, of significant moments or occasions, and that these other two histories will not. I do not mean to disregard moral experience or to belittle the

[3] London, 1956.
[4] 11 January 1957.

importance of moral insight; the concept is already too much neglected in contemporary ethics. In general it is by reason of these moments of deepened vision—strangely represented in current discussion, I believe, by occurrences called 'moral choices' or 'decisions'—that morals can advance. Yet the broad difference surely remains plain: a man may judge rightly and act well, and yet nothing that he experienced on the occasion need in itself be memorable. One cannot appreciate Rembrandt or Shakespeare and experience nothing memorable.

Another illustration may make this plainer. An exhausted or extremely tired person is generally incapable of much feeling; one can be too tired to feel. Now imagine that someone in this state should find himself the beneficiary of an act of extraordinary kindness; that at the time he has little or no feeling of gratitude. That does not prevent him from judging; and if he judges the action, as very likely he may, at its true worth, that is clearly a moral reaction. But in aesthetics such a case is impossible. There is a sense, perhaps, in which one might still make an aesthetic appraisal, but one would not have an aesthetic experience. I have heard of a journalist who, having handled comic cartoons all his life, could pick out a good one infallibly, but he could no longer laugh, or even smile, at any of them. A connoisseur, in the state I have spoken of, might be shown a work of art, and might even evaluate it rightly; further, it might be the formal features of the work which he uses. But it is still true that he would not be appreciating the work of art, just as the journalist was not appreciating the cartoons. If he felt nothing, experienced nothing, that would not be an aesthetic response.

Kant rightly insisted that aesthetic reactions must be first-hand. But one may go further: to appreciate a work of art we must respond to it each time that we see it as if it were the first time. That is not true in morals or elsewhere. Certainly our first reaction may include the thrill of discovery, which is in no way distinctively aesthetic, for there are all sorts of things that are thrilling to discover; and later readings or viewings may deepen our insight, and show us much we had missed. But each is still essentially new. Elsewhere it is generally true that the more efficiently we respond the less we feel, for if our responses are immediately right, there is little room for feeling: the reverse is true here.

An aesthetic reaction, it appears, implies a certain heightening of, or dwelling in, our experience. I am not wholly satisfied with either phrase, but I cannot do better. We cannot talk of attending to our experiences, for that suggests a withdrawal of attention from their object. It is clear, at least, that in some sense the experiencing of the thing—one may say, experiencing it as fully as possible—is here what matters. Certainly much of what we experience in face of works of art, our thrills or exultations and the like, are in no way special to aesthetics; all sorts of objects may be thrilling. And the visual imagery suggested by poetry is variable and generally unimportant. None of this need be denied; for all this is not part of the experience of the object itself, of the work of art. Philosophers writing on art, impressed by such considerations, have lately shown some inclination to hustle the notion of aesthetic experience out of the picture altogether; art-critics and literary critics, they say, are concerned with the objective or real qualities of the work—even visual depth and the like can be so thought of—not with the throbs and thrills and arbitrary associations of the spectator. Bad criticism, it is further urged, largely derives from this introversion of the critic's attention; his interest is in his own emotional states and he watches those, and not the play or the picture before him. All this, I believe, is both true and important; and to find examples of that kind of emotional criticism would not be hard. But we must hold on to both sides of the truth: both that a work of art must be, in some special sense, experienced: and also that the experience must be of the work itself—that the experience must consist in a heightened awareness of the thing.

'Of the formal features of the thing', so Urmson says, and many others with him. I should answer—Not necessarily. These features, it seems to me, lend themselves to this kind of experience: this is, in a way, the simplest or the most obvious form of aesthetic reaction. It stands in our way; the things are there—shapes, colours and sounds—they invite our attention. Yet even to these, we have seen reason to think, it is possible to react in a manner that is only in a minimal sense aesthetic; such a reaction, at least, is theoretically possible. But whether or not we can react non-aesthetically to pure forms, we can certainly respond aesthetically (the change of verb is not through inadvertency) to other things. The truth is, it seems to me, that not only any perceptible form but any object or quasi-object that can be seen as external, may be regarded aesthetically; even an abstract object, say a mode of philosophising or a system of ideas, certainly a person's character as presented in literature, admit of this attitude in spectators. It has always been said that in aesthetics our responses concern appearances; and hence a seeming or quasi-externality serves as well as the real. But it is true, as I have said, that the requisite attitude is generally easier to adopt where a concrete, sensible object is presented, which really stands before our eyes.

Let us take the case of aestheticism in philosophy, which is a familiar field. Surely it is possible, apart from intellectual evaluation, to relish a manner of philosophising for its own sake: say the Moorean manner with its infinite taking of pains, or (though the taste is now out of fashion) the strange intellectual imagination of Hegel. One may take pleasure in the austerity and formalism of one philosopher, and the exciting depths and deliberate amorphism of another. If the response is aesthetic there is no conflict: one may admire both Chaucer and T. S. Eliot. But supposing these responses are allowed; surely, it may be said, in so far as they are genuinely aesthetic, they are also responses to formal qualities. In a sense it may be so. But 'form', I suspect, is now being given its meaning as whatever can be made the object of an aesthetic response; Urmson means to define it with reference to the senses, as a matter of how things look and sound.

I do not think that this notion of form can be plausibly stretched to cover more than half the ground we usually assign to aesthetics. Kant, it will be recalled, frankly abandoned it when he turned to representational art; he was led to recognise another species of beauty, though not beauty, he held, in the strict sense. (And there is, besides, his treatment of the sublime, which, of course, is much less closely tied to the notion of form; indeed the highly suggestive passage on aesthetic ideas in the analytic of the sublime points to a very different approach.) Urmson admits one important addition to his account of aesthetic reactions in terms of form: we may react to objects aesthetically, he says, in view not only of their formal features as such, but also inasmuch as they appear to have qualities that would be non-aesthetically desirable. Thus stable-looking buildings may be admired. But the example is from architecture, and I am not sure that Urmson means to extend this account to cover the representational arts. A picture of an idyllic pastoral scene may perhaps, in a certain sense, be said to seem to have non-aesthetically desirable qualities; but not all pictures are idyllic pastorals. I see no other way in which this extension of the criteria of the aesthetic will meet the problem before us.

Urmson has, however, one direct reference to representational art. He suggests that there is much that we admire in such works as *Hamlet* that we would admire no less in other and non-aesthetic contexts; much, say, that is intellectually satisfying. These features, though not formal, are also not strictly aesthetic. That seems to me true, and I think also that it needs to be emphasised; but it will scarcely serve to account for the whole difference between representational and so-called formal art. For Urmson the paradigm of an aesthetic reaction is a reaction to colours, sounds and the like; he proposes to fit his account, in the first place, to simple and clear cases, rather than to start with sophisticated and perhaps impure ones. But it is arguable, to say the least, that the distinction here is between two typically different species of object; that what he has done is rather to fit it to one single species, comprising some half of the cases to be dealt with, neglecting the other. At all events I think it clear that there are certain non-formal elements in art that cannot be accommodated in any of his other pigeon-holes, the moral, intellectual and so on. I shall seek to make this plain.

We may find Shakespeare's insight into psychological processes intellectually satisfying; so much is admitted; and one may derive the same sort of satisfaction from the study of psychology itself. It remains true, and indeed a truism, that reading a textbook on melancholia is not like seeing *Hamlet*; that an intellectual statement or a theoretical presentation is different from an imaginative one. I have confessed that I have not done my field-work; but this distinction must surely be one of the commonest in literary criticism. Critics repeatedly find occasion to complain that some character in a novel say, or some state of mind, though analysed and observed with intelligence—our intellectual reactions are favourable—is lacking in imaginative force. It strikes our minds with no concrete conviction: we understand it, we are not made to feel it. We fall back here—critics fall back—on these verbs, to see and to feel. Both must be partly metaphorical, for what we feel, in this sense, is neither a tangible surface nor a feeling, though these play a part, but a character. Now we may say if we choose, that the qualities we lack here are still in a certain sense formal. Perhaps they are, but now 'formal' once again has been given a meaning correlative to our aesthetic responses. I may add that I am far from sure that Housman's response to the 'thrilling utterance' of Wordsworth's poetry was a response to something formal in any ordinary sense.

A great writer, let us suppose, brings before our imagination the state of mind of a man for whom the whole world has gone tasteless; such a portrait we are to consider. To concentrate our attention here is not to indulge a perverse preference for sophisticated and intractable examples; it is to look at something that great art can do, and nothing else can. Any work that shows us such an image is counted as art. To say this, certainly, is only to point to the problem: we have yet to create a language in which to express these notions adequately—and for that reason we are bound to use metaphors. We can only form new concepts on the analogy of those we are familiar with. I claim only that the thing exists, and that aesthetics cannot ignore it.

I have claimed that only art can do this; yet there is a sense in which that may not be true. For we must ask more precisely what it does. I should answer that it creates what we think of as some sort of object—as we think, and also speak, of a poem or of a character in a play as some sort of object—which invites and rewards aesthetic contemplation; it invites us to take up a certain attitude. Yet the attitude does not depend on the object; it is also possible to adopt it elsewhere, though often much harder. It is possible to stand back and regard real people, their characters and lives, as we normally regard men on the stage; to make them objects of aesthetic contemplation. To do so is usually difficult, because, as has so often been observed, the attitude implies a certain detachment: we are generally much too involved. Yet sometimes we find ourselves doing so, when life seems to stop like a play, even involuntarily. An aesthetic response, if my account is right, implies no more than a heightened present awareness of the qualities of an external or would-be external object; and any object may be looked at in this way. Even the material we find in the psychological textbook admits of aesthetic contemplation. It is true that, thus regarded, it will be found to be rather meagre and bare; the terms it is written in, adapted to their own purpose, are not calculated to give the keenest immediate feeling of the thing described. For clearly to say that all objects allow of our adopting this attitude is not to say that they equally reward it. But the attitude itself is no more than the full experiencing of any given thing. And I may add that I believe that what I have said of it is not much removed from what Croce meant—despite a widely different philosophical idiom.

Urmson's criteria of an aesthetic reaction, if I am right, are on the one side too narrow; on the other I find them far too wide. He includes not only sounds and visible qualities, but also smells and even feelings and tastes. I have the impression that he does so with some hesitancy: for he says that he sees no reason to disallow the experiences of the gourmet and the connoisseur. On the face of it this ruling declines to countenance as aesthetic the pleasure of a normally hungry man eating boiled eggs. I suppose, too, that he excludes somatic sensations, tingles and the like. Now my own account admits only our response to external objects; and it is, I think, in accordance with established usage to treat only the two distance senses, sight and hearing, as definitely aesthetic. Smell, it has been thought, is a borderline case. No doubt there are pleasing tactual sensations; but I never heard of the beauty or sublimity or other aesthetic excellence of tangible surfaces. One can dwell in one's sensations of all sorts, as in any sort of pleasurable experience; that alone, of course, does not make the experience aesthetic. It must be allowed, however, that critics find occasion to speak of the sensuous qualities of certain sorts of poetry and painting; and our reactions here may approach the character of mere sensations. In analysing a passage of poetry, one might wish to show how a merely sensational effect was being played off against a more abstract or ideal one.

It is hardly satisfactory to leave the matter thus; but I cannot but feel that Urmson is here the innovator, and that the onus of justifying his innovation rests with him. I find, moreover, that I have need of the distinction between aesthetic and merely sensational pleasure in other parts of the subject, so I am unwilling to give it up. To these I shall briefly turn.

A social psychologist or anthropologist would, I imagine, class together the audiences at the Grand Guignol and the Old Vic, and perhaps also the audience at the circus. Whatever the similarities, for our purposes they are very different. The choice is open to us denying that the addicts of melodrama are responding aesthetically at all, or of admitting it, perhaps with the qualification that their taste is bad, that their aesthetic responses are untrained or perverted. I should prefer to follow Collingwood, who distinguishes between amusement-art and art proper. The line he draws is much too hard, it seems to me; and further, adopting one point of view, he ignores the possibility of others, from which the two things are very like; but his treatment of the whole matter is still the most illuminating I know, and I shall use it, adapting it to my own purposes.

The pleasures of melodrama and the like are similar to sensational pleasures. The object functions primarily as the stimulus of a certain feeling, namely fear. The appeal of the tightrope or the lion-tamer is the same in kind. People like being frightened, so long as there is no real danger, at least to themselves. I do not deny that it is always pleasing to see a feat of great precision and skill finely done; but who would go to see tightrope-walking at a foot and a half from the ground? The skill is the same. The more frightening a melodrama the better; to say so, at least, brings out by parody the direction in which melodrama tends, and so points the difference between melodrama and art. Broadly the difference is this, that our response to a work of art is always, as I have said, an awareness of something; whatever part emotional elements play—a question of some complexity which I must leave on one side—the mere feeling of some sort of emotion is not here an end in itself. So far, I gather, Urmson would agree. But elsewhere it is. The simple aim of exciting certain feelings is clearest in the case of pornography and of the many shows and varieties of respectable pornography that fill the theatres in the West End of London.

The distinction, however, must not be too sharply drawn. It is certain that any competent dramatist must know how to work on the feelings of his audience; how to vary tension with relief, to hint at fears, to lull them and to let them loose. The cauldron scene in *Macbeth* is meant to be frightening, and will fail on the stage if it is not. All this gives us some justification for thinking of the theatre as less purely aesthetic than the other arts; although all these factors are also found, if less markedly, elsewhere. But the difference remains too; it is still true that a spectator who responds aesthetically is not merely feeling but seeing something; a good critic, we have already said, must direct our attention to the real features of the work.

The difference between melodrama and art is broadly analogous to the other difference I have spoken of, between aesthetic pleasure in sights and sounds, and merely sensational pleasure. A sensation is something in ourselves, like the emotion of fear, though its source may be external; and what we value here is rather a kind of experience than the experience of an object of a certain character. To say this points the difference in a broad way, ignoring complexities and qualifications; for the analogy must not be pressed too far, nor, in either case, the distinction too sharply drawn. The variousness of the types of situation and response we call aesthetic needs to be emphasised, as well as their generic likeness. Further, the term 'non-aesthetic' is not, clearly, a general condemnation: all pleasure in itself is good, and sensational pleasures no less than others.

An account of an aesthetic response must distinguish it from a moral or intellectual one; and must distinguish, too, aesthetic from merely sensational pleasure, and melodrama and the like from art proper. I have sought at least to outline the way in which this, as it seems to me, may be done. But it may be asked whether any such account can be thought secure or satisfactory so long as it includes no treatment of evaluation, which Urmson puts in the centre of the picture. I shall add a few final words, though I can do no more than indicate the approach I would adopt.

If what I have said so far is right, we may distinguish broadly between two kinds of reason why people will disagree in their evaluations of works of art. First, one spectator may see what another fails to see; from want of attention or of training in certain art-forms, or from other causes, we often miss much of what is before us. Secondly, though both see the same, they may react differently, one favourably, the other unfavourably. Where our concern is with works of representational art, where ordinary feelings and attitudes are expressed, such differences are only to be expected; but they occur elsewhere too. Our reactions may be appropriate or inappropriate; and I imagine that there is no object which it is theoretically impossible to react unfavourably to, though such reactions must in some cases be very rare. I have yet to meet someone who dislikes daffodils. Yet, given appropriate conditioning from an early age, if say, a child were pinched hard whenever a yellow object appeared in his field of view, no doubt the reaction could be set up. (Perhaps Vincent van Gogh underwent the opposite conditioning process.) And I presume that the same is true of intellectual reactions; that in a similar way unfavourable reactions to all sound or valid deductive or other inferences could be conditioned;

though the subject would probably go mad.

Roughly the situation is this. First, of course, there is more to see, in the aesthetic sense of 'see', in some objects than others; and these we rightly value more highly. But where we fail to appreciate aesthetic objects, it is either because we fail to see what is there, or else because, though seeing it, we react inappropriately. But here, I fear, I finally part company with Urmson. When Troilus in the council scene in *Troilus and Cressida* asks rhetorically, 'What is aught but as 'tis valued?' Hector replies,

> But value dwells not in particular will;
> It holds his estimate and dignity
> As well therein 'tis precious in itself
> As in the prizer: 'tis mad idolatry
> To make the service greater than the god . . . (Act ii, sc. 2)

We commend things, in other words—works of art, people or arguments—because we suppose them to be commendable. Shakespeare's argument seems to me sound; and I suspect Urmson of the sort of idolatry in question. He holds, I believe, that there is nothing either good or bad but grading makes it so. But in this I am perhaps misrepresenting him grossly. At all events, here, at the edge of vast issues that lie beyond aesthetics, it will be well to stop.

3

Morality and the Assessment of Literature

At the beginning of *The Principles of Literary Criticism* I. A. Richards complained of the chaos of critical theories—a complaint that we hear pretty often, generally from theorists about to add to it, each making his small contribution.[1] Richards' own contribution was a plan for reckoning the merit of poetry in terms of the more or less organised psychological state that it serves to induce in its readers: for poetry, he held, organises our 'attitudes'—a term that may be taken in different ways. The theoretical picture that Richards connects with it, a vivid enough picture in its way, is of a kind of stock exchange of neural impulses; but perhaps in his practical criticism the word reverts to its ordinary sense. And surely the practical criticism, not the neurological speculation, is what has served to keep Richards' work alive. This is the aspect, at least, to which I shall confine my attention here; my concern is with the use of these and similar concepts in the practical business of criticism. For here we have a critical approach, a technique and an orientation, that has in point of fact increasingly established itself. And the fact is one, surely, that aesthetics cannot ignore; a general theory should take notice of practice. But if this is only to add still more to the notorious chaos, I cannot see any alternative course short of abandoning the subject altogether; and that alternative, at least for those who are instinctive theorists and generalisers, is an impossible one.

Our problem is set, then, by two things: first, the overtly moralistic terms in which so many critics now approach their subject; but beside it we must put the philosophical commonplace, as it surely is, that the ethical and the aesthetic modes—whether we say of experience, reality or language—form different categories.[2] Modern philosophers, for instance, tell us that if we are to evaluate the same object under both headings we must point to different features or aspects, or perhaps use

[1] I. A. Richards, *The Principles of Literary Criticism*, London, 1924, ch. 1.
[2] These critics also insist that their concern is, as they say, with the poetry as poetry. That must be borne in mind, too; however, it only sharpens the puzzle of this sort of two-in-one evaluation.

different sorts of argument. But those of traditional schools have been
no less sure of this radical distinction. Aesthetic theory and critical
practice are no longer simply out of touch, which would be
unremarkable: rather, they are in collision, and that is new. This may
perhaps seem hard enough but we shall find that there is more and
worse to follow; the problem has yet another side to it. For there is non-
representational as well as representational art to consider. For it seems
natural to suppose that our basic criteria, moral or non-moral, will
have some application to both; but if so, what are we to say of the
moral significance of a Chinese pot? If we find in poetry, as one great
Victorian critic found, higher truth, higher seriousness, and the
criticism of life, it would seem fanciful to look for these things in
abstract painting. To be sure I can imagine a critic of a certain sort
who, looking at a porcelain vase, should exclaim 'How true!' or 'What
moral insight!'. But I fear that I should not wait to hear how he would
go on.

The business of literature, to be sure, is never downright moral
instruction. Its moral significance appears in the vision that it shows us
or makes us see; in what it makes concrete or embodies, not in rules or
lessons that it inculcates. When Arnold spoke of the criticism of life his
concern was not didactic nor, in any narrow sense, moralistic. His own
examples put that beyond doubt, whether of works that qualify or fail
to qualify for the highest place. Rather he meant to speak of the
seriousness of complete commitment that excludes charlatanry even at
its subtlest—and no less excludes deliberate preaching. It seems he had
in mind the sort of speech, or use of language, that can so concentrate
the sense of deep experience as to make it felt, perhaps, in half a dozen
words. Moreover we find that he proceeds, 'The superior character of
truth and seriousness in the matter and substance of the best poetry, is
inseparable from the superior diction or movement marking its style or
manner'.[3]

Eloquence or earnestness, the ring of truth—this, for a starting-
point, would give a rough or rather crude notion of what was in
Arnold's mind. Suppose someone speaks of difficult, serious or deep
issues: we can recognise sincerity of tone even in ordinary speech, we
have tests of a man's really meaning what he says—and really
understanding the meaning of it. To poetry the same tests apply—with
this difference, that their application is intensified tenfold. Now, later
critics have extended this notion rather than rejected it or gone back on
it; all aspects of moral maturity, all evidence of subtle and living
values, are now sought in the texture of poetry. This is the sort of
approach, the sort of assumption, that philosophical aesthetics has still

[3] Matthew Arnold, *Essays in Criticism* (London, 1888), p. 22.

to take notice of. We have to re-examine the relation of art to morality in view of the development of critical practice; and we have, secondly, to relate what we find to non-representational art. For if we grant to start with, that non-representational art has some specific excellence of its own—call it organic form, pattern, harmony, or what you will—it would be puzzling if we should find nothing corresponding to it in literature. Yet we are told that here form itself, the form of literary works, is inseparable from their seriousness and truth.[4]

These, plainly, are far-reaching questions. A comprehensive aesthetic, it seems, would have to take account of at least three different sorts of things that we praise and value in art. First we admire mere form in non-representational art; next, turning to representational art, we use what seems to be a separate criterion, namely 'truth to life'; and thirdly (connected with this last but distinct from it) we find the moral approach that we have been speaking of; and here we look for a true and significant vision, for adequate attitudes or feelings organised and embodied in literary work. It is, no doubt, an unsatisfactory plan to seek to put the pinnacles on the spire before the body of the church has been erected; but here I must take most of this for granted. I shall say nothing explicitly of truth to life. My main concern is with the third of the three approaches. But as to the general value that we find in formal pattern or harmony, I shall seek to sketch in a few outlines—to set up some scaffolding that may serve provisionally in lieu of a nave.

Our task, then, is twofold. We are to ask, first, what, if anything, we can significantly say of the value of non-representational art; and secondly, given some account of that, how we can extend it to cover representational painting and literature. Let us take for a start any of those seemingly unpromising notions that I have listed; harmony, form (in an emphatic sense) or pattern—the term I prefer. I suppose that we know what a pattern is, in some sense at least—though the word is presumably undefinable, or only definable ostensively. For imagine that we are dealing with someone who is genuinely ignorant of its meaning; I cannot see how else we could teach him. A definition in words seems unlikely to do more than offer a synonym instead. There are, however, distinctions to be made. For in one sense every object has a form, and every set of objects forms a pattern. This usage, plainly, will not help us; our claim would on this account be left vacuous. We shall do better to distinguish, as we commonly do, between things hav-

---

[4] We must not ourselves be tempted, however, to win the point too easily, as we may be exploiting the ambiguities of the word 'form'. Every work has some form—distinguishable from its content or theme. Not every work has a harmonious form.

ing form or pattern in some emphatic sense, and those that are formless or patternless. Again we can always make a pattern, a mechanical or regular pattern, merely by repeating a given form; patterns on wallpaper, for instance, are mostly of this sort. These play a large part in art, especially in architecture, and their relation to patterns of other sorts would be well worth enquiring into; but here I must leave it on one side. Our concern is with free patterns, those we recognise as such, though we could point to no rule, could formulate no principle, in accordance with which they are constructed.

To say this may so far seem unilluminating. In picking out this special sense of 'pattern', it may be said, I have virtually made it synonymous with 'work of art'—or at least with 'non-representational work of art'. And while there may be no harm in exchanging the one term for the other, there is no obvious benefit either. But the truth is that our use of 'pattern' is much wider. We find patterns in argument, for instance, and in all modes of enquiry; and patterns in individual character and sequences of historical events. A proper working-out of the notion, along with an analysis of these differences, might serve to give us a more-than-vacuous account of non-representational art. For if aesthetic patterns could be distinguished from other sorts the notion might be turned to some account; we should have a definition by *genus* and *differentia* which, formally at least, ought to suffice.

I have said that I do not mean to undertake that task here. Yet failing a few further words, I fear that the notion that I have introduced will seem too large an innovation—something altogether too far-reaching to be accepted, as it stands, without a murmur. For in what I have said I have run together aesthetic and intellectual things, and have treated this notion of 'pattern' as playing a central part in both. Not that this use of the term is quite unprecedented: John Wisdom, for instance, adopts it and seems to feel no special need of justifying or explaining it. He tells us, for example, of Newton that—unlike those who find a ready-made intellectual pattern—he 'had to cut out a pattern in order to show connexions in a whole which no one had ever apprehended as a whole. We are given the conceptions of energy and gravitation.'[5] And similarly Wittgenstein, in expounding the notion of a mathematical proof, speaks much of what he calls its 'surveyability'; a proof, it seems, is a memorable figure that serves to present the material in a form that our minds naturally grasp.[6] That, I believe, comes pretty near my own notion of a 'pattern' and of a work of art.

I can approach the notion by way of a distinction that we may draw in the face of any situation that we find and seek to make sense of—of

[5] John Wisdom, *Philosophy and Pscyho-Analysis* (Oxford, 1953), p. 253.
[6] Cf. *Remarks on the Foundations of Mathematics* (Oxford, 1956), e.g. i. 77–8, ii. 42.

any set of phenomena or data. Sometimes we stand bewildered or defeated, but otherwise we seem to know where we stand; the data may present themselves as unmanageable, as merely fortuitous or arbitrary, or again they may form a coherent order. All this may be granted: yet to make these distinctions, it may be said, is to presuppose some system of concepts; we must appeal to already established principles of explanation or causal laws. Now the opposite, I believe, is the truth: the distinction I have been speaking of is essential to any thinking thing, and exists at a primitive level before explicit rules or conceptual systems emerge.

We respond and adjust to our environment from the first. One may imagine a primitive organism with nothing but its own innate tendencies: it re-orients itself in face of what it meets, preparing for new experiences accordingly. Experience of a given sort touches off certain roughly determinate expectations: hence the next experience, whatever it may be, falls into something like a ready-made scheme; it must either harmonise or conflict with it. To say this is to say that—given our responses to the world—certain things or appearances that confront us, are, so to speak, acceptable; they are seen from the first as mutually fitting or natural, while others are mutually repugnant. We cannot rest in face of the latter until we establish some new viewpoint that removes the discrepancy, showing us the same things in a different light. One might say—in a psychological or perhaps Kantian vocabulary—that some forms of things that we meet are pre-adapted to our faculties of cognition. But then again, as a matter of philosophy, we are bound to put some trust in those same faculties as a condition of our thinking at all.

The construction of languages and conceptual systems, I have said, is not presupposed by, but presupposes, this basic distinction. One could not say that Newton 'cut out a pattern' in his material if anything might equally count as a pattern. We know the difference between pattern and what is patternless. Our languages also form patterns; for logic alone could set no limit to the possible ways in which men might speak. Philosophers have come to talk in recent years of the 'logical behaviour' of words—which is also the behaviour of people who use them. And there are no a priori limitations on the ways in which people might behave; there is no conceivable pattern or want of pattern that we can rule out in advance. Yet not all of them would pass muster as 'languages'. Some are acceptable, our minds grasp them; they prove to be learnable and teachable. And, getting a clear view of their working, we can see what belongs to them and what does not: some would-be parts of the pattern might, perhaps, in a philosophical survey—'assembling reminders', or setting the matter in a new light—be shown to be idle or functionless.[7] They have no proper place in it; others are integral and essential. And this distinction is not a consequence of our possessing other norms, it is involved in our speaking at all. For if any possible usage might pass as an intelligible pattern of language then we could say anything or nothing.

One further word before passing on. If what I have said serves to prove anything, a critic may object that it proves much too much. For it seems that we distinguish between pattern and want of pattern in material of very different sorts, abstract as well as concrete: in scientific theories and language-forms no less than in colours and shapes. Now, if so, the question may arise why theories and language-games should not also be called works of art; for they seem to possess all that is requisite. We shall ask only for a pattern or, say, a system of the right sort—a complex system, and at the same time clearly systematic—and the material would seem to be irrelevant. To this there is a short and simple answer: the conditions being fulfilled, the conclusion holds. Undoubtedly theories admit of aesthetic assessment and contemplation; they, like anything else, can be held up to view and merely contemplated as organised systems of forms. And where they also reward this viewpoint, we shall find that scientists do not hesitate to call them 'beautiful'. There seems no reason to doubt that they are often right—but there is one further crucial qualification. The pattern or system which we find must be something which our minds can hold and grasp: art is a thing to be experienced. For a system might be rigorously coherent, its coherence appearing with perfect clarity as we follow it out step by step. But to satisfy us aesthetically as well it must be something we can view as a whole; we must be able to focus on the general pattern. But for the rest, the inference is legitimate: any sort of object combining what Wittgenstein calls 'surveyability' with richness and complexity in its material will be rewarding to aesthetic contemplation. But the simplest material, of course, consists merely in shapes, colours and sounds.

I have promised no more than a sketch—what I have given is, I fear, of the sketchiest—of a view of non-representational art. But it may suffice for my immediate purpose, which concerns representational art and literature. I wish to ask how far the embodiment in a work of literature of some sort of moral vision or point of view can be related to a general approach to aesthetics. First we must see how the present rough account may be extended to accommodate this new feature, representation, once it makes its appearance.

[7] Cf. Wittgenstein, *Philosophical Investigations* (Oxford, 1953), i. 5, 109, 126 and passim.

Broadly we may say this, that here one pattern is superimposed on another. The process may be simply illustrated by the difference between a black-and-white and a coloured reproduction of the same picture—supposing, what is presumably logically possible, that the colours do not travesty the original. We have, so to speak, two patterns at different levels, one of shapes and the other of colours; and then, when the two are fused in one, we shall have a third as well, a new pattern that emerges with their fusion. That is one way of thinking of it, at least; the pattern of colours in reality is not something that we could detach or present separately. But we shall find this abstract distinction useful when we turn to the relation between the two factors, ideally separable, that make up a representational painting: for we may attend first to the representation itself, to the aspect that the object presents seen in this way, and secondly to the colours and forms that in some sense underlie it. The picture might always be looked at as no more than a pattern of coloured shapes: perhaps a Martian visitor to the National Gallery, recognising none of the things represented, would see nothing else in it.

Our position so far, then, is broadly this: we start with the common opinion that strictly aesthetic excellence consists in some sort of harmonious pattern or form; or again in 'organisation'—this latter being the more natural word to use where we think of a work as a complex thing. So far as we speak of non-representational art it seems hard to say anything other or, indeed, much more than this; and what I have attempted here is only to develop the view by relating it to other uses of the same concept. But if this is accepted the next step follows; there seems no reason why we should not speak of representational art in similar terms—in terms of pattern. There may or may not be other ways of speaking as well, but this must be possible: we can organise representations no less than non-representational forms—as I shall shortly seek to show in more detail. If so, what sort of thing will it be, this organised pattern of representation? Here at last we come to the main issue: we have to examine the relation between organised representation and the kind of moral vision that I spoke of earlier.

This relation is easiest to see in examples from drama and the novel; but just for that reason, perhaps, it will be as well to touch on poetry too. Poetry, we may broadly say, organises words—but words, of course, are not merely noises. They are noises impregnated with meaning; and here I intend to speak psychologically, for it is meaning as something that we experience, not merely as 'use' within a system, that we are concerned with in aesthetics. The mere sounds acquire a new character in virtue of their previous role—as they have passed from hand to hand, or tongue to tongue. They play different parts in our lives; the meaning that we feel them to have reflects their non-literary functioning.

Here again, then, we must distinguish two levels: it is not with the relatively primitive matter of bare sound that poetry operates. Out of sounds-as-meaningful it makes patterns. Now if meanings reflect practical doings, then an organisation of meanings, a particular way of grouping and holding them, will amount to an attitude, a stance taken up amidst all the flux of the practical. That is to say that, in a wide sense of the word 'moral', a poem reflects a moral point of view; it embodies a viewpoint or attitude to some given aspect of life, or perhaps even to life as a whole. But this may be easier to see if we turn from poetry to the novel and to drama; and in a brief exposition it may be best to set to work with the simplest case.

I shall proceed to this task directly. But another question requires our attention first, at least briefly. Otherwise I fear that I should invite protest; for art, it will certainly be said, has some close connection with emotion—and poetry, perhaps, most or most plainly of all the arts. A powerful tradition in aesthetics, as well as in popular thought, identifies art with expression: everyone knows, Collingwood says, that what art does is to express emotion. Now whether what 'everyone knows'—or what ordinary people, if they know it, mean by 'expression'—is the same as what Collingwood himself or Croce meant, is perhaps less apparent: for to express something, in the usual sense, is to make it public, to bring out what is already present in thought or feeling. But even at the cost of some digression, this view, or its bearing on my own, requires a few words.

Now certainly I have not denied that poetry may serve to express emotion, as other activities and other forms of behaviour do too—screaming or weeping, for instance. A given line expresses given feelings; so we rightly and naturally say. Now suppose, for instance, that Alexander Pope wrote the line, then whatever feelings it expresses will probably be expressed to the utmost. Nothing arbitrary, then, remains in it, nothing contingent; every feature and form is gathered up, subserving the controlled movement of the whole. What gives unity to the 'intuition', Croce says, is the feelings—and so far we think that we are understanding him. At least in the common sense of the word 'expression'—perhaps not Croce's—we shall say, no doubt, that Pope's line expresses certain feelings: feelings that might also have been expressed in other ways, perhaps by a look or a gesture, or might never have been expressed at all. Those other forms of expression would be far less adequate; yet in our ordinary ways of thinking we certainly distinguish the feeling itself as something separate, that may or may not find expression. Art broadly, in Croce's account, serves to crystallise and give form—perhaps we may say, organisation—to previously indeterminate material. And that I am far from disputing. My difficulty here is twofold: first I cannot see why this formative process should be called 'expression', which usually means something quite different; nor, secondly, why the material formed in this way should necessarily be emotional. Any other material might undergo the same sort of process and issue in the same sort of coherence.

But if ordinary readers and critics think of art as expressing emotion, it is 'expression' not as the learned but as the vulgar understand it: the externalising of what was previously private, embodying it in visible form. Now in these terms the view is plainly unacceptable: apart from its aesthetic expression the emotion itself would mean nothing to us. We are not seeking some sort of telepathy or extrasensory awareness. It is these forms, thus moulded or organised, these feelings only in so far as they are made the imminent character of objects or visible forms, that we value as art. A rightly appreciative response does not seek, as it were, to get beyond them, to penetrate to the emotion behind. Perhaps we may sometimes abstract, separating the two things in thought: we may speak of the emotion as if it were something like the inward side of those objective forms—or, better, their unifying centre. It is, so to speak, the magnetic point in virtue of which—and towards which—all our different compass needles converge.

But our aesthetic interest is in the convergence itself, the unified pattern—and extends to the emotion that it 'expresses' not as something beyond but only as something visible. Yet expressionism has an element of truth, or at least it serves to point to a truth. Let us remove this one factor, the emotion, and it is true enough that the whole substance will disintegrate; the unifying pattern will be lost at once. We have a given piece of poetry, a pattern of words: the emotion that they express is not felt as something distinct but as something integral to them; it colours and qualifies their whole character. The various tones are all altered, so that they harmonise where they would otherwise clash. Yet it is the whole product, the harmony, that we see and value as poetry.

Now mere expression, if the emotion is to be expressed with the sort of completeness and vividness that we demand of poetry, already implies an organisation of some complexity. In drawing on language to express himself, a poet is implicitly drawing on whatever has given language its meaning; for words, we said, have the meanings that we hear in them in virtue of the part that they have played in the ordinary business of our lives. The emotion itself may be simple, say, wholehearted and unqualified love or anger; the analysis of its expression is still complex. Here, I believe, we need a distinction that critics have not always been careful to draw. The plain fact is, after all, that the vivid expression of feelings—feelings that are intense but not subtle—is something quite possible; this alone will organise the resource of words, yet without presenting any finely organised attitude. That sort of attitude, however, is what the critics whose work I am concerned with look for in poetry; they would never be satisfied with a poem that did no more than express the poet's feelings. A poem will always embody some response to situations outside it: now they would require that that response should be adequate in itself; neither sentimental, for instance, nor—the other side of sentimentality—blindly or self-defensively tough; neither merely negative nor yet merely emotional and uncontrolled.

This is the main claim that we are to assess; but to take the simplest case, I have suggested, we will do better to turn to fiction or drama.

What in the first place these art-forms make or embody is, of course, a representation of life. Now a representation in itself need not exhibit any distinctively unitary form or pattern; we may have what reviewers used to call a slice of life—which will be no less, perhaps rather more, of a representation. The frame of the looking-glass or the window, drawing an arbitrary line, determines the edge of the picture.[8] Now let us leave out of account the value of representation in itself, and ask how, given this sort of material, a unitary pattern is to be formed. There are many ways, some not far to seek. The simplest and most primitive, perhaps—and also the loosest bond, the slackest unity—will be that of a picaresque novel or an episodic plot, such as Aristotle deplored. And he was right, of course; we have here a mere string of happenings, and not, in any significant sense, an organisation. A truer integration begins with a sequence of events causally linked, with a natural beginning and an end; and we take one step further, again, when the sequence in question has a central point and springs out of the character of the main protagonist. Here we approach a deeper unity, and a different kind of unity too; one that involves implicit comment, or at least the highlighting of one sort of personality in its relations to others. Or again—another principle of organisation—instead of being built round a character a story may be built round a moral, this time, perhaps, quite explicitly. We may be shown the

---

[8] It is arguable that, unlike a photograph, any representation in words, where the representation is vivid and concrete, must carry implicit commentary too. For language embodies attitudes, and merely in stating or showing things in words, we are, whether we will or no, presenting them from a particular point of view. An adequate representation, then, that shows them as they are, will embody an adequate point of view. This, I believe, is what critics have held; I hope I am right in attributing some such position to Leavis. If so, I do not mean to dissent from it; but there remains some sense—and a pretty commonplace one—in which a representation may be true and at the same time entirely chaotic.

rake's progress or the reward of true virtue; we may, in a different sort of work, be told or taught that an individual truly finds himself in identification with a political or national cause.

All these are possible sorts of theme; but it is plain that in knowing this we know little of the aesthetic value of a novel that uses them. Even a good theme does not ensure a good book; the central character may be conceived and presented mechanically, or the moral which the action is meant to point may remain merely general and external. If so, it is little more than a repetition to say, the work can have no close-knit or binding organisation; its parts or elements stand in no deep or, so to speak, interanimating bond. But imagine now a story told in such a way that its moral hardly needs to be pointed—or needs it at most to make explicit or sum up things that we have already been plainly shown. We have been made to see and feel them, it may be; the mere presentation suffices. Imagine, for instance, certain typical human characteristics presented on the stage: arrogant self-will, the regal power that says 'Do this', the infantilism that cries 'I want', capable of imagining nothing but that its wants will be supplied. And we are shown next the catastrophic consequences of such egoism; and again, out of that catastrophe, of as degraded a human condition

> As ever penury in contempt of man
> Brought near to beast,[9]

comes some groping towards newer insights and wider sympathies. In saying this, the reader will perhaps notice, I mean to indicate, in rough terms, certain central themes of *King Lear*. A rough, summary statement will suffice, at least to indicate the ways in which imaginative literature points its morals; the moral significance of what we see reflects the quality of the presentation itself.

A playwright or a novelist, I have said, organises various material—words themselves ultimately, but also the things that he makes out of words: representations of scenes and people, and emotions, thoughts and events. These he must so organise and integrate that each separately is enriched by its setting, and all, seen together, form a single whole. He presents a vision of a segment of life, tells a story and implicitly adopts an attitude. The substance or strength of the whole, its quality of meaningfulness or depth, can only reflect that of its elements—along with the order in which they are united. And it may fail for various reasons: perhaps because the whole is loosely knit (though of course there are works that we value, yet value rather for

---

[9] *King Lear,* Act ii, sc. 3.

their continuous texture or their separate passages than for the whole scheme that emerges); or because the parts of a tightly knit whole are weak and inadequate in themselves, the vision not being realised or made concrete; or because, in presenting a picture that is vivid and real enough in detail, the author himself adopts or demands a general view that that concrete detail fails to bear out—the moral is forced on the facts. [10] In all this, to repeat, a general view—in effect a view of life—is to be worked out and borne out in detail; and any faults in the picture that emerges will be moral faults and aesthetic faults at once.

To say this is to do little more than restate much that current criticism takes for granted; but aesthetics has still to recognise and find room for it. What is less familiar, I hope, is the connection—towards which these reflections may lead us—between the moral evaluation of literature and the purely formal value that we find in other art-forms. I began by distinguishing pattern in general from patternlessness. What we seek throughout is a sort of focus, a point of view that will show us the material in a form that we can assimilate and grasp. Our minds reject a world of bits and pieces; objects of any sort are meaningful to us in so far as they form an ordered pattern or an ordered whole. Now as to representational art: in a picture of life, or of some given aspect of life, to present a pattern or unity of this kind is to adopt a particular point of view. An aesthetically significant vision will be morally significant too. But suppose, again, that the same point of view—for the purposes of abstract statement it is the same—is presented yet presented externally, with no vital conviction, so that it never becomes part of a concrete whole: if so, it is a fault in the object; the work, at least to a searching gaze, is no longer an integral whole.

Now let us ask how much this contention involves. First I shall be asked, no doubt, what sort of connection we have here: is it, for instance, logically impossible that better morality should make worse art, or vice versa? Doubtless it may; for, anything else apart, there may be other variable factors to consider. I have not said that we find only one sort of value in art. Suppose that we have a vividly life-like representation which critics value for its own sake, I do not see how we can call them wrong—though we may, no doubt, count this as a less significant thing than a work of the sort that I have been discussing. But again, what is more relevant, we must be clear as to what we mean if we speak of better or worse morality. Suppose, for argument's sake,

[10] All these aspects must be simultaneously emphasised, and in an ideal work of art no one would be sacrificed to any other. All actual art involves some compromise; local vitality, for instance, normally requires some measure of autonomy in the parts. Critics have come in recent years to look for evidence of organisation down to the last image or adjective, which even in Shakespeare (let us say) would hardly be compatible with the real life of art.

that we agree in preferring the kind of life that Spinoza believed in to the kind laid down by Calvin. Plainly it does not follow from what I have said that of two literary works presenting or embodying these two views respectively, the former will be better and the latter worse. A good man need not be a literary artist. Suppose that he attempts to portray the vision that he sees, the life that he believes in; he may lack all power of making it concrete—yet he may still know how to live it in the concrete. What we shall be committed to is this, that where the imaginative realisation is equal then better morality makes better art. And that is a thesis, I believe, that can be argued on other lines too, and perhaps more rigorously.

I shall assume that there are ways to be found of assessing the relative merits of moral views. It is true, of course, that some philosophers deny it, but for them the present issue cannot arise. In principle, then, I shall take it, people who actually differ may be brought to agree; they will agree in so far as they are rational. They may be brought to see disputed issues in the same light, so that their judgments may fall into line. We can say so, in morals as elsewhere, without prejudice to the actual limits that ignorance and different forms of irrationality are bound to set; and again, we can claim to make certain definitive judgments without claiming that every question that can be asked admits of a single precise answer. Here, as in other fields, we may have to be content with a range within which the right answer is to fall.

Suppose now that our general thesis is denied: what a critic will need, as a counter-example, will be a work of literature at once embodying a false morality and presenting a subtly coherent and rich organisation of its material. The material, I suppose, will be human life, for otherwise no moral questions arise (or if a poem or a fantasy treats of the life of spirits or animals, they will at least be interpreted in human terms). Now if the morality is false its meaning must be such that it can be shown. Something must be suppressed or distorted, acts or characters set in false light—which a different presentation would correct. For otherwise we are not in a position to call it false. Our problem, then, is to establish a point of view: argument in general, and in particular moral argument, apart from straightforward inconsistency and verifiable factual error—both of which presuppose conceptual systems or points of view already established—consists precisely in this. Features previously obscured are brought to light: we 'cut out a new pattern', as Wisdom says—and that must be what we shall attempt here. If, then, we are to succeed in establishing that the morality offered us in the work is false, we must show that some feature is falsified; some aspect of the situation, as the picture stands, is glossed over or misrepresented. But if so, we must ask how we can know it. It cannot be only from our knowledge of life apart from this representation; if something is lacking, as we are supposing, it is lacking within the work itself. But to say that is to say that the picture is internally incoherent; some particular aspect must jar with what—on the strength of the rest—we claim a right to demand. And here the moral fault that we have found will count as an aesthetic fault too.

It is sometimes said, and not without reason, that in approaching a work of literature we should first—as it were hypothetically—adopt the author's own point of view; we should set aside our moral commitments and seek to see the story as he did. This, I say, is a reasonable approach; some initial detachment of this sort is the precondition of any free receptivity. It has also its limits, however. Some judgments must be possible on any view, and some works will be condemned as incoherent. But let us ask in what terms that could be said. An advocate of this uncommitted approach, of moral neutrality, might answer that we must first identify ourselves with the author's outlook, see the picture in his terms, and then judge. We may find it discordant after all, but we shall judge it from within and not without. That answer may sound plausible; and I suppose that there need be no special difficulty in discovering the outlook with which we are to identify ourselves. But let us ask how we are to do so. Doubtless we may use biographical or historical aids, but there is no need to argue that in the last resort we must find it within the work itself. What we find there may very well not agree with views generally current at the time, nor even with the author's own views expressed elsewhere. Now our hypothesis is that the work fails; the view or the vision that it presents proves to be internally faulty, the picture is incoherent in itself. But in saying so we appeal to our own vision: in the last resort we are bound to appeal to it if we are to make critical judgments at all. For the fact that we find a discrepancy where, in the author's own view, presumably, none existed, will otherwise indicate no more than that we have failed to see the picture as he did: we have failed to identify ourselves with his point of view. If so the very notion of a discrepancy disappears—and with it the notion of coherence or organisation too.

I shall only add a few reservations. First I have not said that aesthetic and moral value always coincide, only that where they diverge other reasons are required to account for it. Again we must bear in mind that a sound or even a profound moralist need not possess the literary gifts to embody his vision in concrete form—though this, certainly, leaves much still to be said of the relation of abstract to concrete moralising, or of the possibility of abstract moral truth. For I have no doubt that this possibility remains. More also needs to be said of the specific excellence of representation, namely truth to life, and of the relation of true representation to moral judgment or moral perception: I do not mean to minimise these problems. Finally let me remark that human life is not such that widely different points of view may not be adopted and expressed by equally serious and honest men; and we may value the imaginative embodiment, the aesthetic projection, of each alike. A similar situation will be found in another no less familiar field—that of philosophy itself.

4

Milton and Critical Method

The most interpreted book in the world is, I dare say, still the Bible; but its lead is no longer as sure as it used to be. Since English got a place in the universities and the new race of academic critics, not long after, mastered the ancient art of interpretation, the picture has changed; the classics of modern literature, Shakespeare first and Milton gaining, must challenge it before long. Joseph H. Summers's book is called *The Muse's Method*; for students of the critic's methods it is at least equally rewarding—and Jackson Cope's work presents us with the same sort of method only carried rather further: about to the limit, I should say. Against both we may set the work of H. R. Swardson, whose critical approach is relatively conservative, and whose findings stand directly opposed to theirs.[1] He gives us, that is to say, a very different impression of *Paradise Lost* itself, as well as of the right way of studying it. It would doubtless be easier if we could separate the two issues; it is hard to discuss 'meta-criticism' coolly where the critical points themselves are already so controversial. But, of course, they are really inseparable. Milton, in some quarters, has been pretty freely denigrated in recent years, and his champions, understandably, feel strongly; moreover there may always be religious as well as literary issues involved. But we should gain nothing by shirking these difficulties or glossing them over. For Cope and Summers offer a defence, or rather an apotheosis, of a poet in whose vision of God, sin, justice and unfallen humanity flaws have been noted, discrepancies brought into view (Swardson spotlights some of them); and they defend him by critical methods that, roughly speaking, can accommodate anything. The poet, it would seem, can do no wrong; worse, he can write nothing insignificant; every word bears its triple metaphorical and metaphysical load. Equipped by modern criticism with the tools—this for us is the issue—they read the works of Milton, where faults have been found in them, in the spirit in which Pope read the works of God:

[1] Joseph H. Summers, *The Muse's Method. An Introduction to Paradise Lost* (London, 1962); Jackson I. Cope, *The Metaphoric Structure of Paradise Lost* (London, 1962); H. R. Swardson, *Poetry and the Fountain of Light* (London, 1962).

All nature is but art, unknown to thee;
All chance, direction, which thou canst not see;
All discord, harmony not understood;
All partial evil, universal good.[2]

Since Milton, even the flawed original Milton, is a very great poet, there is some call for protest; quite apart from any question of critical method.

To begin with Summers—whose work, incidentally, is much the better of the two: his lucid English is a pleasure to read (Cope's is a kind of quagmire); more, he brings real sensibility to the poetry, and cares for it as poetry, not simply as suitable material for interpretation to work on. He writes excellently of the qualities of Milton's verse, of its variety of pace and movement, of direction and tone—all pivoting on his miraculous syntax—which make it inexhaustibly surprising, permanently readable: so that Pope in *The Dunciad* quotes it as Bentley's grand achievement that his unwearied pains 'made Milton *dull'*—as though that were to do the impossible. 'Miltonic' ought not to mean 'sublime'—or not that only: it ought to mean sublime, lyrical, tender, colloquial, terse—above all, various. But to satisfy the twentieth century it is perhaps best to stress the colloquialism, a quality which has been said to be wholly foreign to him—which we find, however, above all where it properly belongs, for instance in the mutual recriminations, after the intoxication has worn off, of the fallen Adam and Eve. Summers has a fine analysis of the evening hymn in Book iii, with its woven themes of rising and falling (here the method brings real rewards) and he writes well of the psychology of Adam's temptation and fall.

With his treatment of the allegory of Sin and Death his distinctive method—or the new method in general, for it was earlier used by Arnold Stein—appears more clearly. Milton has been censured for mixing substantial figures with allegorical ones, Satan with Sin and Death. Satan encounters this pair, his child and grandchild as he shortly learns, early on his journey, at the gate of Hell. Death stops his path and everything is set for a heroic conflict, when Sin intervenes—rushes between them clamouring, according to Summers, with all the sentiments of an operatic heroine. And the ludicrous effect is intentional: 'the sudden reduction of the action from the civil, military and mythological to the domestic is essentially comic' (p. 46). (Incidentally, why on earth? The involvement of public with private themes, one would rather have thought, is eminently typical of the heroic style.)

[2] *Essay on Man* i. 289–292.

The story Sin tells is grotesque too: she refers in delicate circumlocutions to her incestuous relations with Satan and her subsequent rape at the hands (or other indistinguishable members) of Death, her own unnatural progeny. She is, unlike Adam and Milton himself, prudish and nice; she professes fine filial sentiments to her father-lover. Lastly, she anticipates, with the success of his voyage, the glorious time when Satan shall reign—Milton is certainly working out his hellish parody of Heaven—with her at his side: 'At thy right hand voluptuous, as beseems/Thy darling and thy daughter, without end' (ii. 869–70). With which lines (we are told) 'the high point of comedy' is reached (p. 53)—the high point, I suppose, like Falstaff's famous: 'Why, hear you, my masters, was it for me to kill the heir-apparent?'—though the comedy is a shade more elusive, perhaps. Her final grotesque appearance (in this episode) 'towards the Gate rouling her bestial train' (ii. 873) is claimed as endorsing this reading.

Milton is not heroic here but mock-heroic: it did not need Pope to deflate him; he had already, subtly and consciously, done the work of deflation for himself. The heroism of Hell, the grand debate, and the splendour of Satan's defiance to which we responded in Book i, all this, with a sudden change of perspective, is dwarfed and made ludicrous. So it is from a true transcendental viewpoint; Satan is an impotent and unreal goblin, breathing empty defiance. God has him 'in derision', we shall learn, and securely 'laughs at his vain designes' (v. 734–5). This is the moral, then: the Christian view transcends the heroic. Arnold Stein, as I mentioned, defended the war in heaven, the self-healing spirituous bodies which tickled Pope ('Fate urged the shears, and cut the sylph in twain,/But airy substance soon unites again') by similar manoeuvres. It is all a heroic mock-battle, a battle fought—though the rebels blindly refuse to see it—against an omnipotent opponent. As to the mixing of allegory with history, Summers has a still more ingenious reply: Satan himself is half unreal, '*all* the inhabitants of Hell [not only Sin and Death, that is to say] approach non-entity: they represent a denial of proper being, perversion as well as unfulfilment' (pp. 54–5). I think it is in support of this metaphysical reading—though his comment is somewhat obscure—that Summers quotes a passage from Book ii (which we may well be grateful for having recalled): the description of the infernal exploration, 'o're many a frozen, many a Fierie Alpe', which penetrates a region,

> A Universe of death, which God by curse
> Created evil, for evil only good;
> Where all life dies, death lives, and Nature breeds,
> Perverse, all monstrous, all prodigious things,

Abominable, inutterable, and worse
Than Fables yet have feign'd, or fear conceiv'd,
Gorgons and *Hydras*, and *Chimeras* dire. (ii. 620–8)

I am not sure that I really understand the suggestion that Satan
'approaches non-entity'. Indeed there is a metaphysical doctrine that
error and evil are unreal—ultimately unreal, being only the fragmenta-
tion in finite minds, or constituting finite minds, of a vision that is
unified in the Absolute, in a Spinozistic *Deus sive Natura*. How the
eminently personal deity of *Paradise Lost* can inflict unreal (though eter-
nal) torture for unreal sin, is harder to see. Milton, of course, may have
meant it, but if so he was a pretty bad metaphysician; and I challenge
anyone to read *Paradise Lost*, keeping hold on the vision actually shown
us, and think of Satan as a fragment of God's mind. Besides, we have
seen those tortures and we know better; inhabitants of Hell are rightly
unimpressed when you tell them that evil is unreal. And not being
unreal, it is not ludicrous.

We had best honestly add that Empson is plainly right; that tortur-
ing your helpless enemies and laughing at them—even unrepentant
sinners—is not a sort of behaviour usually thought of as human, far
less divine. Milton himself calls it 'justice', but which theory of justice
will support him? Not a utilitarian theory, obviously; nor a deon-
tological one either. Even if, with David Ross, you claim to know intuitively (an intuition that some of us lack) that wrong-doers ought to
suffer proportionately, yet no sin is proportionate to endless suffering.
The difficulty is flagrant enough; and one sometimes wonders how far
those critics who find a perfect moral vision, a perfect harmony orches-
trated in *Paradise Lost*, yet never mention it, can be in earnest about the
problems that they seem to treat as most serious.

I have selected the episode at Hell Gate as typical of Summers's
work. The scene as he depicts it is made so lively, the detail chosen and
pointed with such skill, as to send the reader—one reader at
least—back to the text, wondering how he could have missed anything
so obvious, where, alas, the impression dissolves: it just won't read
mock-heroically. The tone is continuous with what went before; the
passages Summers re-sets with apt epithets—with vivid glosses such as
'Sin is incapable of being low; she modulates immediately into injured
innocence' (p. 49)—fall back into place. I have played the same trick
back on Summers, somewhat unfairly; but the only alternative would
have been to quote both Milton's passage and his commentary in full.

Of Cope's work I shall have to confine myself to a few samples of
approach and method. I have read somewhere the complaint that
Waldock insists on reading *Paradise Lost* as if it were a modern novel.

Cope insists on reading it as if it were *Finnegans Wake*. This is not just a jibe, an irony of mine: he virtually says so himself. At least he appeals to the analogy to rebut Tillyard's 'linear', 'progressive' and Aristotelian reading. (Tillyard has the fine remark that Milton 'domesticated' the heroic poem, making the climax the reconciliation of Adam and Eve. Cope will hear nothing of a *climax*. Whatever you are, don't be linear and Aristotelian.) By an odd trick of imagination, it must be, I keep finding myself thinking of Thomas Gradgrind; I can hardly resist adapting the first sentence of *Hard Times* . 'Now, what I want are Images. Teach these boys and girls nothing but Images. Images alone are wanted in literary criticism. Plant nothing else, and root out everything else . . .' What is really wanted, I fear, is less throwing about of criticial machinery; less talk of the modern mythic consciousness and metaphoric what-have-you and the realising of time in spatial terms; more ordinary all-round literary sensibility, and a sane right-way-up approach to the poem as a whole. Some of the *impedimenta* might also have been left behind—I mean the baggage-train of learning—or only brought up when something really relevant was to be got from it. It is sad to see so much learning with so little light.

I proceed to examples. At the unfolding of the gates of Hell, Sin and Satan first look out upon Chaos, described by Milton as 'a dark/Illimitable Ocean without bound' (ii. 891–2). An image, one might feel, in itself unremarkable: of course no other poet could have written the whole passage as Milton did, but whoever wrote it the comparison of Chaos to an ocean must surely have suggested itself. Cope's view is different. 'The old metaphor of the raging sea should alert us,' he writes (p. 55); (Cope being easily alerted where images are concerned, trigger-happy, one might say. Milton, incidentally, never says a *raging* sea; he only calls it 'dark' and 'illimitable'.) The moral we should draw, it would seem, is that Chaos resembles Heaven in one respect: that space and time are concepts we cannot apply to it. 'Having validated icons by looking with self-idolatory into the mirror provided by Sin, Satan has validated also the medium in which icons must exist, the medium in which his spiritial distance from the "Most High" must be perceived in the image of the fall: space' (p. 56). All this so that 'the structure of the divine irony can finally be realised': to wit, that God said—but could not really have meant—that He created Man to replace the fallen angels. Man was set upon the earth; earth is spacial; and space, apparently, is the proper element of Satan. But God will turn it all to His glory.

We were speaking just now of unnatural births, chimeras and prodigies. If this writing were merely exceptional, an isolated freak in modern criticism, I should not quote it; but it is representative of what students are given who come to universities to study literature—of one large class of criticism at least. A good course, perhaps, will be to contrast it at once with the legitimate pursuit of similar interests; and happily there are better things in Cope's book as well. What we need, to treat imagery as symbolic—to justify such treatment and, more particularly, to test given readings—is some extrinsic evidence to appeal to. Now *Paradise Lost* is certainly a poem about the Fall; and hence the recurrent imagery of rising and falling is the most promising strand. It seems further that the paradox of the 'fortunate fall', so popular at the time, was never far from Milton's mind: it is hinted at early and towards the end, through Adam's mouth, made all but explicit. So far we are on fairly firm ground. Yet criticism does not end here: it does not suffice to gather images, though images be as plentiful as blackberries, nor even to interpret them; we are studying a poem, the whole imaginative projection of a vision, and we shall want to know how they contribute to it. To see that we must look beyond imagery. The paradox is of rising through descent, of spiritual gain through humiliation. We know, also, what humility sounds like; we think, for example, of *King Lear*. Only at rare moments, it seems to me, notably in Eve's great speech in Book ix and her final words in Book xii, does Milton convincingly catch that accent; he commands every other human tone, but rarely this. (It may be that speaking through a woman's mouth, whose lower status he so firmly insists on, he was able to draw on a part of himself, a layer of his own personality, not otherwise open to him.) Imagery has significance in a work such as *Paradise Lost*—poetic significance—so far as it takes up and echoes what is embodied in the main action and the characters.

I have not space to deal properly with Cope's refacing—plaster for brick—of Milton's God. Like Summers he welcomes Stein's interpretation of the war in Heaven, and seizes on the method—which is indeed a godsend for critics of this sort. But he rather surprises us by rejecting, though he finds it 'impressive', the view that God speaks non-rhetorically, tonelessly, to symbolise His unique status, His omniscience and godhead. Here Cope's scholarship serves him well; for the passage, he shows, is thick with rhetorical figures. Still, it is worth noticing as a warning of where interpretation can lead; and our interest is more in a critical style than in individual critics. (The staginess of Edith Dombey, which critics complain of, has its place, for all I know, in the mythic structure of *Dombey and Son*; it symbolises her essentially unreal, unidimensional or theatrical role.) Cope's own view is that God by a 'decorous synecdoche' becomes a metaphorical—all-seeing, all-generative—eye: which, so far, may be true; but how it helps us with that all-too-recognisably human voice, sometimes jeering and sometimes grand, but bent mostly of self-vindication, is not clear to me.

We turn finally, perhaps not without relief, to the work of Swardson; as one might descend from a switchback to stand again on the familiar steady earth. His treatment of Milton is only a single chapter in a book devoted to a wider theme: the divided heritage, the Christian tradition and the classical, which seventeenth-century poets strove to reconcile. Milton among them—in this like his great opponents in the public sphere, the English Catholics—inherited the problems of a dual allegiance: Milton more than anyone, who made it his task to write a Christian epic, a Homeric or Virgilian poem on the Fall of Man. He surely knew the nature of his undertaking, 'above heroic' he calls it; complaining too—though here doubts suggest themselves—of the traditional battles, races and games and other epic subject-matter: 'the better fortitude/Of Patience and Heroic Martyrdom/Unsung' (ix. 31–3)—doubts, I say, because this description squares so imperfectly with the actual content of *Paradise Lost*. He constantly invokes, with careful qualification, the 'fabl'd' or 'feign'd' gods and goddess, so that their ideal glamour may invest the sacred, historical action. In spite of everything the two traditions fall apart; such is Swardson's contention. For God, the invisible author and omniscient mind of the universe, put into a heroic poem can only appear as a generalissimo, the chief of one great party—whose side we are on, so to speak. A heroic poem must be filled with 'martial bustle' (Swardson's phrase). Even before the revolt in Heaven it is much in evidence; we hear, for instance, of 'Ten thousand, thousand Ensignes high advanc'd' (v. 588); and later we find the 'unarmed Youth of Heav'n' seeking recreation (despite Milton's sneer in Book ix) in 'Heroic Games' while 'Celestial Armourie, Shields, Helmes, and Speares' hang nearby (iv. 551 and 3)—all which, surely, makes little or no sense in Christian terms.

Incongruities such as these, of course, are just what the new art of interpretation—or new application of an old art—is used by Stein and Summers to remove. Meanings are everywhere, and allegorical meanings where literal ones fail. Milton has deliberately 'placed' the heroic tradition: hence the war in heaven, which is calculatedly absurd. Now we have found Milton not always very accurate in his own programmatic statements; but for the rest Swardson has no difficulty in showing that if military activity is absurd in a Christian Heaven, God is no less implicated than Satan. There is military show in abundance before Satan's revolt. And later we hear, for instance, how Raphael was sent 'Squar'd in full Legion (such command we had)' during the creation of the earth to watch the gate of Hell and ensure that no evil spirit broke out. This was God's order 'Least hee incent at such eruption bold/Destruction with Creation might have mixt' (viii. 234–5). God, it would seem, being interrupted, might spoil His own work in a fit of temper (you always have to be careful with the Boss); which is no more meaningful in Christian terms than that Omnipotence should need Raphael to prevent it—which latter point Milton recollects; but hardly mends matters by turning the expedition into a military exercise designed to test discipline. Yet another mock-battle in the cosmos. Or take Gabriel defying Satan (who has been discovered in Eden):

> who more than thou
> Once fawn'd, and cring'd, and servilly ador'd
> Heav'ns awful Monarch? (iv. 957–60)

Now granting that this is a lively description, that epic encounters which wholly eschewed such writing would be hard to manage, we may still ask how far—*Paradise Lost* being a Christian poem—we are to take it seriously. If we do, we must try to give meaning to servile adoration of God—adoration which can hardly be pleasing to Him. Perhaps we can. But Satan is to be thought of as fawning and cringing—watched contemptuously, perhaps jealously too, by Gabriel and others—before the Throne. How, then, did the Monarch respond? But it only gets worse the farther we go; Milton has slipped into the notion of an earthly potentate.

Milton's interpreters, it appears, have matter to keep them occupied for a long while yet. I wish rather to ask, not how to manufacture interpretations—that no longer presents difficulties, the greater danger is overproduction—but how to test them. It is a curious thing, surely, that in a period in which methodologists elsewhere have been occupied—almost obsessed—with problems of tests and controls, falsifaction and so forth, so many critics seem never to have heard of them. The first general point to be noticed is only this, that the human mind is an interpretative instrument; this is its instinct and bent, it looks everywhere for pattern and meaning—and, generally speaking, it finds them. It finds them in prophecies and biblical texts; in flights of birds or leaves left in tea-cups; in imagery from dreams or from Milton; briefly, in whatever material you offer it. In fact we can generally find not only one pattern but half a dozen; which, of course, is precisely the snag, for we so far have no way of choosing between them. And this is the end of the story, the farthest we can get, unless we can find other tests to appeal to.

So with the interpretation of poetic imagery: there is no problem in combing texts for images, and no great problem in 'interpreting' them—that is, assigning symbolic values. Our tolerance here is pretty wide; we have no rigorous criteria so there is generally a fair range of things with an equally reasonable claim to be counted as the meaning of any image. Last, manipulating these counters we must work them into some pattern that can be read as tantamount to a 'statement' or theme; and this, given the elastic rules of the game, presents no great difficulty either—at least, not once you have learnt the general trick. What you have, then, is an interpretation that fits—fitting being defined as above—the original data: and this, so far, constitutes no achievement in criticism whatever. We might, rather roughly, compare it to an untested scientific hypothesis.

I have already indicated one place at least in which we can look for further tests. We should start with what is not in dispute: *Paradise Lost* is certainly about the Fall of Man, and at least two passages refer, pretty explicitly, to the paradox of the 'fortunate fall'. In a sense the best we can do with imagery is to tie it to the main action; if we find recurrent imagery of rising and falling in a poem of this sort, it is no great stretch to give it a special significance. But of course it can acquire it in other ways too. Images may have a symbolic significance, ready for use, outside the poem; a symbol may be the common property of a culture. Or, failing that, a writer may pause or work on it to give it significance; he may establish his symbols within the poem. (Or we may find both: the river, symbolising time, in the *Dry Salvages*, is in effect a public symbol; and Eliot also fixes it, as well as deepening it, within the poem.) This is not to say that poets never write in what we may call a private symbolism, without working in this way to establish their symbols; on the contrary, in our time especially, it has been rather common. But if so, what they write is bad poetry; for poetry must exist as a public object or not at all.

One further distinction. Imagery undoubtedly makes up a large part of the substance of poetry: it works on the reader's sensibility along with rhythm, tone, structure, for instance, or the interplay of mere sound and meaning, contributing imperceptibly to the whole effect. And this is the normal use of imagery in poetry: a thing radically different from the use of explicit symbols or symbolic images, which have to be interpreted to be understood. These latter can only exist—that is, exist objectively, in the poem as distinct from the poet's intention—where their meaning is fixed, where they are more or less pointedly focused or underlined.

The problems raised by Summers's reading of the episode at Hell Gate are more elusive; and, of course, there is no ultimate test other than the text itself, carefully re-examined, and sensitive reading. 'Ultimate', however, needs to be stressed; we need not yet abandon hope of further guiding principles anywhere. We can, for one thing, make explicit the principles which any particular reading presupposes, and test them by looking at the consequences of applying them elsewhere. And, naturally, we can look within the poem for other passages bearing on this; we can try out our reading there too. In the present case we have, in effect, tried and got the results of that test already: Summers finds a special account to remove one anomaly; Swardson points out half a dozen others. What is still more convincing, his explanation is general; they all flow from one cause, namely the tension between Milton's Christian material and classical form. Summers's account, then, cannot be generalised; Swardson's can.

In Summers, however, there are two distinct positions to be distinguished which have an air of lending each other support and conversely, perhaps, lean on each other too. The fall of either might bring the other down with it. He finds first, in this episode, a shift of tone—from the heroic it moves abruptly to the mock-heroic—and secondly a metaphysical parable. At least the former, surely, it may be said, calls for no special comment: a poet can move from one key to another, or a critic point out such transitions, without being asked to cite special methodological principles. And examples could easily be added, though examples (our opponent will go on) seem somewhat superfluous. It is just part of imaginative writing; Shakespeare's plays abound in such changes. *A Midsummer Night's Dream*, for instance, moves between three worlds, those of the courtiers, of the fairies and of the 'rude mechanicals' of Athens. Or Plato's Socratic Dialogues, with their play of tone, their shifting level of seriousness, might serve to provide examples of similar differences less explicitly drawn.

Even so the case before us seems to me to deserve a little more scrutiny. The transition Summers finds is pretty radical—from black to white, in effect; the heroic style is turned inside out; and further, it comes wholly without warning. The verse is continuous, and so is the action. We simply follow Satan on his voyage. The different worlds of *A Midsummer Night's Dream* are each well established, with their own characters and even their own style of language, verse or prose, before they are allowed to overflow. And as to Plato, though particular shifts come without warning, yet we are repeatedly warned to beware of Socrates; we know of his irony; and in difficult cases, as in the *Gorgias*, another character may serve as a sort of chorus to help us out. The myths are always clearly marked off; and in the *Republic* we are explicitly warned when the goddess speaks 'mysteriously and in jest'. In the *Ion*, I suppose, we need no warning: Socrates explains that during his own oratorical performance he was literally inspired—that is, mad—and hence cannot remember what he said. Plato may have been half in earnest, half in jest, in his theory of inspiration; but if Summers could point to anything as clear or nearly as clear as this, I might acquiesce in his reading. But the lines 'Retire, or taste thy folly, and learn by proof,/Hell-born, not to contend with Spirits of Heav'n' (686–7) do not seem to me very plainly to 'verge on the comic' (p. 47).

Summers, however, goes much further: his reading not only requires a sudden and absolute reversal of tone; Milton, with the introduction of the allegory, is supposed to break through the very form of his own poem, using the form, and the break in the form, to make a substantial metaphysical point. Now the objection here is first the old and obvious one to any critic who imports, from his own intellectual stock, material which is not actually in the poem at all. Recondite metaphysical theses are to be touched off by obscure hints—as Cope was 'alerted' by the word 'ocean'. Milton's weakness was, if anything, an overfondness for pointing morals; and he is at pains to let us know his metaphysical views, where they are relevant, through the mouth of Raphael or of God. His standards, in other words, of what constitutes poetry—publicly or objectively constitutes poetry—seem to have been rather different from Summers's. And rightly. The great passage describing the 'Universe of death' does not say that evil is unreal or only half real; it says that in this region 'nature breeds/Perverse, all monstrous, all prodigious things'.

But, after all, the thing is possible: an artist may break the illusions—like Groucho Marx with 'This is a bright red dress, only technicolor is *so* expensive'—which his own art presupposes. But there, of course, the effect is comic and meant to be comic; and we know what is happening. In general the trick is easiest to play on the stage, where the wall between actors and audience, between make-believe and reality—an invisible wall—is so evident and, as it were, clear-cut. Elsewhere to play such a trick, to play it without warning, with a serious not a ludicrous intent—this seems to presuppose a wonderful understanding between artist and audience, a perfect *rapport*. After the action in Hell we follow Satan on his flight, and first meet allegorical figures—described vividly enough to be real. Now it seems that we are meant to feel the jolt; to guess that since Sin is unreal (allegorical) Satan after all, who encounters her, cannot be wholly real either; finally, recollecting our metaphysics, to see the deep propriety in the anomaly. The point is not that all this, as a matter of historical fact, is extremely unlikely: it is that poetry as a public thing—and otherwise it is nothing—presupposes certain elastic, but not wholly elastic, conventions or rules. This sort of interpretation, consistently applied, would take from us the conditions that make poetry possible.

Beardsley, examining criteria of critical interpretation, makes the suggestion that we should accept whatever reading of a passage makes the best poetry out of it.[3] Now whether Summers's reading really improves the episode at the gates of Hell may be doubted; but at least it removes the anomaly of mixing allegorical figures with 'real' ones. This, then, might be claimed for it; but the proposed criterion, it seems to me, is unworkable anyway. Take any passage of crude rodomontade such as the Restoration heroic drama abounds in; to make the best of it we might treat it as pastiche. It would not make it good, but it would make it better. But on this showing anything can be anything; and, once again, poetry as a recognisable entity disappears.

But to examine this device, a work of art that breaks through its own conventions, the best place to look is in Milton himself; he uses it in *Lycidas*. The voice of St Peter foretelling 'the ruin of our corrupted clergy then in their height' breaks through the pastoral convention, which Milton afterwards re-invokes, closing the interruption with the words,

> Return *Alpheus*, the dread voice is past,
> That shrunk thy streams; Return *Sicilian* Muse.

No doubt he was sailing near the wind, and knew it too. He takes care to let *us* know that he knew it: the change of tone is abrupt and unmistakable, and the poem leaps out of Arcady into contemporary England. Not satisfied with that, Milton gives us explicit notice of the end of the break (in later editions he added a note to the title as well). If any of these features were paralleled in the passage from *Paradise Lost*, the interpretation could claim some basis; the notable thing is their absence.

Criticism is, or should be, a serious discipline, a different thing from advocacy. The high point of the advocate's art is so to present his case as not even to draw attention to its weaknesses by defending them; to state the issue so as to bypass them from the start. The whole poem for Summers, I have said, is a great moral parable: a thousand visions, shifting perspectives, contained and harmonised within a single vision. His ear, moreover, is so finely attuned that not even inaudible harmonies pass him by. Now most readers have been shocked by certain painful discords; and here, all of a sudden, he is wonderfully deaf. He only keeps hold (he might perhaps answer) of the plain moral structure. Which is, as far as I can find, that God is God, because Milton says so, and good, presumably, because he is God. Further, he is omnipotent and laughs at his enemies, being 'secure'; so what Satan does, and what Sin says, is most laughable. The question to ask here, I would

[3] Monroe Beardsley, *The Possibility of Interpretation* (New York, 1973).

suggest, is how the poetry sounds. Gabriel defying Satan sounds exactly like Satan defying Gabriel—or defying Death. They are just on
different sides. Sin complains that God calls his vengeance
'justice'—which must be absurd, since God is just. Yet oddly enough
she has the poet's own authority; for God allowed Satan to rise from
the burning lake so that he might first seduce Man, only to see Man
forgiven,

> but on himself
> Treble confusion, wrath and vengeance pour'd. (i. 219–20)

So it is vengeance after all; moreover it sounds like it. The devils in
Hell, we are told, hold firm concord and rejoice 'in their matchless
Chief' (ii. 487, 496). What is Summers's comment? 'Every emotion
except pure love of God can be corrupted. . . . Parodies and distortions of most of the theological and cardinal virtues can be found in
Hell' (p. 28). Parodies and distortions seem pretty much to the point: a
miraculous balance that comes level whatever the weight of the goods,
a bendable yardstick that adapts—this truly is a critical find. I do not
mean that such a judgment could never be right; a detective might explain a crime where the explanation involved six separate coincidences
and yet be right. I mean that explanations of this sort require—to put it
mildly—special care, suspicion and scrutiny; they are not to be tossed
around like a juggler's balls. Critics, it seems, require to be reminded
that such a subject as methodology exists.

Let us finally glance back at the poem: must we conclude that it is a
bad poem, that Milton after all simply failed? He certainly failed to
project that flawless image which some admirers have hallucinated; but
then, it may be, he never meant to. He failed elsewhere, too: in his
presentation of God, in the war in Heaven, where the heroic fuss, as
Empson observes, is mere fuss, because it is about nothing. Yet we do
not say the same of the action on earth or in Hell, of Satan's defiance or
his despair, of Eve in her physical presence or Eve penitent. What the
action in Heaven chiefly lacks is any credible *mise-en-scène*; it is not
subtle parable, but a morally and metaphysically avoidable lack of
props. We are not allowed to imagine what any personage does
between whiles; we have no detail to fill in the set. (Only compare the
beginnings of conspiracy, angry words and smouldering discontent, in
the first act of *Henry IV, Part I*.) Milton cannot touch on such themes:
Satan, after a single brief speech (whispered to Beelzebub), hurries his
legions under cover of night 'to the quarters of the North'. 'The North'
is not precisely a vividly realised locality. One more short speech, and
that is all we get; emptiness seems to gape all around. But Hell is quite

different: it is a place that we learn about concurrently with Satan himself; and the material setting and martial style do no harm here. There is further perspective too: a background, sufficiently suggested, of a heroic campaign undergone under Satan's leadership—his voice 'heard so oft/In worst extreams' (i. 276–7) cannot fail to rouse the legions—which gives us all we need. (It is only later that we learn that a single day made up all the real fighting; the second being a cannonade, and the third, when the rebels 'all resistance lost', merely a rout.)

Milton's greatness is to be looked for, it seems to me, not in any subtle play of suggested meanings, of moral perspectives; rather it is a gigantic straightforwardness. It is this, that his mind baulks at nothing; every vista of ordinary experience—ordinary, though on a huge scale, and this is his strength—is entered into with tremendous whole-heartedness. The passage quoted earlier is a fair sample, describing the region in Hell which 'God by curse/Created evil', populated by monsters and freaks. Summon Dali or Kafka: the twentieth century has nothing on this. But in a twentieth-century author it would have been all of a piece, his whole range; the rest of the material would have matched. The same poet who described this land of death also described an earthly paradise and celebrated the beauty and mystery of wedded love. All which is no doubt humdrum praise, and old-fashioned, compared to the great coherences recent critics have found: better to be humdrum, I think, and praise things that are really there.

Dryden makes Charles II pray

> From plagues and agues Heav'n defend my years,
> But save me most from my petitioners.

Change the word to 'interpreters' and you have a form of prayer suitable for poets expecting immortal fame.

5

Cleanth Brooks and the New Criticism

There are two reasons that might serve as justifying the close study of a particular thinker; either his weight and importance in himself or the width of his influence on others. And both, I suggest, are relevant to some special examination of the critical theorising of Cleanth Brooks. Brooks has been ungenerously characterised—I recall seeing the phrase somewhere—as a man with a keen nose for a fashionable idea—which is, if you like, true enough. But, I think, the same point might have been put rather differently: his work incorporates and sums up a large tradition, indeed, sums it up and sets it forth systematically; he also quotes and carefully answers his several critics. Brooks, in other words, consciously theorises—among writers in the field a relatively rare and welcome merit. (The great exception is doubtless I. A. Richards; but Richards's ambitious theorising or, to be plain, his preposterously bad pseudo-scientific psychology has little or no connection, as has often been noticed, with his real and great merit as a practical critic.) True, there are theoretical suggestions to be found in Richards too; his would-be neurological model admits of reinterpretation. And Brooks, in fact, has amply acknowledged the debt. His debt to Empson, I shall seek to show, is equally clear. Lastly, the tradition is still much with us, even though Brooks's *The Well Wrought Urn*[1] (the fullest and most orderly setting-forth of his position), which I shall concentrate on, appeared a long time ago; thus Wimsatt, even in his most recent book, *Hateful Contraries*, still declares his broad adherence to the 'tensional' theory, as he calls it—which means in substance, I suppose, the theory of Brooks.[2] It subsists, in a large sense, as the reigning orthodoxy. (Of course Leavis and his powerful following remain on one side, but that would be a study for another occasion.)

At the bottom of it all, in a way—and perhaps as the most acceptable part of it—I possibly ought to notice a looser view; one best represented, I think, by a couple of sentences from the preface to the second edition of Empson's *Seven Types of Ambiguity*:

---

[1] London, 1949.
[2] William K. Wimsatt, Jr, *Hateful Contraries* (New York, 1972).

What I do suppose is that, wherever a receiver of poetry is seriously moved by an apparently simple line, what are moving in him are the traces of a great part of his past experience and the structure of his past judgments. Considering what it feels like to take real pleasure in verse, I should think it surprising, and on the whole rather disagreeable, if even the most searching criticism of such lines of verse could find nothing in their implications to be the cause of so straddling a commotion and so broad a calm.[3]

That we are here in a region of important and potentially fruitful insight need hardly be doubted; though as to its common application some reservations will appear in the sequel. But this at least I shall take as plain: it hardly suffices to talk merely, say, with reference to Burns's or Blake's lyrics, of their 'wonderful simplicity' and nothing more. Thus 'The Cat is on the mat' is wonderfully simple. Something deeper must be moving within or underneath that simplicity; informing it, so to speak; and, I suppose, Brook's account of those further forces is broadly familiar. Underneath lies a tension, and harmonisation, of conflicting—or at least potentially conflicting (a difference I could have wished Brooks to pay more attention to)—or diverse views, feelings or attitudes.

Exposition presents obvious difficulties; I must assume some familiarity with Brooks's work, at least with the poems that he discusses. He himself, as I emphasised, goes to work commendably systematically: first quotes a number of poems, or samples of poetry, in fact nine, from Donne and Shakespeare to Tennyson and Yeats; secondly offers careful analyses of each; and lastly proceeds to theorise, generalising on the basis so thoroughly laid. At most I can attempt to recall briefly one or two of his more typical analyses—analyses, it seems to me, varying greatly in quality: that of Wordsworth's *Westminster Bridge* I find the least satisfactory, and much of Gray's *Elegy* pretty dubious; but that on Herrick seems to me largely excellent, and still more, what I shall give my main attention to, the discussion of Pope's *The Rape of the Lock*.

Our themes, once again, are to be these: conflict, ambiguity (Empson's word), irony and, of course, harmonisation. So to the present case. I recall the *bon mot* with which Disraeli shortly settled the then raging Darwinian controversy: 'The question is whether man is an ape or an angel; I am on the side of the angels.' (Whether or not the angels were on the side of Disraeli has, I believe, still to be disclosed.) The question here, broadly speaking, is whether the poet's heroine, Belinda, is a species of angelic creation, a kind of divinity, or a more or less ordinary young woman with good looks and quite her fair share of

[3] W. Empson, *Seven Types of Ambiguity* (London, 1949), p. xv.

feminine frivolity; at least, over-simplifying, that forms a large part of
the question. And if angelic, Pope asks, (through the mouth of
Clarissa) to what end?

> Say why are beauties praised and honoured most,
> The wise man's passion, and the vain man's toast
> Why decked with all that land and sea afford,
> Why angels called and angel-like adored. . . . ? (v. 9–12)

Both views are, let me stress, visible *there*, are things that the poem
makes real to us; and the conflict between them, at least a prima facie
conflict, whatever we hear of 'harmonisation', hardly needs underlining.

Brooks enters into details of all sorts, which I shall have to skirt lightly, but a few words on the recurrent analogy of the sun, which may
either typify the heroine's serene self-sufficiency or alternatively her
self-admiring and easy-going non-commitment, seem in order. It
appears from the start of the action:

> Sol through white curtains shot a timorous ray
> And oped those eyes that must obscure the day . . . (i. 13–14)

(The stock Romantic analogy equating the lady's eyes with that
heavenly luminary.) And again the sun rises 'not with more glory'

> Than issuing forth the rival of his beams
> Launched on the bosom of the silver Thames. (ii. 3–4)

And finally, at the very end of the poem (on the supposed stellar
translation of Belinda's 'ravished hair'):

> For, after all the murders of your eye,
> When, after millions slain, yourself must die:
> When those fair suns are set, as set they must,
> And all those tresses shall be laid in dust,
> This lock the muse shall consecrate to fame,
> And mid the stars inscribe Belinda's name. (v. 145–50)

Brooks's comment here, apt enough it seems to me, is that whether or
not the poet took his heroic wholly seriously, his seriousness in one
particular is hardly in doubt; namely, concerning his own poetic name,
indeed immortality. He made that promise of lasting memory, meant
it, and magnificently kept it. Arabella Fermour, Belinda's original,
died somewhat over two hundred years ago and was buried in a village

in Hertfordshire, in a parish church where not even her monument remains. (The church was remodelled some time during the last century.) But one thing remains, that sable tress, eternally severed from the lustrous profession of its fellowship, that everyone still knows of: 'This lock the muse shall consecrate to fame'.

Brooks deals, too, illuminatingly and at length, with the metaphor of rape written into the poem's very title, and with the war of the sexes depicted in Canto iv, asking how seriously we are in fact meant to take it all. But that issue, which I cannot linger on, leads me to the main point, which for Brooks is the poet's attitude to a certain central virtue, namely chastity. He believed in it, certainly; but Pope, Brooks insists, was a good humanist. He believed in it as a negative virtue; not, in other words, as something meant for keeps. To finish the quotation I began earlier from Clarissa's speech, in which Brooks finds (so far as such a thing could admit of abstraction) the main moral of the poem: to what end serve all this allurement and adornment 'unless good sense preserve what beauty gains'? The point is, doubtless, precisely what beauty gains; in other words the attraction of the opposite sex, and ultimately marriage and motherhood; to all of which, we gather, despite his apparent lightness of tone, Pope's attitude is profoundly serious.

I have hardly begun to do justice to the detail and fineness of Brooks's analysis. Perhaps, just before passing on, it is worth noticing that Pope can afford an eastward glance towards the busy world of the City, where 'The merchant from the exchange returns in peace', and even towards Tyburn, without detriment to his own perfect toy scene set up in Hampton Court. There is no suggestion of callousness in the contrast; his sureness of touch precludes that. Rather the thrills of a game of ombre and the agonies of the rape of a lock of hair are set in vivid but diminutive perspective (one recalls, perhaps, the first book of *Gulliver's Travels*).

But to proceed to our own more proper business, namely the larger theoretical-critical moral that Brooks draws: all we see here, built into the poem, is in effect a whole complex of attitudes; that is many relatively simple attitudes taken together, simultaneous in tension and in harmony; a harmony—the great point—properly to be grasped in nothing short of the whole poem. We may attempt, Brooks himself indeed has attempted, something by way of abstract statement, that is some statement of the same sort of position; such a statement, however, is no more than a skeleton of the thing itself. But I had best, perhaps, quote Brooks's own words, turning to the chapter called 'The Heresy of Paraphrase'. The enemy here, so to speak, is the theorist who distinguishes first poetic 'content' (what *per impossibile* an adequate abstract statement would paraphrase) from, secondly, what the poet presumably—his special poetic expertise—pours or moulds it into; some appropriate 'form'. Now that 'content', on a Brooksian approach, is just one single aspect among others; you can abstract any aspect you please. What matters after all is the whole thing, the poem itself, and the meaning of the poem qua poem, its poetic or imaginative meaning, which inheres in nothing less than the whole—not, in other words, in any abstractable 'content'. Thus he writes:

> though it is in terms of structure that we must describe poetry, the term 'structure' is not a wholly satisfactory term. One means by it something far more internal than the metrical pattern, say, or sequence of images . . . [nor] certainly 'form' in the conventional sense in which we think of 'form' as a kind of envelope which 'contains' the 'content'. The structure is obviously conditioned by the very nature of the material which goes into the poem. The nature of the material sets the problem to be solved, and the solution is the ordering of the material.[4]

And again:

> The unity is not unity of a sort to be achieved by the reduction and simplification appropriate to an algebraic formula. It is a positive unity, not a negative; it represents not a residue but an achieved harmony.[5]

Brooks goes on to recall—I spoke of his place within and virtual summing-up of a tradition, a theoretical movement at least—the variety of terms, more or less familiar, pointing in the same way: Empson's *ambiguity, paradox, complexity* (of attitudes), *irony* (his own earlier favourite), and so on. To extend the list, we saw, Wimsatt has since added *tension*.

One other example, briefly at least, before passing on. Brooks finds in Herrick's *Corinna's Going A-Maying* a crucial tension—what we might expect him to find—between the poet's explicit Christianity and the pagan imagery that none the less runs throughout. So the question is this: Are we innocently and unquestioningly to fall in with the 'harmless folly of the time', or to treat it as—if we treat the poem seriously at all, it is hard not to treat it—something much more than harmless folly? The latter of course yields just the sort of reading Brooks's whole theory demands; and to get the poem's meaning qua poem, once again, there is no way but to read it or re-read it as a whole.

[4] Cleanth Brooks, *The Well-Wrought Urn* (London, 1949), p. 178.
[5] Ibid., p. 179.

Brooks, I said, shows careful and commendable candour in setting out and answering his own critics, the critics of his earlier work; answering them largely successfully, it seems to me (with the possible exception of Winters), inasmuch as, I suspect, they themselves have not quite succeeded in articulating what perhaps underlies their real criticisms. First Brooks quotes from Herbert Muller, who complains that the critic-theorist

> considers only technique, mechanism, outward show. He overlooks the unifying attitudes, the world of view, the quality of mind, the inform-ing spirit—all that . . . enables a Shakespeare or a Goethe to be as simple, forthright and eloquent as he pleases.[6]

Once again I can perhaps do no better than give Brooks's answer in his own words:

> to say that Shakespeare could be as simple as he pleased suggests the poetry resides in certain truthful or exalted statements which need only to be stated simply and forthrightly. But the assumption, as Muller himself knows, is desperate; and on this assumption one could never explain why such a poetic material, when stated in clear expository prose is not poetry, or why only those who are great poets have managed to locate and exploit such 'poetic material'.[7]

But the adjective 'eloquent' is what Brooks chiefly falls foul of: for he sees it as fatally reinstating the vicious dichotomy of 'form' and 'con-tent'. Poetry proper will either reside in mere externals, 'eloquent' form; or alternatively, the other horn of the dilemma, in some suffi-ciently exalted body of moral or philosophical truth, which it then clothes in fitting finery; appropriate poetical 'form'. We can hardly deny that Muller's own language invites some such criticism. Consider his contrast of 'informing spirit' and 'outward show'—tell-tale phrases which reveal his real thought. Another critic dealt with, Donald Stauffer, makes it his main objection that Brooks, fixated with com-plexity, has no room for truly simple poetry, one familiar Romantic ideal; all the stress is on conflict and diversity. Once again I shall give Brooks's answer in his own words. If the statement means

> that a poet may be able to write without giving a sense of pom-posity—that he can give a sense of casual and simple directness—the point may be granted at once. If the statement means that the poet can

---

[6] Quoted in Cleanth Brooks, op. cit., p. 205.
[7] Ibid., p. 205.

make his poem *one* by reducing to order the confusions and disorders
and irrelevancies of ordinary experience in terms of one unifying insight, granted again.[8]

But Stauffer, it would seem, wants simple matter simply stated; and
then, as I said at the start, any child's reading book furnishes an abundance of unimpeachable examples: though I fear that Brooks's own
talk of 'unifying insight' is more like a papering over of the cracks than
a probing for the underlying theoretical strains and stresses that they
may indicate.

To summarise and repeat: the whole poem embodies and unifies a
potentiality of conflicting attitudes, than which anything less is more or
less as arbitrary limitation; for it will not be anything that can helpfully
be called a paraphrase, a statement of the 'content', but an abstract or
aspect and nothing more.

Here, however, Brooks faces a difficulty, and I fear a serious one.
After all, what has he himself been doing, at least attempting, in all
that has gone before—for instance in his analysis, outlined above, of
The Rape of the Lock? He cannot be wholly unaware of it; he is too
scrupulous a thinker. In fact he seeks to meet it—rather, one might
fear, to brush it aside—in a footnote; a long footnote, but important
enough, I think, to quote, at least the first half, in full:

> We may, it is true, be able to adumbrate what the poem says if we
> allow ourselves enough words, if we make enough reservations and
> qualifications, we attempt to come nearer the meaning of the poem by
> successive approximations and refinements, gradually encompassing
> the meaning and pin-pointing the area in which it lies rather than
> realising it.[9]

All this deserves looking at. Let me pick on two words, first 'approximation' (the critic gets nearer the meaning of the poem by 'successive
approximations . . .') and, still more important, that final 'realising'.
But for the former, it is plainly false: criticism can be refined or
developed as much as you like, there is nothing of approximation or
anything resembling approximation in the case. Criticism remains
criticism, its own literary mode with its own function, poetry poetry.
Otherwise we might contemplate our reaching the point where we
should say: 'Having now the advantage of Brooks's analysis (or that of
some later critic), we can forget about that antic eighteenth-century
poet and his mock heroic poem in five cantos, *The Rape of the Lock*';
which, in Euclid's phrase, is absurd. The second significant word I

[8] Ibid., p. 203.
[9] Ibid., p. 188n.

spoke of came at the end of the passage quoted: Brooks writes of pin-pointing the area of meaning rather than 'realising' it. It is not acciden-tal; he needs some such addendum. For why, after all, is Brooks's first claim, at least, as we saw, his implicit claim, foredoomed to failure? Why can criticism, however adequate as criticism, never take the place of poetry itself, or even approximate to it—so that we might ultimately hope to scrap the one in favour of the other? Brooks himself, we find, has unwittingly let us know: whatever, qua critic, he does with those meanings, attitudes, or what you will, what he leaves undone is all very plain: namely, to realise, make them real or else vivid to us. He does not, in other words, bring them home to us; or act, like the poet, on the imagination. More follows: only grant that, and significant conse-quences—significant for the 'tensional' theory at least—immediately appear. What I have described; that is what poetry does—and I fear that the formula will sound disconcertingly simple—at least one thing that it does is precisely to realise its 'content' imaginatively. But, as I say, grant that and you are no longer committed to complexity; for, as Brooks's critics urged all along, what it serves to realise may be as simple or straightforward as you please. It may be. It need not be; and often, of course, it is decidedly otherwise. But then it is not a very startling discovery that those writers whom we value most highly are those who have felt and thought deeply; nor that life, so considered, is unlikely to strike one as simple. In a major work at least you are likely to find prima facie conflicting attitudes, or even really and irreducibly conflicting attitudes. What does not follow is that in all poetry we are bound to find them. I am brought back to Muller's controversial phrase 'eloquent'; let a simple attitude be expressed vividly, if you like eloquently, and therewith we already have poetry—even if only of a relatively humble sort. It would be easy to cite simple lyrics, say of Burns; but for tactical reasons I choose rather to instance Waller's lines *On His Mistress's Girdle*:

> That which her slender waist confined
> Shall now my joyful temples bind,
> No monarch but would give his throne
> His arms might do as this has done . . .

which ends with the couplet:

> Give me but what this ribbon bound
> And take the rest the sun goes round.

Here you have a poem that seems positively cut out for some sort of Brooksian analysis; urbane, witty, consciously 'conceited', very much of the metaphysical tradition—and, of course, it was, in the twenties and thirties, the great vogue and revival of the metaphysicals that underlay this whole critical approach; that to which Brooks's own work belongs. Yet for all that it is basically simple, at least the experience behind it is simple. It is merely one of abandoned and joyful ardour; which, one hopes, less gifted persons must occasionally have been happy enough to have known. It is joyful, hence playful and hyperbolical, even, if you like, ironical; the complexities subserving the vivid realisation of experience (or perhaps expression) with those of the experience itself. Does it follow that I am committing the 'heresy of paraphrase'; that I cannot explain why a plain prose statement would not have done just as well? I answer that I can: that statement in the ordinary prosaic mode might have made us understand, cognise the poet's mood; it might do all that but not 'realise' it for us, not make it imaginatively vivid—which, to repeat, is not to deny that major literary work is likely to embody deep feeling and searching reflection; nor that observers who ponder long and profoundly over human experience rarely find it devoid of complexities—which, however, is no very staggering news. So here I locate the crack in Brooks's theory: the urn, well-wrought as it may be, has hidden flaws, and will ultimately not hold water, even Parnassian water—or whatever other more ethereal fluid.

I spoke earlier of several of Brooks's critics: another has appeared on the scene since the publication of the work I have been dealing with. Murray Krieger in his book *The New Apologists for Poetry* urges two main objections to Brooks—though I shall not spend a lot of space on the first, which appears to me to rest on a plain mistake. I mention it chiefly to shelve it; it is desirable that we should not seem to have left parts of the ground uncovered. The point of the 'contextual' theory, according to Krieger (yet another synonym for the theory for which we have already found so many), is that references are, so to speak, internal or inward-directed;[10] one aspect of the poem, it seems, always referring us back to another, keeping us, as it were, within the poem itself; the poem, then—one old-established notion, one main strand of traditional Romanticism—is its own self-contained object of contemplation; it stands so, rather than as mirroring the world beyond. Now that is just wrong. And strangely enough Krieger elsewhere, as we shall see, shows himself thoroughly aware of what makes it wrong: namely that the precise claim made for this sort of language, of complex, ambiguous poetic language—as it is described—is just what enables it to mirror, and

---

[10] Murray Krierger, *The New Apologists for Poetry* (Minneapolis, 1956), p. 128ff.

alone enables us adequately to mirror, all the shifting complexities of actual life.

I turn to Krieger's second and more searching criticism—which, incidentally, presupposes the falsity of the first (unless the one is invalid, the other can never be launched). He quotes Brooks's own words, and again the passage may be worth reduplicating:

> his task [Brooks writes, that is, the poet's task] is to unify experience. He must return us to the unity of experience as man knows it in his own experience. The poem, if it be a true simulacrum of reality [*pace* Krieger's 'inward reference' interpretation]—in this sense, at least an 'imitation' of reality—by *being* an experience rather than a mere statement about experience or any mere abstraction from experience.[11]

The objection here is obvious enough; a perfect 'simulacrum of reality', one might expect, so far from representing anything like an imaginative unity, a harmonisation or oneness, would be just about as chaotic as the original—whose distressing refusal to conform to our tidy demands or preconception is something that has been lamented often and in vain. Even *Ulysses*, it has been remarked, has more obvious regularity than Dublin. Krieger accordingly treats all Brooks's stress on unification, harmony and so on as a kind of afterthought, an appendage to the essential Brooksian doctrine; which is certainly mistaken. It is not only that we find these terms there from the start, and in one case, italicised, as we saw, but that the concept of bringing together, of somehow reconciling would-be conflicting attitudes, is the centre of the doctrine itself. Yet genuine difficulties remain. At least some of Brooks's phrases, his reference to a 'true simulacrum of reality' for instance, seem rather to suggest what is more humbly called a slice of life; as, say, you might take a cine-camera and start and leave off shooting at some arbitrary point—a technique I suspect some successful, modish directors of adopting—without any unity whatever. It boils down to this: grant that Brooks is right, he is certainly right to stress unity and harmonisation; yet he can only stress it; it remains, on his theory, something which we must take on trust, an uncashed cheque.

Accepting, then, in large part the importance of what Brooks has to tell us, I find it still needs, what I shall seek finally to supply, some theoretical underwriting.

I return to my main original example, *The Rape of the Lock*. Belinda is presented as an erotic, or erotically desirable object; hence, in Romantic eyes, very much more. She gets transformed into an angel or a divinity—which should not surprise us. We are surely familiar with

---

[11] Cleanth Brooks, op. cit., p. 194; quoted in Murray Krieger, op. cit., p. 195.

this tendency of erotic feelings to exalt and idealise their objects—at least where they are not merely animal (a Freudian might suspect, indeed, precisely so as to suppress and deny the animal, that is as a counter-formation; the state described as 'being in love' somewhat resembling a local neurosis). But the present point is simply this: that there exist psychological facts which are as hard as physical facts and as useless to argue with; that it only remains to accept and to live with them. And their acceptance is a main part of common wisdom. Hence few readers quarrel with the idealisation of Belinda, which may doubtless be a little absurd; but the absurdity, if so, is in human nature, about which there is not much one can do. What would certainly be foolish would be to forget or lose sight of the other side: granted she *is* physically very attractive, likely to arouse desire and hence, to repeat, in romantic breasts, adoration; and she is, in all fairness, a genuinely nice, substantially unaffected, charming girl; but also—let us add—very human; which among other things includes carnal. Woman, like man, is a rational animal; hence *a fortiori* an animal. Recall Disraeli's question, ape or angel? Of course, neither. But though decidedly not an angel, yet 'angel-like adored'; and if not an ape, at least as we see a creature sharing the ordinary instincts of animal nature. These things, and both things, are there; I mean that they are there in the poetry; they constitute a part of its complexity. Now first to repeat what I have already argued: to make a poem a poem, to make it more than a piece of analysis, they must not be only and barely there but must also be realised, made vivid or brought home to us. So much for that; but my present theme is harmonisation. The question that faces us—I suggest that faces Brooks, though he never sees it—is how it is that those attitudes, admittedly in conflict, do not merely remain in conflict. We achieve, he says, a 'unifying insight' where what might surely seem more naturally predictable in the circumstances would be a head-on collision. And in fact unresolved incoherence, tendencies that merely jar or conflict, constitute a by no means unfamiliar aesthetic fault; rather something that critics do often complain of.

We must answer, I think, at two levels. And for the first I have already hinted at the answer: life not being simple—and since we cannot make it so—we have no choice but to accept the co-existence of attitudes and the like that we cannot reduce to order—whose acceptance, to repeat, constitutes no small part of human wisdom. True, the theoretical *desideratum* of reducing complexity to order always remains with us; its drive underlies a great part of natural science, but the patient humility of accepting the unreduced recalcitrance of brute facts is something which even scientists—at the risk of blatant apriorism (like that of I. A. Richards)—must also learn to respect and accommodate. Now that, underneath, at the deeper level, is what makes endurable or acceptable the portrayal of such unresolved conflicts; what remains is the question, at the poetical or technical level, of how—as I may say—it is put across.

I propose, without apology, to offer certain humble analogies. Clearly we are most of us much readier, generally speaking, to listen to views we disagree with, even to trenchant criticism of ourselves, which are offered with imagination and tact; which means that they are so offered as to let us know—rather, make us feel—that the speaker also sees, or sees as if from, our own point of view. Thus from a public platform: 'The railwaymen have, of course, an understandable sense of grievance, yet . . .' or: 'I come to bury Caesar not to praise him . . .' but realise none the less that he was a splendid chap.

You may accuse me, in using such comparisons, of denigrating Pope's fine poetic art. Of course I grant this much: so far as he does the same sort of thing he does so in ways infinitely subtler. And here a further point. I am led to reflect on what is surely the most glaring omission in Brooks's whole treatment. Certainly he covers a wide range of poetry, but his method has nothing to tell us of the difference between *The Rape of the Lock* a playful poem, the genre being mock heroic, the heroine treated with amused affection, and the exalted seriousness of some passages ('And hear the mighty water rolling evermore') that he quotes from Wordsworth. His concern is with value; which he always finds in the same achievement, a complex harmony. The poems here are essentially alike and, one would gather, those other differences are things that hardly matter. The achievement, in either case, to repeat, is the projection of a varied vision, comprehensive and adequate; which is serious. Pope, in his basic concerns, is still serious, and serious in much the same way as Wordsworth.

The view I shall offer is the very opposite. What Brooks has nothing to say about might pass for the most important thing of all; I mean what I shall call the poet's tone—playful, solemn, mock heroic and so on. For it is that tone, principally or most often or characteristically, that makes possible the desired effect; it is the tone or the conviction it carries (where it succeeds) that makes conjointly acceptable those apparent incompatibles or conflicts. It serves, if anything serves, to convince us of the poet's real awareness of those conflicting demands; of his awareness at once of the conflict and the necessity of contemplating both; of living simultaneously with both, without our ceasing to be aware of the conflict and aware of it as of something at once deep and real. This Pope achieves, and does so in the mode of the mock heroic. That in principle it might have been done differently I do not mean to deny; but the felicity of his particular choice, given of course his own sureness in handling it, is evident enough. Mock heroically, we are able to see Belinda simultaneously as adorable and absurd, and as angelic—at least to understand those who see her as angelic—and eminently human. (R. K. Elliot has pointed out to me that Byron in *Don Juan* roughly unifies its absurdly chaotic and heterogeneous material—even ranging from comedy to horror—by mere unity of tone; all except, I would add, the lyric *The Isles of Greece*, which does not belong but he evidently felt was too good to leave out.)

The same issue, let me finally observe, might have been differently tackled, approached from a very different angle. I have spoken of what I called 'wisdom'—a high-sounding phrase perhaps calculated to call up some image as of a bearded sage in his cell, having attained the art rightly to number 'every star that Heaven doth shew/And every herb that sucks the dew'; it may, in plainer words, suggest contemplative withdrawal from the world of action. But that is another issue. Indeed often a man of action amidst daily necessities, immediate pressures, must go ahead, choose either this way or that—or, of course, stand dithering and do nothing (this last, however, at least as regards its effective consequences, is no less a commitment, a given course of action, than either of the former). But let us add this: even where the necessities of the case in fact allow two alternatives and two only, we might place more reliance on an agent, a leader perhaps, who still remains conscious of the complexities, conscious of the multiplicity of other possible viewpoints which might in other only slightly different circumstances, have led him differently—even though in acting he of necessity sweeps them irrevocably behind him, puts them unavoidably aside. Alternatively the step may not be irrevocable: such an agent might be readier to revise his views, adapt his course promptly, in the light of small signs that may be warnings, in the light of changed circumstances of new evidence, rather than sticking pig-headedly to it through thick and thin. Now here we place Brooks's 'complexity', I mean his proper emphasis on complexity; it is part though not all of what we rightly value in poetry. And underlying it, as I hope I have been able to show and as critics sharing this broad approach have so often emphasised, but not, I think, wholly succeeded in making intelligible, is our whole concern with the extra-literary business of life. Nature, I conclude, comes before art; and poetry, however valued in itself, supposes a pre-poetic reality, much as monuments suppose memorable acts.

6

The Excellence of Form in Works of Art

I

A work of art is an artefact, something made, and made for particular ends, to be valued, admired or enjoyed, in general to be appreciated appropriately; more specifically, for intensive contemplation. It is true that objects not originally so made can come to be similarly regarded. Such a formula, doing service as a rallying cry—though no doubt poorly adapted to reach deviant or borderline cases, complexities of all sorts—none the less has its use. So I find it, at all events, in the present disarray of aesthetic theory; and therefore I plant my flag here. I begin with this notion of an artist; one who makes things for others to contemplate, that is, merely to read, hear, look at or the like. Certainly they may serve other ends too. A novelist or a playwright, for instance, may also be working off grudges, satirising friends, colleagues or rivals; he may be recouping his bank balance or exploring the depths of his soul. But all this is incidental, even the last; art has, qua art, no further end. Pretty obviously it is not psychoanalysis, even self-analysis, though the two things sometimes touch; nor likewise is it philosophy or engineering, which it also can touch, and perhaps more often and more nearly. Turn from novel-writing, say, to ceramics, and the notion wears its absurdity on its forelock.

I spoke of things made to be contemplated and hence enjoyed. Now features that invite such contemplation, which we value inasmuch as they reward it, are of sorts that vary widely, perhaps indefinitely. As my title announces, my sole concern here is with one, namely form; which is something we often praise in works of art. As I say, we praise other things too; we may also, for instance, praise expressiveness or (in appropriate contexts) vividness of depiction or 'truth'. But I specifically mention expressiveness in order to distinguish it from form; the two things are sometimes confused. And the views I shall shortly be proposing presuppose some grasp of the distinction; a better grasp, I fear, than is confidently to be relied on. In general or intuitive terms one can draw attention to it tolerably easily; 'form', where we use the word, goes along with others like 'economy' or 'fitness', with praise of 'each part in its place and none superfluous'. With 'expressiveness' on the other hand, goes talk of 'serenity', of 'dignity'; and further, and hardly surprisingly, it may bring some reference to whatever we find expressed: perhaps authority or military prowess, perhaps mere natural energy or the like, and sometimes, of course, states of mind. The broad distinction is surely plain, however; things we call expressive can be formless, and expressive in virtue of their very formlessness. Others, I can see no a priori reason to deny, eminently manifesting form, may largely lack the distinctive feature I call expressiveness.

But I spoke of the confusion of the two: consider a 'well-made' play or novel which is likely to be praised for its 'form'. Or again take the old architectural slogan, popular not long ago, 'Form follows function'. Now 'form' here is outward embodiment, which is taken as 'expressing' the function. While it does so, however, in the architect's technical sense of the verb 'express', it may wholly fail to be expressive in ours. Conversely of course it may succeed. 'Functionalism', the old name for that movement, by my reckoning was not a bad one. True, 'functionalist' buildings may have been hell to live and work in; as, I am told, they often were. If so, they functioned abominably. But the point was not that but their expressiveness; they looked, in their bright steel and glass, the shining witness of technical mastery, of functionality (if the context may justify the rather ugly word). Now a building of this sort, or let us note equally, a scientific theory or the like, is one whose outward body, as it were, announces its essence, makes visible the principle of its working, and it is apt to be praised for its *form*; in my view confusedly. We should gain clarity by talking of expressiveness. That confusion may be reinforced by another, namely the assumption that expression is solely, at least pre-eminently, expressive of human states of mind; or, worse still, of human emotion. It may seem a novelty to talk of the expression of functionality, of technical mastery; but the case is essentially the same with buildings bodying forth the power and grandeur of the Barberini or the Medici; their civic virtue and military prowess.

Of expressiveness itself I have written elsewhere; I cannot enlarge on it here. In general I hold (and argue in a forthcoming article) that, say, awkwardness is expressive precisely of awkwardness—despite appearances, no mere tautology. For 'visible' or aesthetic awkwardness is expressive of practical awkwardness. And grace is expressive of its opposite, a certain sure rightness of touch, an easy felicity of handling. One might put it as follows: the present object is more than itself. It is coloured by an intuitive judgment (or quasi-judgment); and what the 'judgment' of is something 'behind' it. And we value or condemn it accordingly. Emotion, introduced here at source, serves merely to muddy the view.

II

I called *form* an object of praise. Only think of the sort of thing one hears said: 'I'll tell you what it's got, it's got form'—a feature, then, that not everything can boast of. But we shall find it a protean monosyllable. 'Form', a correlative or polar term, has its meaning bound up with its correlates. Now the latter prove bewilderingly numerous; hence the former must vary correspondingly. I distinguish, provisionally, the following:

(i)   form as opposed to matter;
(ii) form as opposed to content;
(iii) form as opposed to formlessness.

That, so far, is no more than common usage; but, presently, I fear, we shall need to distinguish two different senses of 'content', and two sorts of formlessness as well. Therefore I add these:

(ii*a*) form, here, as outline or boundary, as opposed to content, whatever it bounds;

(ii*b*) form as something outward, an embodiment; opposed now to what I call *import*, whatever it embodies or expresses.

For the second distinction that I mentioned, at this stage I can only supply labels:

(iii*a*) non-aesthetic form as opposed to formlessness;
(iii*b*) aesthetic form as opposed to formlessness.

I need last of all yet another item, which is really a modification of (ii*b*). But since the notation gets unwieldy I call it:

(iv) form as structure.

To take these in order as far as possible: *matter* is what anything is made of, wood, bronze, plastic, concrete or the like. In critical or aesthetic usage that seems to be the notion employed; but nowadays elsewhere the idiomatic word is 'material', ('matter' itself being reserved for what used to be a secondary sense). But the point is not one that need detain us; I find the sense in question relatively unproblematic. From the fact that Bernini's *St Longinus* is made of marble and Donatello's *David* of bronze no special aesthetic problems seem to arise. We can, of course, speak of 'the same matter' where we no longer say 'the same thing'. Matter is what persists through such changes, which gives the concept its meaning and use.

As to *content*: as a starting point it is often observed that a tin of tomato soup contains soup. It would seem that we think somewhat similarly of an object having visible boundaries, and hence of its shape as enclosing the rest. Oddly, it is unidiomatic to say 'content', though the notion of containment would seem to survive. For certainly we speak of its 'form'. Again, in non-spatial things we can easily conceive a rough equivalent.

I distinguished two senses of 'content', though there is no obscurity as to their common metaphorical root. The soup passes, say, from the shopkeeper to me. And information may be thought of as conveyed, and if not in a tin or a bottle, yet in words, code, gestures, or the like. The same goes for facial 'expression'. Brows may be important with presage; which, conveniently, in my sense is their 'import'. Content here, then, is something expressed, something made accessible; not something encompassed or enclosed.

I have already anticipated my next item, namely, *structure*, which I take out of order. For, as I said, it is really a modification of (ii*a*), form-opposed-to-content—form here being boundary or outline. Now that outline may be regular or irregular. And it may mark out distinct, related parts, which may even be mutually remote, spatially, temporally or so on; yet still placed in discernible relations. It is here that we naturally speak of structure; the usage has, I think, some warrant in ordinary speech. (Not that usage is notably consistent; thus in my sense 'logical form' is a structure.) The parts I speak of may be repeated, varied, inverted and so on. Critics commonly speak, for example, of the structure of *War and Peace*; sometimes of its form—which may or may not (the reader must guess) mean the same. *Form* as structure, it will now be clear, is constituted by a system of relations; and it is opposed to *content*, as what they relate.

I turn last to formlessness—a word that may recall a common remark, namely, that everything, in some sense, must have form. It has form, for we can now be more precise, as outline or structure, a system of boundaries or relations: opposed to content, what they bound or relate. And that form may be no matter how elusive or indeterminate; that, we shall be told, makes no difference. The object has the form that it has; so have bogs, fogs, and the writings of Heidegger. Now these things in another sense are properly and intelligibly called 'formless', or relatively formless at least. (The notion of anything totally formless is one that tender consciences may stick at.) We may say so of concrete things at all events; I confess to being less sure of the form, opposed to content, of the number three.

Now form in this new usage, it seems—*form-as-opposed-to-formlessness*—as yet only in its *non-aesthetic* sense—belongs to things having specifiable features, visibly definite and regular. Contrast, say, a square clearly drawn and such as to stand out from its background with what we would call a 'formless' sprawl. Such things have a special significance for us, a point I shall return to. My present concern is with the distinction between *aesthetic* and *non-aesthetic form*, (iiia) and (iiib), each opposed to its own sort of *formlessness*; a point that proves strangely intractable. The failure of critics to observe this difference, while they go to town with the epithet 'form', leaves half what they say obscure and dubious. What is true is that the one underlies the other, but not that the two are the same. A modern painter may seem to exalt mere regularity, mere order. One, I am told, has exhibited a series of works significantly entitled *Homage to the Square*.[1] The square has a special value or 'meaning' for him, or so he persuades himself. But if so, I dare say, it must be seen in a peculiar light, perhaps a special cultural context. Even grand compact blocks of them, a very plenitude, whole sheets of mathematics paper or chessboards, are not hung in galleries and merely contemplated (not yet anyway, perhaps they may be before long). Such things are indeed ideally regular; which taken aesthetically, however, scores no credits. The same goes for ordinary objects, for objects such as cricket balls, for example; nice clear-cut, discriminable things—for such they unquestionably are. They are virtually spherical, uniformly bright red, hard in outline and stable in shape. They are even movable, too, (which means one can probe them all round). It follows that we know where we are with them; further, that we know ideally well—a state of affairs to be wished for. That distinguishes them from more elusive realities, from wisps of mist, tips of icebergs, the Aurora Borealis and the like.

Yet this sort of merit, to repeat, is not what we ask of works of art. What we admire in a sentence of Jane Austen's or the grouping of the figures in *The School of Athens*, though we properly refer to it as 'form', remains something other and more obscure. It is not mere lucidity and definiteness, not certainly mechanical regularity. Yet the two things are not merely disparate; nor have I spent so long listing all these uses of this monosyllable simply in order to discard them. One must first understand structure and outline, *form as opposed to content*, if we are to go on to understand *form-opposed-to-formlessness*. And one must understand the latter, in turn, that is, *non-aesthetic form-opposed-to-formlessness*, to grasp finally the concept of *aesthetic form*.

[1] Cf. older titles like *Homage to Manet* and Gombrich's comments on Manzu's *Chair with Fruit*, 'Tradition and expression in Western Art', in *Meditations on a Hobby Horse* (London, 1963), pp. 95–105.

Everything has some form, we said; which here is form-opposed-to-content; form, more specifically, as structure or outline. Now in cases like those I have illustrated it also has form, non-aesthetic-form, opposed-to-formlessness; which is, I said, something to be wished for. Briefly, 'good' form-opposed-to-content is form-opposed-to-formlessness, too; it is wished for and is good specifically for the purposes of the intellect. For such things are easily discriminable; or re-encountering them they are easy to recognise, easy to handle in thought and recall. But most basic is the point already stressed; what quite generally we prefer is to know where we are. To think or act at all, I would suppose, one must know what it is one is thinking of. To confine ourselves to concrete particulars, which in any case are basic in other ways, (only through them can we get at abstractions); the ability to discriminate things—'things' emphatically, and not merely formally—in our immediate perceptual environment is what all thought and discourse presupposes. A certain derogatory sound attaches to this word 'formless'; which, I think, ought not any longer to perplex us. It is in the nature of thought to prefer precision. To know more precisely is to know just where you are; possibly, how much you are committed to. It is in itself to know better, which of necessity we value in valuing knowledge at all. (One might add, too, the importance of regularity, I mean, its importance for rational beings; for quite generally, I would argue, explanation depends on it.) I have spoken of perceptual discrimination, of things in our perceptual environment. This, of course, is to talk of the world as our senses reveal it to us. Advanced science drastically reinterprets such common-sense findings; however, it also presupposes them. For maximally discriminable pointers on dials are what a scientist in fact employs and reads; that, discrimination, after all, is what they are precisely designed for.

III

Form, non-aesthetic form-opposed-to-formlessness, presupposes form as *outline*—opposed to *content*. And aesthetic form presupposes them both. But before putting forward my own view of it, I shall attempt, necessarily briefly, to survey others; for several are already in the field. I class them as views of form-opposed-to-formlessness, though of course the label is my own; it seems to be the same thing, however, that is variously characterised as *coherence*, as *harmony* or as *significant form*; indeed even as *proportion* or *order*—misleadingly, as we see, for *order* strictly is mere non-aesthetic form. For convenience I stick to 'coherence'. And for the views I spoke of, I broadly distinguish the following:

(i) coherence as the reconciliation of order (or unity) with variety;

(ii) coherence as a thing *sui generis*, directly 'perceptible' in its own appropriate way;

(iii) coherence as *gestalt.*

Of these, let me say, laying from the start my cards on the table, I myself espouse the first. But I need to distinguish the view I advocate from another, closely related, that I reject. Hence I shall add a fourth item:

(i*a*) the reconciliation of unity and variety, as supposedly exemplified in any structure simply qua structure, in science, mathematics and so on; hence seen as essentially unproblematic.

I postpone the exposition of my own view, and likewise, provisionally, the variant above. This leaves us with (ii) and (iii), coherence as a thing sui generis and secondly coherence as gestalt. The former perhaps has a rather depressingly familiar sound. We have heard before of unique qualities, unique relations, irreducible and unanalysable; things known directly—not of course by 'direct' as against 'indirect perception', that is, sense perception—but after their own special manner. Such doctrines, available pretty widely to philosophers not otherwise provided for, can never be easy to refute. One can at least invoke the name of Ockham, however; with ad hoc suppositions of all sorts, the rule is the fewer the better. Now I shall shortly seek to vindicate the possibility of an alternative, one dispensing with this sort of postulate; which then *eo ipso* must be preferable. Besides, for the present rather ugly specimen, before we lie down with it we should notice certain further inconveniences. For, we shall find, once embraced, it breeds monstrously. (The strange curse pronounced, I think, on ad hoc hypotheses was, 'Be sterile *and* multiply'.) 'Form' as used here, first of all, has an emphatic, commendatory force—though indeed with qualifications to follow. Similarly 'coherent' is a term of praise and 'incoherent' plainly the reverse. Say a critic should recommend Ezra Pound's *Cantos*; we ask 'on what ground?' 'Because they are incoherent.' Very likely; but it is hardly a reason for praising them. Our new quality *sui generis*, it would seem, a quality merely known in experience, at once reveals an interesting further feature; it intrinsically carries commendation. That alone would be puzzling enough; for how should one set out to explain it? We know the thing merely by 'inspection'; but on this point inspection throws no light. Worse is to follow however; for, to speak accurately, what we praise is never mere coherence, but rather what I shall call 'coherence in spite of . . .' So, too, with self-control and restraint, which also, in appropriate cases, are objects of praise. Not elsewhere, however; as Campbell asks,

'Where's the bloody horse?'[2] The suggestion, then, is of something, presumably something pretty strong, that calls for control or restraint. Devils formerly, among other tactics, used sometimes to tempt saints with naked virgins, or with spirits assuming such a likeness. But no devil, I suppose, or none with an IQ over seventy—seeking to pressurise that particular valve—would have taken on the person of an aged crone. So, too, of the potential incoherence that gives significance to mere order in works of art. One may note that even Beardsley, an eminent advocate of this view, off-duty, knows our common concepts as well as anyone. He lapses significantly at one point into talking of a group of shapes as unitary 'despite the variety of hue'.[3] That 'despite', I suggest, is revealing. Coherence, after all, it would seem, is not an irreducible something; we have unity in spite of variety—an approach very different from the one he officially advocates. Besides, as we saw, ad hoc postulates enjoy an unnatural fecundity; and for this present instance, it multiplies, if not beyond necessity, which has still to be demonstrated, at least beyond all reason and proportion.

I turn next—and shall bluntly say with little enthusiasm—to that favourite of some aesthetic theorists, the deep, elusive notion of a *'gestalt'*; a term that proves, intellectually speaking, so valuable a labour-saving device. The intellectual dish it serves to heat contains four ingredients at least, things bearing on our problem very variously, and exuding thick darkness. A *gestalt*, first, is simply any shape—or a body of impressions or the like—that is somehow distinctive and recognisable. Second, a 'good *gestalt*' would appear sometimes to mean the same thing, only with the confusing suggestion that others need not be distinctive after all; but oftener, I think, the new phrase simply serves to pay homage to the square—and other forms resembling the square. That is, it comes down to *regularity*; or, in the usage I have employed to clarify these differences, to *form*, but specifically *non-aesthetic-form, opposed-to-formlessness*. Third, a widely different thing, expressiveness: we have characteristically expressive shapes or contours, say, 'visibly' dejected or agitated; which, we have already seen, is something easily confused with aesthetic form. Last of all comes our own special interest, the very feature we hoped to see illuminated; namely, this excellence I distinguish as specifically aesthetic-form-opposed-to-formlessness. The phrase is a clumsy one, doubtless. By the present step, however, the substitution of the anglicised German word *'gestalt'*, I confess that I cannot feel much enlightened.

[2] They praise the great restraint with which you write
   I'm with them there, of course;
   You use the bridle and the bit all right,
   But where's the bloody horse?
[3] Cf. Monroe Beardsley, *Aesthetics* (New York, 1958), p. 195.

Koffka, the *gestalt* psychologist, tells us that the *gestalt* in a work of art 'determines its part in a sort of hierarchy'; it highlights certain features, subordinates others and so on.[4] In general it organises the material; that, I fear, is all his elaborate account amounts to. Again Osborne distinguishes what he calls 'synoptic' from 'discursive perception'; the latter of which, perception of *Gestalten*, grasps 'a rich intricate complexity as a unity and a single whole'—the object of 'direct intuitional awareness'.[5] To this latter account I shall return directly. But what of that given by Koffka? I find in it a kind of intuitive rightness. But suppose it were simply—shall we say?—'the aesthetic principle' to whose efficacy so much was attributed; or suppose that the form were said to organise the material, or the organisation to give it form. In all this, I fear, what we are offered is little more than a choice of epithets. And as to that, we have found there is already no shortage. But to turn to Osborne's more developed and articulate account; he, I think, faces a dilemma. He tells us elsewhere that *gestalt* theorists never favoured merely regular or symmetrical forms; those manifesting, in my usage, non-aesthetic-form-opposed-to-formlessness—hence including discs, squares, chessboards and the like.[6] As for the historical point, I shall not dispute it. But our question is what their theory requires; or rather, perhaps, how much can be milked from it. Let me borrow an illustration from Wittgenstein: first of a random scatter of dots, and second the 'same' dots, the same number, but now neatly ranged in platoons.[7] There are ten sets with two rows of five, exactly a hundred in all; which is fully apprehensible now, and as Osborne says, non-discursively, 'in direct intuitional awareness'. The phrase is his own technical coinage. We cannot go to existing usage to learn its meaning, and he himself is content to leave it there. We can only apply it where it seems natural, and where, if not here? Otherwise I am left with a verbal formula; in other words, with no notion how to use it at all.

Yet he cannot mean that; we saw, indeed, he expressly denies it. Osborne, it would seem (and if so I sympathise), has no wish to do homage to the square. Suppose he did, however; it would have one merit, that of adding some positive doctrine. Otherwise, what remains to us? Little more than yet another superfluous synonym for all the rest. Or not precisely a synonym, to be accurate; for 'synoptic perception' is not the same as objects of the sort that concern us but rather correlative with them, in favourable cases at least. These then will

[4] K. Koffka, 'Problems in the psychology of art', in *Art, A Bryn Mawr Symposium* (1940), p. 247.
[5] Cf. Harold Osborne, *The Theory of Beauty* (London, 1952), pp. 122, 124.
[6] Cf. Harold Osborne, 'Artistic unity and gestalt', *The Philosophical Quarterly* (1964), pp. 214ff.
[7] *Remarks on the Foundations of Mathematics* (Oxford, 1967), i. 153, ii. 1ff.

manifest some '*gestalt*', or if your prefer 'coherence', or if you prefer 'harmony', or what Reynolds in the eighteenth century spoke of quite simply as *form* (and incidentally saw as deeply puzzling, as something urgently in need of explanation). It is last, I suppose, what Clive Bell, transforming and illuminating everything, renamed 'significant form' – which is presumably what entitled him to be contemptuous of pictorial story-tellers such as Reynolds. (Reynolds, unlike Bell, took himself to be indicating a problem, not a solution.)[8] The upshot is the same as before; the term '*gestalt*' only names and conceals a difficulty. I cannot find that it does anything to elucidate it.

I come finally to my own favoured candidate, the last item on the list that I began with; namely, the ancient formula 'order (or unity) within variety'. Yet here, as I hinted, we must be careful. It is ultimately traceable to the Greeks, and passed thereafter from one facile pen to another; for it reappears in the British eighteenth century (one finds it, for instance, both in Hutcheson and Price), and thereafter in Coleridge, and coming to our own, in Roger Fry. The phrase itself must seem unproblematic; at least none of these thinkers, except Coleridge, reveals the least sense of a problem. Even he only indicates it obliquely, that is, by his use of a single word, with which it seems he simultaneously disposes of it. The word in question, a favourite of his, one that solves many problems for him, is 'reconciliation'. Art reconciles unity and multeity—the latter term making, I think, no substantial difference. But again, Coleridge seems to have liked it. This much emerges, at least; we have to do with an opposition of some sort, perhaps even logical—but if so, surely, hardly such as to admit of being reconciled.

A cricket ball is red and roughly spherical, which plainly are simply two qualities. Nor would it be credited with such an achievement as reconciling redness and sphericality; the two are only different, not 'opposed'. A logical relation, I fear, is indeed what we face; and worse, one that looks like contradiction. Something more orderly or unitary might be thought to be *eo ipso* less varied; pretty much as a nearer place is less remote. And conversely, the more varied is less unitary. Now, how are we to 'reconcile' *p* and *not-p*—at least if we want meanings, not mysteries?

We can translate the point into terms that are more specifically aesthetic. Let me take another example. It seems that for Rudolf Arnheim, likewise a *gestalt* psychologist, 'coherence' is itself a *desideratum*.

---

[8] I confess I cannot regard Bell's work with the seriousness I find in some thinkers, and some I respect. I find it divides neatly into two parts, platitude and folly: the one, that some works of art are to be valued for their form; the other, that none is to be valued—truly aesthetically valued—for anything else.

Now, on these terms, what he ought to admire are sheets of squared paper and the like; in fact he applies it to the analysis of a Cézanne portrait of his wife. (*Gestalt* psychologists, I have already observed, find themselves tugged in opposite ways; first by theorising in such terms; secondly by looking, as they commendably also do, at works of art.) Arnheim's explicit starting-point makes the paradox startlingly plain; he uses an illustration adapted from Klee, which I in turn shall slightly adapt. Let us take two squares, each containing a disc, one placed exactly centrally, the other a little off-centre.[9] Arnheim's avowed purpose is to establish the presence of certain supposed lines of tension in the visual field.[10] But for our purpose the relevant thing is his account of situations answering to the second of my pair of figures. He writes as follows:

> An unbalanced composition looks accidental, transitory and therefore invalid. . . . Under such conditions the artistic statement becomes incomprehensible.[11]

It may be 'accidental' or even 'incomprehensible'; it is also, I think, at least marginally more 'interesting'. A wholly regular figure is, if you like, ideally coherent but a trifle dull. Viewed aesthetically, doubtless, both examples are about equally negligible; but something emerges, at least schematically. The central disc is perfectly regular, equidistant from all four angles; or rather, seen holistically, all four sides—for that is what matters in aesthetics, the overall visual impression. It stands just where it does, then, and not arbitrarily; its position is governed by a rule. And, moreover, to talk meaningfully of rules we also need room for their opposites, for irregularities too. One might perhaps, to exclude Leibniz's trick, say a 'visibly obvious rule'; but we need not concern ourselves with distinctions admitting no empirical application. Regularity thus characterised, however; a 'good *gestalt*', which is all we have so far attained to, is no nearer to anything aesthetic. In the illumination of a Cézanne portrait the concept takes us nowhere at all. (Osborne, more judicious, left his account in general terms; not courting disaster by applying it to the analysis of specific works.) But, I said, something emerges. We can at last state our difficulty in relevant terms, in truly aesthetic terms. On the one hand take unity or regular-

---

[9] Cf. Rudolf Arnheim, *Art and Visual Perception* (London, 1966), pp. 1, 3.

[10] Those in turn call for explanation. But Arnheim's way is not to appeal to the unremarkable truth that we seek—surely for good conceptual reasons—to 'read' shapes as regular. Hence, where in point of visible fact they are otherwise, we see them as it were, explaining them to ourselves, as pulled away or striving back. Arnheim explains them, more scientifically, by certain electrical processes in the brain.

[11] Op. cit., p. 9.

ity (different concepts, of course, but not for our purposes relevantly different). Now they, we find, have the following tendency, they make for coherence with dullness. The converse holds equally: irregularities bring interest and detract proportionately from coherence. We are, it seems, launched on a kind of see-saw. It will, I suppose, admit of a middle point; an Aristotelian mean that in principle we might aim at and hit. But, of course, a middle point would be no nearer a 'reconciliation'.[12]

We have here a dilemma, I think, that we need fairly to face, not to dodge. One approach that I mentioned makes light of it, the one I labelled (iv). It runs as follows: Any theory or structure, we are told, simply qua structure, mathematical, scientific or what you will, works first in mixed, varied materials. Now those materials it serves somehow to order or unify; which is certainly true. But that unity is, speaking roughly, mechanical not aesthetic. Recall Wittgenstein's dots ranged in rows; an illustration, we may note, precisely designed to exhibit for us the characteristic working of mathematics. But it throws no light on works of art; nor was it meant to. In that pattern variety disappears and merely disappears into order; order that in my terminology is form, but non-aesthetic form, opposed to formlessness. Of scientific laws and theories the same holds; we begin with a diversity of phenomena which, certainly, they serve to order or unify. But they themselves are metamorphosed in the process. We started, I said, with phenomena which were qualitatively various as well as numerous. What emerges is a system of laws, along with their colourless instances; still a plurality, doubtless, but in no other sense a diversity. And hence what emerges, viewed aesthetically, is no longer 'interesting'. What we seek is a sort of coherence that serves, so to speak, to hold and focus together both diversity and unity, and hold them simultaneously and lastingly.

To say this is of course not to echo romantic denigration of science. For, I believe, good theory is a joy for ever, and may also, incidentally, be a thing of beauty—no less than things 'fickle or freckled' (a point I noted in speaking of expressiveness). But another perspective exists too. The celestial bodies 'for ever singing as they shine', but a Newtonian chorus—and, let us note, 'in Reason's ear'—may indeed proclaim aloud their great Original. That was said at one historical moment. For contemporaries of Addison they stood newly revealed, their marvellous

---

[12] A complication that some years ago a student in Kansas drew my attention to: one extreme, which would be merely arbitrary randomness, is no nearer to qualifying as 'interesting' than its opposite, namely drill-square regularity. What we need for the latter, it seems, is rather this: order in some degree, but imperfect, somehow dislocated but still discernible; so that one given element or a few elements can be seen as being 'visibly' out of place.

order made manifest; it arose from the fury and the mire, from sublunar contingency. There exists a distinctive perspective in which science or scientific discovery captures something of the quality of art. We have, it seems, two viewpoints, the scientific and the pre-scientific; the muddy process and its crystalline product. Now suppose by some fortunate chance that they present themselves to our awareness simultaneously; we are given both variety and order, and visible coalescence of the two. In favourable cases we find theories that somehow invite us to focus both. They 'visibly' manifest their own workings, which gives them expressiveness. They combine unity and variety, which gives them form. And such theories are rightly called beautiful. But for science in general the case is different, and its value is different; the order that emerges is mere order. It is form opposed to formlessness, but non-aesthetic form; order educed from variety, the latter, as it were, dying in childbirth. That, of course, is not 'reconciliation', which would seem to be as far distant as ever—at least as concerns works of art.

IV

To reconcile unity with variety, or to make clear the possibility of reconciling them; that and no less was our project. But surely a preliminary task it suggests is some analysis of the notion of unity; which is one, to the best of my knowledge, that earlier aesthetic writers neglect. Now once we explicitly turn to it certain main points must be tolerably plain; first, unitariness is a matter of degree, and is itself not a ground-level feature. It depends on or arises out of others. Hence different considerations carry weight. Unitariness, let me stress, need not cease itself to be a unitary concept, though its 'criteria' (following R. M. Hare's usage) vary systematically from case to case. And not only that: in any one instance such criteria, by which I mean considerations that we rightly appeal to, are not all of a piece but divergent. It follows—a point I shall return to—that they also prove potentially conflicting. Take a unitary shape, for example, and suppose it is regular too. Regularity alone enhances unity. But to describe it in these terms at all, as one shape, a unitary shape, it must also be homogeneous and distinctive; that is, unlike its background and—taken internally—like itself. Imagine, say, a uniformly black disc set on an indeterminate or mottled ground; its unitariness is sufficiently evident. But suppose, on the other hand, that it loses its internal uniformity, that is, it itself becomes mottled; it loses its unity proportionately. Carry the process to the limit and it ceases to exist as a distinct entity, or *a fortiori* a unitary one.

Here, then, we find diverse factors which, I said, potentially conflict. And that is a point on which to pause. To develop the example, however, I shall turn to a unitary group (this, purely for expository purposes, I find it easier to handle). Take a group of shapes, say, yellow triangles, and let them be so arranged as to form together a larger triangle set close together on a grey ground. There you have an 'obvious' group. You have regular forms themselves regularly related, and qualitatively identical too—like each other and unlike their surroundings. The effect of all this is pretty plain. Two concerns which I earlier referred to belong essentially and basically to rational beings: we seek 'things' in our immediate environment: that is, for any obviously distinctive item to pick out. We need, as it were, a *pied-à-terre*, as something that we can subsequently work from. And secondly we value regularity, which all explanation depends on. Hence the group I have described demands attention; it is emphatically a group, and as such unitary. It still remains a group, if rather less obviously, supposing that we weaken the relevant features.

We might move our triangles farther apart. Resemblance and regularity still suffice; they join hands, so to speak, across the gap. But imagine a more radical change. We shall add a new feature, wholly new, unlike all the others already given; a black circle to enclose the whole group. We found that resemblance enhances unity, but then so does outline or self-containedness. What results is a group whose several members are dissimilar, 'interestingly' varied; and yet one no less unitary than before.

To turn back from flat shapes to solid objects: consider a clump of trees or a row of columns. A 'row' will be regular already, its members are all alike, evenly spaced and finally form a straight line—or at least a smooth curve. A clump of trees may be spoken of as a group; it is less obviously or eminently a group. Let me vary my example once again, at least provisionally; instead of columns I shall take a row of pilasters marking out bays along a facade, hence evenly spaced, as before, and forming a regular series. Such a series, we learn from mathematicians, is one satisfying the following conditions: each element stands related to its predecessor as, in turn, its successor stands to it. In each case the relation is the same. I described our example as regular; but the regularity, we must note, is less than perfect. The sequence we specified is finite; it ends at a given point, and ends arbitrarily. It 'ought', one may feel, to go on—which would satisfy the demands of regularity, or what I shall call the inductive expectation (perhaps simply a species of the same thing). That moreover, taken psychologically, is merely a matter of fact—whatever else some philosophers say of it. As to perfect regularity: unless we look beyond the world of perception, say, to scientific laws, what we need will be circular forms; say, returning to the architecture, a colonnade forming a *tempiello*. But as to a finite series other than a circle or the like, that is, a series of which some given item forms the last, it is *eo ipso* irregular, or, as I said, less than perfectly regular. A circle, the symbol of eternity, has no final item. That item is what offends against the rule, having of course a predecessor but no successor. Now where a feature, at least an obvious one, is formally irregular it tends aesthetically to be felt as anomalous. To return to our example of the colonnade: in fifteenth-century Italy, I imagine, the thing was never analysed explicitly; but we have good enough evidence that it was felt. There emerged a new feature, familiar enough since; namely, the doubling of the terminal pilasters, (or, of course, columns); a full stop, so to speak, to end the row. It effectively mitigates the anomaly; that is evident intuitively and immediately. But our own analytic concern is with the underlying principle of its working.

The last term was previously irregular, related differently to its neighbours from the rest. It is still irregular, perhaps even more so, two pilasters where one was the rule; a point to be emphasised. The modification, whatever it achieves, is no mere return to regularity, in my usage, to non-aesthetic form. Yet, I said, its rightness is at once obvious. It is an irregularity that 'visibly' fits: precisely that is the phenomenon to be accounted for. Now in other contexts all this is familiar enough. After all, it has often been noticed that works of art contrive to set up expectations; whose nonfulfilment, in general distressing, is sometimes precisely the reverse. It is a problem that I. A. Richards consigned to what he called 'the jungles of neurology'; Richards being, like Arnheim, a prospector of would-be scientific psychology—I use the term advisedly, for, I think, a speculative gold mine is an image more apt than a jungle—who would have done better to try logical analysis. I said that we feel it as 'right'. And it is so, surely, not only from what may operate—a response such as Freud notes in a different context—that one good irregularity deserves another; or perhaps that is where if you must break the rules you had best break them conspicuously, and get away with it. All that which might mitigate our malaise, could hardly suffice to remove it, far less positively change it to satisfaction. Our concern is with regularity and unity; an irregularity was what drew our attention. Here, then, not in speculative neurology, I find it reasonable to look for an answer. Now unity, we found, is enhanced by not only regularity but also outline; the facade with its arbitrary final item was partly irregular before. Now, with this further anomalous feature, it is barely more irregular. Further, what it loses in regularity it makes up for in outline. So in that respect the score remains even. What it gains on the other hand is more 'interest'. In brief, it gains more than it loses. It is more 'interesting',yet as unitary as before. So we reconcile unity with variety, yet without violating logic or talking nonsense—even elevated Coleridgean nonsense.

The illustration, of course, is only schematic. We are speaking of aesthetic effects; and rules such as admit no exception are things that it is useless to seek for. And so with the requirement of emphasised endings, for coupled pilasters or quoins. Gropius at the Bauhaus and elsewhere lets the glass wall run on round the angle (and was, I believe, the first to do so). He moved the upright away, visibly detached from the wall, which then, as critics point out, is seen as emphatically not load-bearing—no longer a formal feature but an expressive one, expressive of function. That itself, perhaps, may 'justify' the irregularity. It is interesting, like all irregularities, but doubly so here, in the visible detachment of the glass wall, its discrepancy from the load-bearing uprights. Doubtless more might be said; however I return for the present to schematic examples.

The row of columns, we found, form a group. So, for that matter, do half a dozen matchsticks similarly arranged, or lines drawn on paper. But here we can proceed as before, varying our picture with a new feature, a significant addition. So far we have verticals only; my addition shall be two horizontals, at the top and the bottom respectively. Or alternatively, to return to the colonnade: we add first—to carry the columns—a continuous plinth, and secondly an entablature to crown it. Being different, and emphatically different, the new feature will be an object of interest; and yet, we find here as before, without detriment to the unity of the whole. But the factors at work are more complex. Once again there is a clear gain in outline; however, more emphatically than previously. We must take account of what I call 'implicit movement' (a phenomenon, qua phenomenon, sufficiently familiar; nor is this the place to embark on an analysis). Columns, as we always say, 'rise'. But that upward 'movement', before merely lost itself, so to speak, remained unintegrated with the rest; made no part of what now—no longer, I hope, as a mere vacuous slogan—we can speak of as a 'significant form'. The entablature, we see, serves to 'stop' it, redirecting it to keep it within a whole. A rectangle too—if less markedly than a perfect square—itself registers as a regular form; less, as I say, than a square, yet more so than the rows it replaces. So the outcome is the same as before; enhanced 'interest' without loss of unity—perhaps, indeed, rather the reverse.

Our response to stone columns on solid earth, carrying capitals of one or other classical order and a moulded entablature, is one thing; I should grant that it does not greatly resemble any natural attitude to flat patterns of matchstick-like lines. And, let me add further, that it is only a repeatable motif, not in itself a work of art. The schema, however, does its job if it serves intellectually to clarify—the better by its very abstractness—what the real thing effectively, if obscurely, makes manifest; what it embodies, enriches and brings to life.

A final example of this sort: the process is to be the same as before, the addition of an 'interesting' feature which, we see, means an irregular one. As well as the horizontal at the top we are now to draw in two converging diagonals, the whole therefore forming a flattish triangle. In our culture, doubtless, a pediment is a thing far too familiar to be marvelled at. And its function is basically simple. What on one theory it meets is the basic need for a gable-end, of which (it has been said) the pediment is only the Greek refinement—yet if so, one that has proved, and not for nothing, hardly less durable than the syllogism or Euclidean geometry. We have, first, as before, a new feature; the triangle which is strikingly new, is proportionately an object of interest. But secondly, we have coherence, which is simultaneously preserved, indeed is strikingly enhanced: the entablature, we saw in our previous example, served to 'stop' the upward movement of the columns. It stopped it with a sheer collision, however; certainly an effect, in an appropriate context, that could serve as contributing to expressiveness. It hardly could contribute to coherence. For, plainly enough, the two movements of horizontals and verticals strain vigorously in opposite directions; the whole mass, more specifically if you strengthen the outline, is at once held together and torn apart. But turn to the temple front, or even its reductive two-dimensional counterpart: here, as if miraculously, the conflict vanishes. It follows that the mood changes, too; for expressive factors and formal ones interact.[13] (We find, too, for instance, that an upright, which formally is merely a vertical, may gain a new salience as a support.) That 'movement' is now gently carried on, continued though modified, in diagonals leading up to the apex; we have now not a counterweight but a consummation. The pediment sits lightly on its base; it possesses, one might say, its own principle of levitation—whence, too, in large part (to return to considerations of expressiveness) its own distinctive quality of serenity. The apex, we can hardly fail to note, has a further significance, it brings a new quality, namely symmetry—or visible symmetry, at least. Formally, doubtless, a row of six columns is symmetrical; however, what matters for aesthetics is symmetry such as is evident to the eye.

[13] And doubtless much else as well. I should perhaps stress yet again that I am deliberately isolating a single aspect.

Symmetry I call regularity about a centre, whether the latter is actual or ideal. This, perhaps, for our purposes will suffice. (Given appropriate technical machinery, I am told, the term admits of an exact mathematical definition; which might appeal to philosophers of some schools, those who prefer such statements as 'The cat is on the mat' rewritten in logical symbolism.) What matters for us about symmetry is its service to variety and unity; for, it will be noticed, I defined it in terms of regularity. What we have are two 'wings', as one may name them, identically related to the centre; those relations, then, are 'rational' or rule-governed. We get as much as we got from an outline, yet with no need for that sort of emphatic marking. By way of coherence, to repeat, the coupled pilasters achieve no more; but what they yielded they only yielded by dint of a new irregularity. With symmetry then, we gain doubly, we gain both 'interest' and coherence; with this further difference, however, that here the latter gain is unqualified. We dispense, too, with the hardness of an outline; the eye travels out to either wing, and back to the centre and out again, never finding any need to reach beyond.

V

My last venture must take me, I fear, to fresh fields and perhaps darker woods; where one professionally a philosopher might be wiser not to tread. In formal aesthetics, I used to hold, however we theorise about art, we should keep clear of concrete examples; my own, as I have stressed all along, were intended as no more than schematic. Yet it is a hard thing to institute a self-denying ordinance without some time being tempted to overstep it. Let me at least insist on this: what follows, namely practical application, may of course fail; if so, however, my general argument neither stands nor falls by it.

My findings, I believe, which I have illustrated from architecture, at least from architectural motifs, admit of wider application. We are to speak, as before, specifically of form; but analysis proceeds by abstraction. We have already seen how form and function interact; and of literature, still more plainly, the same holds. The first of my concrete examples is a very brief but well-known passage of Bacon's, the first sentence of his essay *Of Death*:

> Men feare *Death*, as Children fear to goe in the darke: And as that Natural Feare in Children, is increased with Tales, so is the other.

My concern, of course, is with form opposed to formlessness, which can roughly be identified with style. It is with aesthetic as against non-aesthetic form; hence not only with order but order reconciled with variety—and therefore with 'interest' as well. But our problem here presents itself rather differently. For the latter (indeed skating over certain complications) can be treated as given. An orderly form is educed in material already and intrinsically manifold. To proceed then: the broad lines are obvious. The first main division of Bacon's sentence taking it as far as the colon, is divided in turn in two parts, each of which serves to balance the other. It begins, let me note, with three monosyllables, the sort of feature a poorer stylist would have made nothing of. But Bacon is alive to such niceties. A monosyllabic noun or verb invites emphasis; which here it receives, and each singly. We begin, then, with a self-contained unit consisting of three heavy beats. To make the point explicit, perhaps laboriously and superfluously (also modernising the spelling for convenience): 'men' gets its emphasis in retrospect by contrast with 'children'; 'fear' by straightforward repetition, and 'death' being, if not repeated, varied by the final phrase, 'to go in the dark'. But not only by the phrase as a whole: 'death' and 'dark', the two alliterating terminal monosyllables, related both in meaning and form, impose a second pattern on the first. For the rest, it is sufficiently obvious that the first short sub-division both balances and contrasts with the second. And the second main division of the sentence repeats the general pattern of the first. But it may be worth noting the final throw-away phrase; a weak ending, as it would seem, trailing-off, were it not for its coolly dismissive tone, a slight hint of contempt. (The Lord Chancellor, I assume, being orthodox, believed in damnation; Francis Bacon, the essayist, leaves room for doubt.)

For my final and most ambitious example I return to architecture. The comparison I mean to attempt, though with warnings as to its inevitable sketchiness—given the few, rough-hewn tools I have had no space to shape adequately—is between two great domed cathedrals of Europe: St Paul's, London, and Michelangelo's last masterpiece, St Peter's, the Vatican.[14] Now the contrast, you may say, is sufficiently obvious; it will probably be drawn in terms that, in my sense, are not formal but expressive. And if so, I have no notion of challenging it. The majestic repose of Wren's dome—dignified but cool, unimpassioned—contrasts vividly with the character of Michelangelo's; with that uprush of energy, yet concentrated and constrained, that seems almost bent to take heaven by assault. But something may also

[14] I say Michelangelo's: for us questions of ascription are irrelevant, though the upshot of James S. Ackerman's discussion in *The Architecture of Michelangelo* (London, 1961), pp. 100–2, may be taken as less radical than it seems. What we have broadly—allowing that the handling of the detail is partly della Porta's—represents Michelangelo's earlier rather than his final intentions. That anyway ought not to prejudge our verdict as to questions that are purely aesthetic.

be got, I think, from a merely formal analysis, or the outline of such an analysis.

To talk first of the feature I referred to, the giant upthrust of the dome of St Peter's: it is half broken by the lunettes between the ribs, impediments it none the less overwhelms, paradoxically reinforced in the process. It grows greater in swallowing opposition. And doubtless those prominent ribs themselves, so salient a feature, serve largely to contribute to it; and they take up the colonnade of the drum. Aligned with them too, the projections of the broken entablature with its massive coupled columns supporting it, makes it look less over all like an ordinary colonnade than a circle of formidable buttresses. The same design repeats itself in the lantern, and the two, namely lantern and drum, are joined by the ribs of the dome—those, as I said, being aligned. But the lantern not only repeats it on a reduced scale, as it must, but is more compact too; so that the energy, generated below, seems now concentrated, bound in a tighter grip. I cannot pursue the analysis or attempt to apply my general findings (they would concern, broadly speaking, unification implied in contained energy). My concern is the contrast with St Paul's.

Now the unity of a continuous upward movement is precisely what Wren's dome eschews. Its lucid distinction of part from part accounts largely for that first striking difference, its relative coolness and restfulness. And that is a matter of expressiveness. The unbroken line of the entablature, surmounted moreover by a balustrade,[15] divides dome from drum; the smooth contour of the former, with its light ribs barely echoing the colonnade, unpunctured by lunettes, preserve the same clarity of precision. Nor again does the lantern echo the drum; the contrast with Michelangelo is extreme, for nothing invites us to relate them. Indeed it is further worth dwelling on: Wren's lantern is taller but slenderer; with less of vigour, more of grace, than the squat, weighty mass that crowns St Peter's.

I have dwelt, so far, on discontinuities; the mutual distinctness and unlikeness of the components of the dome of St Paul's. Their expressive character is evident enough; but here our concern is their form. The question that seems forcibly to arise is how they are united at all. Well, after all one remains; the feature most people will think of first of all perhaps as peculiarly distinctive to Wren's dome. That smooth outline of which I have spoken is neither semi-circular nor yet oval; its line is entirely its own, first steeply rising, then levelling relatively sharply—the impression being further accentuated by the height of the

---

[15] Perhaps, however, contrary to Wren's wish. His comment, following his dismissal from office, on the main balustrade is well known: 'Ladies,' he said, 'like nothing without lace.'

attic above the drum; indeed it is accentuated yet again by the small, almost playful lantern-dome, a subdued climax, capping the whole, whose squarer contour reinforces, even mimics, the main effect.

The chief datum of any domed building, or its outline, to reduce the thing to manageable terms, is the simple juncture of a vertical and an arc. The peculiar contour that Wren devised—however clearly legibly, as we saw—yet follows no regular curve; hence it is proportionately 'interesting'. But our previous analysis invites this question: how is it so, yet without loss of unity? Now the first step is easy enough: to the problems it later gives rise to—which for Wren were to prove opportunities—I shall return directly. It is plain that this steeper initial slope relates the whole dome to main verticals below; first to the colonnade of the drum, ultimately to the rest of the building, the side elevations of the aisles. Yet that steep curve must shortly change course; it levels off relatively sharply—sharply and arbitrarily, too—an anomaly requiring 'justification'. Variety again must recover unity. It is at least a deviant or distinctive feature to be left as such or further exploited. But genius appropriates what it finds; art, Aristotle wrote, favours lucky accidents, and accidents co-operate with art. What we find is the following: the weight of Wren's lantern, being taller, though relatively slender, defines, as it were, a focal point. The convergent ribs are held down as, turning, they level towards the centre. The lantern, then, secures them in place and thereby 'explains' the distinctive contour.

These are, of course, only the barest pointers; nor have I spoken at all of the manifold subtlety of Wren's lantern, which defies even the pretence of a short analysis. But one question inevitably poses itself; why he chose, to speak loosely, a rectangular solid, a novel, 'unprepared' form, to one roughly cylindrical—such as that with which Michelangelo echoes the drum and he himself used in the Great Model. For of course it might still have been slender, so as to concentrate its weight on the precise centre. But let me look momentarily elsewhere: it is worth noting the strange, concave feature surmounting Michelangelo's lantern, hence at once inverting and continuing the main curve of the drum beneath. The upward movement is both broken and unbroken; but Wren's building is earth-bound and self-sufficient. His lantern, differentiated from the drum, serves a function analogous to the coupling of the terminal pilasters in my earlier example; that, namely, of a sort of marker, indicating a limit. First, plainly, as to expression: that right-angled outline, in contrast to the sweep of a circle, makes for stability. But great art works by condensation or telescoping; each member, and each at the same time, plays many parts. This expressive role doubles with another. The 'felt' weight of the distinctive lantern, its downward pressure, makes the eye still relate it to the rest. Note that, no less plainly, the revolving 'move-ment' of a circular colonnade, with strong circular horizontals, base and cornice, would run counter to it; it would weaken it—(too much or not more than it could absorb? That could only be a matter of judg-ment; or for an architect, planning, of trial and error). So their regularity required for a 'marker' is doubly 'justified' in the whole economy of the building: the lantern with its own mini-dome is half a key, half a linchpin.

People speak of the analysis of works of art; what they mean, I fear, is something rather different, the noting of a few salient features. Literary criticism at least is no longer supposed to be impressionistic. But the difference remains one of degree. One may suspect that an ex-haustive analysis would run to such inordinate length as to defeat its purpose; mere boredom would repel potential readers. And as to my own attempted analyses, both more and less schematic, let me add lastly that they all of course have been *ex post facto*. I know of no mechanical procedure for artists to apply, any more than there are mechanical procedures for finding new and interesting theories or the like in science or mathematics itself.

7

Expressiveness in Visual Art

Children of the imagination, like 'all our fathers', worship stocks and
stones; for what else is the *David* of Michelangelo but a block of inanimate marble? So, too, the reclining *Venus* of Titian and
Brunelleschi's Church of Santo Spirito are only concoctions, artifacts
of stone and plaster or canvas and pigment and the like. But, of course,
to art lovers and connoisseurs they are infinitely more. Expressiveness
in objects of sense seems rather as spiritual grace has been thought
of—as something never wholly or properly their own, descending and
investing them, yet visibly and miraculously manifest.

I confine myself to only one sort of aesthetic excellence, one thing
that we widely praise in works of art; nothing I shall say precludes the
recognition of many others. There exist, so some theorists tell us simply
enough, a third class of property to be found in things not traditionally
taken account of, so-called tertiary qualities, over and above those
familiar 'primary' and 'secondary' qualities (a problematic distinction,
irrelevant here). Verbally, if you like, the suggestion may pass as a
harmless one; every adjective can stand for a property. More must be
at stake, however; and, at least phenomenologically, we shall be told,
the account simply answers to the facts. We do just find all these things
and 'see' them: we 'see' respectively grandeur, serenity, or dignity in
St Peter's, in a Brunelleschi arcade, or in St Paul's dome in London.
(Complex balance, or what we call 'form', is something we find too;
this consideration, however, would belong to another inquiry.)

And they are all, at least prima facie, 'out there'; they are, one must
stress, qualities of those objects, not, certainly, emotions either aroused
in us, or, still less, putatively attributed to their original designers or
makers hundreds of years ago. The latter can be summarily ruled out;
no such question need ever enter our heads. And for the former the objections are barely less familiar: a man looking at a rival or a colleague
might see him unhappy, see 'visible' wretchedness written all over
him; and, far from sharing it, might secretly enjoy his discomfiture.
We first 'see' something, which we then may respond to, and respond
in different ways without 'seeing' anything different.

Now first the main point, which I shall put barely and boldly; doubts and reservations can follow. It is this: expressive things are typically characterised in terms whose primary application is elsewhere. We look at stone or ferroconcrete and call it *bold*. We ascribe *gaiety, serenity,* and the like to colonnades and facades; terms, in the primitive sense, applied to people, their actions, and so on. The ascription, at least on the face of it, must seem odd, somewhat as if one should ascribe *colour, taste,* or *smell* to the square root of nineteen. 'The gesture of the two-wide embracing one-storied colonnades of Ionic columns is irresistible' (Nikolaus Pevsner's description of Park Crescent, Marylebone, London).[1] Mumford, comparing an embassy in a foreign city to the problem facing 'a lecturer from another country addressing a foreign audience', goes on to say:

> Our London embassy presents a cold unsmiling face, a face unfortunately suggesting national arrogance and irresponsible power. . . . One has yet to be persuaded that this blank, bureaucratic-military mask is the true face of America.[2]

Before proceeding, I must pause to take stock; one possible basic objection to my whole approach, to this whole way of presenting the problem, would be the mere denial of its starting-point; that secondary status, namely, that I have made the hallmark of aesthetic vocabulary (not all such vocabulary, perhaps, but a large and significant part of it). Let the critic have the floor, then, and speak. Now surveying some number of facades, suppose we find them to share some common feature, some 'visible' quality, which Mumford, perhaps, labels 'arrogance'. But our critic will advocate another course; we are, henceforth, neutrally, to call it Q; and again what Pevsner calls 'reticence' (ascribing it to Wood's excellent Corn Exchange in Bristol), which we shall refer to as Q', and so on. All these qualities, it may be objected, are those that a learner might well have trouble in picking out—I mean, in default of those imaginary helps that our secondary, 'metaphorical' language supplies. Such questions, however—questions, that is, concerning a priori conceptual distinctions—are not to be settled by appealing to differences in individual psychology; some learners will be quicker, some slower. And, as things in fact stand, there exist some terms that most of us do master, and without any great difficulty, which, on the face of it, are primarily 'aesthetic' terms, for instance *elegance* and *grace*.

[1] Nikolaus Pevsner, *The Buildings of England. VI London* (Harmondsworth, 1952), vol. 2, pp. 348–9.
[2] Lewis Mumford, *The Highway and the City* (London, 1964), pp. 148–9. Looked at less 'physiognomically', the facade of Saarinen's building presents an odd combination of weighty, angular forms with restlessness and movement.

These issues, I fear, are far-reaching, and not to be settled out of hand; but broadly, the case is as follows. We can coin terms in any field we please, an easy course, always available. We can ad hoc postulate qualities, unique, irreducible qualities, hardly explanatory perhaps, but serving at least to stop the mouths of questioners—or such questioners as prefer words to explanations. Not only qualities, incidentally: we shall also need unique relations, unanalysable relations, which soon follow. But, I take it, the rule here, one for which we can cite authorities going back to Ockham, is, briefly, the fewer the better. At least before resigning ourselves we may look about us for alternatives; I mean, before submitting meekly to lie down with so decidedly unattractive a thesis and from it, all too probably, engender more offspring resembling their parent.

But what else might one offer by way of an answer, or urge against such a permissive linguistic policy? Well, at least we can nibble at corners, though most likely, I fear, educing on the other side with every new difficulty, a new ad hoc proviso to meet it. The qualities in question, one may argue, are strangely unstable and shifting, and hence, perhaps, calculated to arouse suspicion. (Very well, we meet the answer, so they may be. Why not? They form a special new sort of quality.) Or take the 'arrogance' we 'see' in a facade and call expressive, or that we 'see' in someone's bearing, or impatience in a gesture. Now its source, we are to note, lies further back; these things, first of all, are states of mind. (Very well—so the quality Q, the unique tertiary quality, may, in its own unique way, resemble ordinary arrogance or impatience, which is given and must be accepted; a sheer matter of fact, after its fashion, perhaps, it may be added, somewhat as certain sorts of sounds, usually shrill sounds, are said to resemble bright colours.) And so on. Let us raise whatever difficulty we like: an ingenious enough apologist, on such lines, will always find some countermanoeuvre to deploy and win, if not a paper victory, at least a stalemate.

But, as I said, nothing prevents our looking for alternatives, alternatives less roundabout and more economical, which if we find them, we shall plainly have a reason for preferring. Now the alternative I propose is, I think, a fairly obvious one: precisely to reverse our critic's manoeuvre. He reads words like *boldness, arrogance* (that is, terms that as applied to works of art prima facie might otherwise count as derivative), on the analogy of pure aesthetic terms, that is, of nonderivative terms such as *elegance* and *grace*. And, on that basis, he sets out to coin and put in currency a whole new aesthetic vocabulary. Now we can precisely proceed in the reverse direction; reading *grace* or *elegance* on the analogy of those derivative terms, of terms like 'aesthetic arrogance' and the rest; reading them, in other words, as expressive, and therefore looking behind them for qualities of another sort, those, on this view, that they will serve to express.

First of all, let us look closer at the former: *graceful*, at least in one very obvious way, is unlike *yellow* or *noisy*, which are qualities simply 'met' in experience. To call something graceful, at least in normal contexts, is to praise it; *graceless* and *inelegant* are terms of disparagement. One can say so in general and pretty confidently, I repeat, barring special qualifications or contexts and, further, without pre-committing ourselves to any one theory of value. These are truisms, however one goes on to account for them, that any theory of value whatever must start from; we stand so far, I hope, on non-controversial ground. But what of our would-be new-found qualities? They suggest strange analogies. 'Desirable yellow'—as opposed perhaps to its complementary, 'undesirable blue'—seems a curious quality merely to meet and wholly know in experience; or is that, perhaps, a further sheer fact? We do merely value or condemn such things—further evidence, if so, of what I spoke of, I mean the monstrous self-multiplication of ad hoc postulates.

But to pursue my suggested alternative; rather than *grace* I shall start first of all with its converse, which I take to be *awkwardness*, eminently an aesthetic or 'visible' quality, though doubtless a negative one (for words such as *ugly*, of course, no less than *beautiful*, are used for expressing distinctively aesthetic views). As to *awkwardness*: we 'see' it in movements in arms and legs, their restriction or jerking, and again in the stiff carriage of bodies, as plainly as one could desire, and possibly as painfully. But, we ask, what lies 'behind' that impression, its non-aesthetic *archetype* (I shall call it), that we set out to look for? The question virtually answers itself. The very word *awkwardness*—and indeed *arrogance*, too—functions equally naturally in either role as describing either a quasi-sensible aesthetic impression, or something practical, a kind of bearing or performance, at least an attempted performance; in fact, often enough, both at once. What lies 'behind' awkwardness, that is aesthetic awkwardness, is of course plain clumsiness; it is bodily ineptitude. And, I am led to reflect, it would have been hard to hit on an unhappier example of a would-be pure tertiary quality as subsisting apart in its own aesthetic realm.

Grace of movement is nowadays perhaps admired, or at least explicitly spoken of, more often in women than in men; and yet it has, perhaps, its masculine counterpart. Whatever holds the twentieth century, or fails to hold, we often find women novelists of earlier times praising in their male characters a quality called 'military bearing'.

Traditionally man governs and fights, while woman presides over domesticity. And small things can be seen as significant. The performance of easy tasks, absurdly easy, which we hardly call 'tasks', such as taking a few steps across a room, lifting something and putting it down again, may suggest likely performance or failure laced with harder ones. Grace of movement suggests sureness and gentleness, the doing of whatever needs doing, but with no commotion, no strain or the like. The poet Richard Lovelace who, one recalls, 'loved honour more', and protested to his Lucasta—who may or may not have been reassured—that otherwise he could never have loved her so much, affirms that he embraced yet more fervently 'a sword, a horse, a shield', which was evidently admirable and very masculine. But consider a woman's typical tasks, perhaps tending a baby, moreover, importing life, not death. We might here prefer a different sort of touch. Grace, again, is to be connected with poise, the latter being less movement than readiness to move, therefore promptly, towards any occasion. The word functions like *awkwardness* either practically or aesthetically; that is, it names either the actual state of readiness or again the vivid quasi-visual impression, the 'visible' appearance of it. Doubtless language may blur these distinctions, which remain possible, none the less, and for these purposes, important. That impression, precisely—the impression of present alertness, quiet and vivid—is what theorists call a 'tertiary quality'. Further, our main point: underlying the aesthetic judgment, the aesthetic impression (impressions being intuitive judgments), what we meet is an ordinary judgment, a judgment, one might add, in which Thomas Gradgrind himself could have found nothing to object to—though he perhaps, or his modern disciples, might prefer to arrive at it otherwise, less 'intuitively' probably, by EEG measurements of tension. Now, similarly, with the quality of grace: 'forced gracefulness' is virtually a contradiction. It is one, like the quality of mercy, that can never be strained. It presupposes a state of mind, and with its a state of musculature, all carrying, of course, their obvious practical implications. They are things that we recognise 'intuitively', and, lastly too, recognising them, generally value.

Here other related notions converge or overlap: add to *grace* the suggestion of reserve, add the consciousness of worth, and it becomes *dignity*. Still more of the same makes it *arrogance*. I take *elegance* for sophisticated grace, at least in social contexts, something probably acquired, less simply spontaneous, a shade nicer. On the other hand, applied to scientific or mathematical theories, the term suggests apparent and visible economy, as where different things, that look totally disconnected, fall together, fall aptly into place, as if it were on purpose to suit us. True, grace itself suggests economy, but never what we call 'rigid economy'; grace, rather, carries a little further, with a hint of amplitude, even space to spare, something like leisureliness. Again, in inanimate things—in arches, pediments, lanterns and the like—gracefulness is still closer to poise, the suggestion being here of exact balance, at once near the edge as it were, yet very safe, a stance whose felicity lies in the combination of economy and ease.[3]

All I have done so far, in fact, amounts to little more than expanding on certain suggestions of Gombrich's:

> For there is indeed such a thing as 'physiognomic perception' which carries strong and immediate conviction. We all experience this immediacy when we look into a human face. We see its cheerfulness or gloom, its kindliness or harshness, without being aware of reading 'signs'. Psychologists such as Heinz Werner[4] have emphasised that this type of 'global' and immediate reaction to expression is not confined to the reading of human faces and gestures. . . . These reactions testify to the constant scrutiny with which we scan our environment with one vital question: 'are you friendly or hostile?' a 'good thing' or a 'bad thing'? It may be argued that the answer to this question is as basic to the survival of any organism as are the answers to the questions of other perceptual probings, such questions as 'what is it?', 'where am I now? ', 'how do I get from here to there without bumping into things?'[5]

'Behind' tertiary qualities, it seems—or anyhow one class of them, those we call 'expressive', including not only *boldness* and *arrogance* but also *elegance* and *grace*—we find other things of a different sort, such as

---

[3] The encyclopaedic F. E. Sparshott has assembled a whole series of interpretations of grace (cf. *The Structure of Aesthetics* (London, 1963), pp. 75–6). The authorities agree in finding it expressive of qualities of character and the like; but Schopenhauer, who happily thought of seeking light on gracefulness by way of its opposite—'wooden stiffness' or 'meaningless bustle' as he calls it—has the truest account, it seems to me. He speaks of 'every position' as 'assumed in the easiest, most appropriate, and convenient way'. Reid, I should say, is near the point, but not quite on it, in speaking of 'perfect propriety of conduct and sentiment, in an amiable character'. For, I think, other things would seem to express amiability more clearly, for instance *charm*, though doubtless charm and grace go naturally together. But by 'propriety of conduct' he most likely means its fitness for practical purposes, which would be a naturally eighteenth-century usage; and if so his account is pretty near our own. Spencer echoes Schopenhauer's attention to 'meaningless bustle', stressing economy; but having got to that point, he gets no further. Mechanical and mathematical economy, in human movement at least, is the very antithesis of grace, for it implies a tense and rigid self-control, whereas grace can always afford to overflow. 'Goodwill, like grace,' says Halifax, 'floweth where it listeth,' and so too of visible gracefulness.

[4] Heinz Werner, *Einführung in die Entwicklungs Psychologie* (Leipzig, 1956), p. 47. [Gombrich's note]

[5] E. H. Gombrich, 'On physiognomic perception', in *Meditation on a Hobby Horse* (London, 1963), pp. 47–8.

skills, dispositions, and the like. One example, taken from *King Lear*: Lear, returning from hunting and finding Kent disguised as a poor man, waiting in his hall, asks him who he is—'A man, Sir', Kent answers (characteristically)—and what he wants: 'Service'. The dialogue proceeds:

> Lear: Who wouldst thou serve?
> Kent: You.
> Lear: Dost thou know me, fellow?
> Kent: No, Sir. But you have that in your countenance which I would
>   fain call master.
> Lear: What's that?
> Kent: Authority. (Act 1, sc. 4, 24–30)

The authority Kent 'sees' in Lear's countenance is, even literally, physiognomic,[6] yet, it seems, not something different in kind from the visible 'arrogance' manifest, according to Mumford, in the facade of the embassy in Grosvenor Square. Kent reports an immediate impression, something 'seen' and not 'contemplated' or dwelt on. The aesthetic attitude, theorists tell us, is contemplative; Kent here is eminently practical. The judgment he makes, or pretends—but only half-pretends—to make in the character he is playing, is briefly this: Lear, he says, is a man to be obeyed. Such impressions, doubtless, are notoriously deceptive, but it remains true that the greater part of our practical conduct, especially under pressure of time, inevitably rests on them. And it remains astonishing what complexities of feeling and attitude a really intuitive observer can 'read', reliably and at once, in looks and movements. Kent, to repeat, passes a practical judgment, to qualify it further, an 'intuitive' practical judgment, not one (presumably) he would offer or be able to verify or do anything like demonstrate. (I shall henceforth drop the quotation marks enclosing *intuitive*, for, I think, to handle the word we no longer need forceps.) So-called physiognomic perception is in reality not perception at all, but nearer judgment, intuitive judgment. Its objects are not sensible, but mental—namely, skills, dispositions, and the like. It is in fact intuitive judgment, but based on a present perception. We may call it, in a certain sense, 'confused perception'; but the word *confused*, here, need imply no disparagement. Doubtless clarity, in appropriate theoretical contexts, is something we value, along with rigour, precision, and

---

[6] Though commentators make *countenance* mean, not just face, but more generally *bearing*, the verb *to countenance* in *Macbeth* (Act 2, sc. 3, 81) means simply *face* or 'Look in the face', confront; and other examples abound, for instance, what of 'A countenance more in sorrow than in anger'? The question two lines earlier had been, 'Then saw you not his *face*?' Nothing, however, in the present argument turns on this point.

above all consistency. Nothing follows elsewhere. The flat surface of a looking glass, for instance, is not only hard but virtually impossible to distinguish focally, to see separately from whatever it happens to reflect. So here, too, we find a kind of confusion, one of course which need involve no intellectual confusion. And it is something we deliberately create; we should be worse off, not better, without it.

So-called physiognomic perception runs together two distinct kinds of object—those of sense perception, faces and facades, and others that, we say, lie behind them—which properly speaking consists in this. We infer these from those, or rather we quasi-infer them. For (among other qualifications to follow) strictly to speak of an 'inference' you need two things—evidence and conclusion; they are first distinguished and subsequently related. Here, precisely, we take everything at once. Let us more accurately say that, if that quasi-judgment were a true one, we should infer it; we should do so, in other words, if it were not holistic and intuitive but explicit. In the case before us, what we find is this. The latter presence is less inferred than 'sensed' or 'felt'; the two things are not identified separately. It is that failure that, in certain aesthetic theories that have gained considerable currency, is called 'fusion', fusion of percept and concept, for instance, or alternatively is obscurely hinted at in Elisco Vivas's paradoxical references to 'felt meanings' in poetry and the like.

In a facade, it seems, we 'see' arrogance; menace, in storm clouds. Phenomenologically, at least, theorists insist, we experience such impressions 'objectively'; we experience them as qualities of things. Certainly, if so, they are tertiary qualities. But it might be truer to say, in somewhat Sartrean language, that we experience them as qualities haunting things—a further something about them, but neither explicitly distinguished nor firmly grasped.

Of these two kinds of object, to repeat, one is merely thought of, but suggested by the other, actually perceived. And a further confusion is this: it is quasi-inferred, not only as present, but also (at least most often) as good or bad; or, if not most often, for obvious reasons it is such impressions that chiefly interest us. Thus, in our example, fitness to command is something we have reason to value; and we found similarly that poise and grace of movement import valuable qualities. There are, then, properly, two judgments and essentially separate, but all grasped in a single impression—one of value, the other of existence—of something, that is to say, both as present and as good. But we find that our aesthetic impressions distinguish neither one from the other, nor yet the synthesis of both from their common basis in things literally perceived.

Hospers, writing of what he calls 'expression'—I think, the same thing is what I have been calling 'expressiveness'—refuses to identify it with beauty. Expressive things, he points out, in a simple argument, but surely conclusive, are often not beautiful but ugly.[7] He himself speaks of 'whining adagios', mentioned by Hanslick; but simpler examples might serve. Awkward movements are expressive and ugly, their ugliness and expressiveness being indeed exactly proportional. Our appraisal of what we 'see', of the so-called 'tertiary quality' reflects our appraisal of its archetype; or rather, more accurately, it is simply one and the same thing. Admiration for appropriate skills—or, conversely, its reverse in the case of their opposites, say, physical ineptitude or clumsiness—makes part of a single impression and one precisely which contains in itself no distinction between what I see and what I 'see'. Thus, we naturally find things at once expressive and ugly, where, judging intuitively, we judge what they express to be objectionable or bad, that is, where we 'feel' it to be antipathetic.

It follows, too, that various people's judgments will differ and not only because they first differ, although of course they often do, as to what sorts of non-aesthetic things are good and bad. But further: a voice, for example, that I hear as authoritative, as firm, a better judge may hear rather differently, as pitched a little too shrill, perhaps, as straining after authority, not quietly or confidently possessed of it.

I have spoken so far of skills, dispositions, and the like, of different sorts of mental quality to be found 'behind' aesthetic impressions. But, let us note, our argument need imply no such restriction; it requires nothing more than a further object of thought, one whose presence we first 'infer' and then secondly respond to favourably or unfavourably, approve or condemn. Tools and instruments, for instance, have functions to fulfil, which they do well or badly; we commend or condemn them accordingly. Those, so far, of course, are 'straight' practical judgments. Now in aesthetics we conversely seek vivid impressions and seek no further; viewing instruments too, then, we may judge on occasion, not how they function in fact, but how they look. It would be nonsense to say—what perhaps no functionalist ever seriously said, or literally meant—that a perfectly functioning building is *eo ipso* beautiful. But suppose that a building looks 'visibly' functional, that the impression is immediate and strong: now our stance changes; to say that is certainly to make on its behalf an aesthetic claim. For we are now judging what we 'infer', what we quasi-infer, in what we immediately see; and at least minimally we should prefer it to look not shaky or top-heavy, but firm and stable. For underlying the aesthetic preference, here as before, there exists a practical one. Anything else

[7] John Hospers, *Meaning and Truth in the Arts* (Chapel Hill, 1946), p. 70.

apart, we have, in Professor Nowell-Smith's terminology, a pro-attitude to buildings that stand up.

Let me add a last kind of expressiveness, rarely recognised as such, namely this: where theories in science or mathematics are recommended, as they often are, of course, in aesthetic terms, as *elegant* or *beautiful*, not only as *valid* or *true*, then their aesthetic excellence, one must insist, is in fact a form of expressiveness. Theory, doubtless, no less than practice, has its own values, intrinsic values—theoretical power, rigour, coherence. It may have them, however, without showing them—I mean, without making them visible or obvious; but where the clothing, as it were, expresses the body, where the mere form of the theory vividly reveals its own workings, we shall find not only such theoretical values, but aesthetic value too. Similarly, a last case, with a sportsman: say a cricket batsman, who not only stays in and scores—our primary, as it were, 'practical' evaluation—but one whose strokes, whose very movements, also express their own function, as he cuts or drives with vividly 'visible' command. Now here once again, on the same principles as before, an aesthetic appraisal supervenes.[8]

Kent's concern, I said, when he read authority in Lear's looks, is not primarily aesthetic. He does not dwell on the impression for its own sake—yet, in saying so I find myself pausing. For surely the words Shakespeare gives him, with their brusqueness, their vivid aptness, hint at more. We are made momentarily, before the dialogue hurries on, to notice and enjoy the possibility of a face that 'has that something in it' that one naturally obeys; it is at least a first budding of the aesthetic. Now once we remove practical pressures, the unremitting requirements of action that drive us hourly on, the rest follows; spontaneously a purely aesthetic interest will open up.

To repeat, Kent's interest is practical; but where our interest is strictly aesthetic, no practical question arises. Indeed, if it did, there may be nothing 'there' for it to judge. The 'wide-embracing gesture' of Park Crescent, described by Pevsner as 'irresistible', is immediately and visibly 'seen'; and gestures, of course, bona fide gestures, do certainly express attitudes, hostile, friendly, or neutral. But what of a terrace of houses? Bricks and mortars, certainly, are not friendly or hostile—a point, let us note, on which the admirer of Park Crescent

---

[8] I have attempted no examples from literature which raise large problems of their own, and problems I cannot adequately explore here. Language, roughly, in virtue not only of its visible or audible forms, but also of its syntax and vocabulary, acquires a kind of quasi-publicity. We have, at least in a certain sense, one object, more accessible, 'coloured' by others less so, that 'lie behind' it. And clearly we have pro and con attitudes to ideas and emotions that language is made to express. Or sometimes, without actually sharing them, we feel bound to take them seriously none the less—often, too, certainly, admiring the extreme vividness of their expression itself.

need be under no illusion. Nor can Lear's countenance, his face or bearing itself—though it may have authority 'in' it—be fit or unfit to command. One passes a make-believe judgment, and is unlikely to mistake it for a real one; a judgment that becomes, roughly speaking, 'if that *per impossible* were a gesture, it would then be a warmly open and friendly one.' Toy guns, to take an analogy, are made to play with, not fight with, and are assessed for their merits accordingly. Further, play is an activity *sui generis*, yet an activity that in default of the notion of real guns—those that kill people—would be inconceivable.[9]

Art, once again, is both continuous and discontinuous with life. We can either merely dwell in impressions, or seek alternatively to clarify or transform them. They are, of course, fallible, and accordingly call for clarification, though not generally for practical purposes, and under the pressure of the moment, beyond a certain 'reasonable' point. Perfect clarity, certainly, is one thing to aim at; it is not the only thing. Let us recall another, no less requisite, and still for practical purposes, a strong sense or sure intuition of qualities immediately 'seen'. But once we leave practical preoccupations behind, two developments lie open beyond them. We can dwell in impressions for their own sake, now seeking mere heightened sensitivity, which has become pure aesthetic sensitivity; or, alternatively, we can seek for sheer clarity, clarity and intelligibility for their own sake, proceeding, in other words, into the alternative region of pure theory. Neither serves any practical purpose—neither pure science, nor pure art; both, then, are in that sense gratuitous; and both are valuable.

I spoke earlier of better judges and worse. Let us return to our earlier example, the would-be 'authoritative' voice, the voice that different hearers hear differently, that rings true in my ears but not in yours. That, though so far a practical issue, brings us to the edge of problems that are more specifically aesthetic. First of all, in an instance like this, we need not differ in our primary attitudes; in those we may call pre-aesthetic. We both want to see power in good hands—firm, competent, and trustworthy hands. But turn next to the corresponding quasi-judgment, now an aesthetic judgment. Parallel differences, of course, appear, which naturally we should like ways of resolving. Now those, in one sense, we inevitably lack; there can be no *experimentum crucis* or the like. But that, of course, is anything but exceptional, by no means confined to aesthetics; most fact-statements state only probabilities. The weather forecast, for instance, predicts rain; but of course the non-appearance of rain does not show that the forecaster was wrong. He went on the evidence, perhaps rightly; it was indeed highly probable.

[9] See Wittgenstein, *Philosophical Investigations* (Oxford, 1953), i. 282.

True, this failure, along with similar predictions which subsequent events prove false, might certainly have some tendency to show that the forecaster is wrong. So far, then, the judgment we have been speaking of, concerning someone's fitness to command, whether based on the sound of his voice or on other, solider evidence, is no different in principle. In theory, you may say, it could be put to the test, if the owner of the 'authoritative' voice, presently gaining a position of authority, were to succeed or fail. But the test, plainly, is anything but decisive: success or failure, notoriously, is contingent on a thousand factors; and winners (we generally observe) are wonderfully lucky. But, at least, verificationists will insist, we still know what to 'count', what to reckon, in such cases, as confirmation or disconfirmation, as relevant evidence.

Hence, the next step, it may seem, is the dubious one; we pass from judgment proper to what I have called quasi-judgment. To those quasi-judgments—judgments which precisely are no longer practical—the truth or falsity of any subsequent event cannot be relevant; no such question can arise. Therefore nothing, it would seem, even tends to confirm or cast doubt upon them. Suppose we say so; it is doubtless a possible way of speaking. So that whatever I hear as authoritative is *eo ipso* 'authoritative to me'. It is, none the less, not the only one, nor in point of fact how we ordinarily talk. I may after all still be what we call a bad judge; and in regard to that possibility, why should evidence be lacking? True, it can only be evidence, strictly speaking, of my practical judgment, rather than my aesthetic judgment, my judgment of authority in people, for instance. Set the two things side by side, however: the analogy between them is pretty striking, and if there are differences as well, who is to declare their logical relevance self-evident? It seems that certain statements, certain judgments, are to be allowed; they pass and gain the status of being 'meaningful'. (Or 'science' by a line of 'demarcation' is distinguished from inferior non-science: presumably inferior, for otherwise what interest attaches to the demarcation?) What we still need to know will be principles that lay down for us just where to draw the line—what principles, and again, how to justify them.

Unless here, as elsewhere, one simply 'decides': one can draw it, if he likes, precisely here. Those judgments are empirical and meaningful; these others are pseudo-judgments, void of content. What follows? We on our side can 'decide' differently, using the same logical prerogative, or existential prerogative, which is one way of settling philosophical difficulties. Indeed, verificationists show wonderful ingenuity in devising different sorts of strong as against weak, and direct as against indirect verification, so as to let in and keep out just what they want. Ingenuity, I fear, cannot make it less dogmatic; and with a dogmatist the right course is to steal his clothing. Answer a dogmatist according to his dogma, lest he be undogmatic in his own conceit. We answer then that we are verificationists too, but more thorough, more comprehensive verificationists. We take account, not only of 'direct' and 'indirect' verification as hitherto recognised, but also of 'secondary indirect verification' (or 'oblique verification') hitherto overlooked.

But after all, I shall doubtless be asked, what is this new method, this 'secondary indirect verification'? I have already said. One treats the pure aesthetic judgment as if it were practical, intuitively practical, ignoring extraneous information, judging not what the thing is, but how it looks; so far there is nothing peculiar to aesthetics. The judgment 'Those clouds look like rain' is intelligible, surely, and may be true, yet concerns appearances, only appearances. Further, I should not withdraw it, should not judge otherwise, even though I may happen to know that nothing but perfect weather lies ahead. I know it, perhaps, by special divine revelation or by private radio communication from the stratosphere. I may say that a man sounds authoritative, that any competent judge would agree, though I myself know him, from some special acquaintance, in fact to be singularly foolish and vacillating, incorrigibly timid and inept.

Larger issues, I fear, lurk behind; and I can only indicate roughly where they lie, can point out the appropriate area, not properly explore it. All empirical findings presuppose judgment, and judgment itself not empirical; you must recognise green things where you see them, to test empirically whether some substance, perhaps immersed in acid, turns green. We assign individuals to given classes, which seems not to be hard. Not in that instance, certainly, but elsewhere the case changes. What are we to say of an 'inflationary trend' or 'negligence' (John Wisdom's example) or—something that may matter in its own way, whose classification may matter, at least, as determining its liability to import duty—a 'work of art'? Decisions here, or judgments, are less straightforward. Or is neurosis rightly classified as disease?—'Mental illness' says Thomas Szasz, a shade dramatically perhaps, 'is a myth'.

We must go further; such judgments often presuppose others too, and others that differ in kind. We have to do with interpenetrating dimensions; notions can, so to speak, cross our ordinary logical boundaries. Thus, streams of energy are like streams of water—like them, yet radically different. Or light that travels (Stephen Toulmin's example), and travels in straight lines, is like a travelling vehicle or a flying stone. Certain questions that in the old context we ask naturally and legitimately—the question 'Travelling fast or slowly?', 'A stream of energy flowing or dammed up?'—remain equally appropriate here, and they are carried over automatically into the new. But, no less evidently, others are ruled out. That latter stream, for instance, carries with it no quantity of sand or sediment, nor flows between low or lofty banks. We have here a new judgment of likeness, if you like a new sort of class intrusion, though one that embraces or straddles other radical differences. From one perspective the damming-up of energy and of water are things of the same kind, though a kind that also cuts across others. Again, in regard to the whole procedure: the legitimacy of models and metaphors yields questions enough to argue over, both in detail and in general. What we lack, and inevitably lack, is any short or simple way of settling them.

Children's stories paint a world in black and white. At least they used to; nowadays (I believe) psychology has got hold of them. And it seems there remain sophisticated theorists whose logical perspective is much the same; who long to hear a clear, conceptual bell that either strikes—suppose we only hit hard enough—or else fails to. They long for 'decision procedures', for answers that are final and unquestionable. We may indeed wish for them, but our actual searching inevitably proceeds mostly among shifting shades of grey. It seems that the harder balance to hold involves recognising ideals as ideals, neither merely relinquishing them, nor mistaking them for accomplished realities. Precision, like economy and completeness, has its place among regulative principles, among ideals. And, meanwhile, all those problems remain and confront us obscurely and actually, which we must either blindly legislate out of existence, or else accept and make the best of as they are. But to go further: different questions arise at different levels. We can ask, for instance, first and generally, whether energy (or whether libido) may be conceived on the analogy of a stream, or light can be conceived as the kind of thing that travels. Now say that we answer affirmatively. To do so straightaway lets in a whole new range of questions that could never arise otherwise. Suppose someone looks tired or inert. Now given this new way of thinking, we shall naturally ask other questions in turn. Is his energy, his real energy, dammed up, in technical language 'repressed'?—and if so we next ask 'Repressed by what?' Or is the original supply, the source or spring, in some way deficient? So much in general. Turn now to specifically aesthetic judgments or quasi-judgments; we shall find that the formal analogy holds, indeed holds exactly. To ascribe *arrogance* or *authority* to a facade means to treat it, roughly speaking, like a person, to assess it after the manner of a man's looks, his voice or bearing. And that is the first step, one, however, that easily gets taken for granted, though without it the rest would be nonsense; it would be no less nonsense to apply the term 'authoritative' to a building than to call it, say, the square root of nineteen. Now the initial 'seeing-as' plainly involves a certain exercise of imagination, and here already it must be possible to fail.

Two distinct steps are involved, to repeat: we first see a facade as a face, which we can then see as authoritative or arrogant. The former is imaginative 'seeing-as'; the latter is, basically—and odd as the account may sound—a judgment of class-inclusion. Now not all such issues, once again, can be plain sailing; they may or may not be decidable out of hand. Some, perhaps, we must also acknowledge, may never be decidable at all; and everywhere we shall find a certain indeterminate fringe. Both, none the less, are things belonging intrinsically to rational thinking—the one at all levels, the other at all but ground level. Moreover, both are often presupposed—the first, indeed, not often but always—in any final appeal to empirical facts. Now take this sort of question comprehensively. To expect simple procedures for settling them would be naïve. And again, in default of such procedures, it would be, not naïve, but wrong-headedly sophisticated to dismiss them as meaningless.

As to intuitive perception, if only to make it clear that we need to go deeper into these regions than merely de facto psychology, let me add this: we are speaking of something that lies in our nature as rational beings, something intrinsic to it, not accidental. I need not speak of omniscience; I leave that on one side. I speak, then, of fallible beings, learning progressively, and ignore, too, some would-be progressive learner, one in whose mind new truths start out independently, say, like cards in a card index; each, in other words, being wholly self-contained and self-sufficient. For it is a description that no fact can answer to, inasmuch as each item is, as it were, bound to point to and admit of modification by others still perhaps to follow; in brief, any one suggests others. What remains is as follows. Everything, each single object, among those passing before us incessantly, perhaps in the daily perceptual stream, can never totally focus our attention which, once again, would be a feat only for omniscience. Each one, then, will carry its suggestion of others, suggestions half-clinging to it, and 'colouring' it, which are then grasped intuitively, grasped as things lying 'behind'.

Now any mere exercise of our faculties, let us say—though these, I must grant at once, are large issues, and issues impossible properly to explore here—is its own end and justification. To act is to choose to act, and what we choose *ceteris paribus* we think good. We may be wrong, doubtless—wrong in any instance. But the presumption necessarily is otherwise; not everyone can be perennially fooled. And so much is necessary, an ineluctable assumption, for thought to be possible at all. Next then, if their mere exercise is good, their fuller exercise will be proportionately better; and art, in one aspect at least, if the previous argument proves acceptable, exercises certain of our faculties—namely, our intuitive faculties—to their fullest.

A couple of final points—points, I hope, that we can deal with more briefly: expressiveness, I have implied, is pervasive. Watching, walking, or talking, we make intuitive judgments all the time. Now works of art differ, of course, but differ in degree, not in kind; they differ, more specifically, in their vividness or concentration of expression. In poetry, it has often been remarked, words seem, as it were, charged or even surcharged with meaning, far beyond their ordinary quota; and visual art, too, presents objects that seem fuller, richer than mere objects, as if they had acquired a new depth, indeed a new dimension of depth. It is a difference that is essential, certainly one, so far as possible, I do not wish to play down. Here, however, I shall not seek to explore or account for it, not, certainly, that it need be unintelligible or inexplicable. But the analysis of particular effects, the means of heightening particular impressions, I take to be the proper business of art criticism and literary criticism, not the business of the philosophy of art, though the fact, which paradoxical or not, certainly is a fact—that their effects can seem positively more vivid in their 'aesthetic' presentation than its archetype, the thing itself—might repay exploration on another occasion.

Lastly, a point dwelt on, and not only dwelt on but fully and brilliantly illustrated, by Gombrich. Expression presupposes a context; we bring expectations to works of art, that is, to particular works, holding comparisons at least implicitly in readiness, normally, no doubt, unconsciously. Now we see them accordingly then, say, as reticent or exuberant, as joyful or calm; and with a different background or set of expectations, the expression, too, may startlingly differ.

The difficulty is certainly real, but I think more practical than theoretical. First, as to works from some alien culture, wholly alien prehistoric works, for example: they have, in fact, I have very little doubt, been often quite wildly misjudged. And, of course, if we come to judge them better, it is by learning more of their background, the culture to which they belong. With conscious innovators, however, the case differs; with innovators like Caravaggio or Wordsworth, who were still part of the culture they rebelled against. And as such they felt themselves rebels. True, there must be some things, some aesthetic effects, that history has all but obliterated. Thus, for instance, early baroque nowadays, to our eyes, can never be quite what it presumably was to its contemporaries. We compare it, unlike them, to what followed and not what preceded, not to mannerism or the renaissance, but to high baroque—that is, to just the same sort of effect carried further. For us, then, inevitably, its impact, its emphatic drama, will partly be muted. At most we can hope and strive, with historical aids, progressively to approximate to an appropriate point of view, which we do more or less anyway in all sorts of historical study. Or alternatively, what seems to be the sole obvious alternative—which some theorists, in ethics, too, appear to revel in as perfect freedom, though one might rather think it perfect meaninglessness, making responsible freedom impossible—we can give ourselves leave to see anything as anything.

8

Presentational Objects and their Interpretation

The work of artists is to make works of art, and of theorists theoretical works. In our ordinary dealings with such things, elusive as ontologists may find them, we seem to know well enough in either instance how we should regard and handle them. Ontological questions are none the less raised: what species of entity may they be? It is a question, I confess, to which I could never respond with much enthusiasm. My own interest in art is more ordinary; I care about paintings and poems, about what serves to make them good or bad, about how we should look at or read them. Yet it may prove after all that the two issues are not wholly unrelated.

'Grammar,' says Wittgenstein, in one of those dark teasing dicta of his, 'tells us what kind of object anything is.'[1] Where an air of obscurely charged potency clings to philosophical utterances it seems to affect different readers differently; but perhaps we can ignore that, and seek simply to get at the issue. At least this present saying seems to me to reward the labour it demands.

First, presumably, there may be objects of all sorts: people, pebbles, propositions, works of art. The parenthesis 'Theology as grammar' suggests that Wittgenstein himself would have added the Deity. These are things which we speak of in different ways; which for example we grasp or avoid as we do material things, at least those of appropriate dimensions; or which we blame or expostulate or fall in love with, these of course being attitudes proper to people; which again, in the case of propositions, we affirm, doubt or write on blackboards; which we pray to or worship or blaspheme against, in the case of God. Here, I recall a saying of John Wisdom's which, I think, proves helpful and relevant; namely that ontological and epistemological questions prove ultimately to be one and the same. Philosophers of the past used to ask what was, say, a table in itself—behind 'the veil of appearance', the real thing. The veil in question however proves to be a kind of net. We have the criss-crossing of forms of speech and forms of conduct and talk of appearances among them. Together they define our different concepts. And the whole complex, it would seem, can hardly sensibly be thought

[1] *Philosophical Investigations* (Oxford, 1963), i. 373.

of as interposing between us and objects; for it itself serves to establish the latter and marks out their logical contours. In general it defines for us our different notions—notions which would otherwise be vacuous. Perhaps however I need not labour the point; all this by now, I assume, is tolerably familiar. There are, I said, objects of all sorts; yet a twofold distinction exists too.

We may use the word first to accord 'ontological status' to favoured candidates (I use jargon deliberately to leave open the issues it obfuscates). But there are, secondly, intensional objects, for instance objects of concern, or thought, perception and the like. Now as to the 'furniture of the universe', in Russell's phrase, there will presumably be diverse items of furniture. And footstools, ontological footstools, will differ from ontological armchairs; which, where 'object' is used intensionally, no longer holds. For what I merely think of, you may see; what I worship, perhaps the brute image of Dagon, you in your righteousness may abominate. Here we have objects that differ as objects of intensional attitudes, but which are, ontologically, the same. Yet this difference at a certain level grows less clear. Ontological objects, I suggested, are defined by appropriate attitudes; by the ways in which they are known or may be known, and perhaps others too. Chairs and tables may be seen as well as thought of; they cannot be affirmed or denied. Propositions, precisely conversely, are things that can be doubted or believed; this lies in their nature; but they cannot be seen, smelt or tasted. The upshot is this: when we are speaking not of actual but only possible attitudes, and again not of individuals who see or think of things, but of people quite generally, the pattern changes. Here kinds of ontological objects are kinds of object for cognitive and similar attitudes too.

I am of course by devious tackings, and through waters not wholly untroubled, approaching my own objective; works of art. A work of art is a thing *sui generis*; so much can be said tolerably tamely. As a convenient formula to summarise these platitudes—namely that these things are known, viewed and valued precisely thus, as we all very familiarly understand them to be known, viewed and valued—I shall speak of them as presentational objects; though I use the phrase rather differently from Richard Wollheim, from whom I have stolen it. (In philosophy, perhaps, one may innocently play at Robin Hood; in other words, theft becomes excusable when it is taken as serving the general interest.)

Wollheim opposes this theory to another that he himself advocates; works of art, with certain qualifications, are to be identified with physical things. What should one say? I find the whole notion a perplexing one; what sort of identity can be in question? Certainly I can imagine possible contexts for it. 'That statue,' one may say, or even perhaps 'that piece of marble is—is identical with—Bernini's St Longinus.' I dare say with ingenuity one might even imagine some odd context for 'The physical object is Bernini's St Longinus.' But in fact he asserts it wholly generally. And of course the trouble is that it looks at face value patently false; I mean that it looks like the false assertion that what Wittgenstein calls the 'grammar' of the two concepts—the sorts of discourse and 'forms of life' that sustain them—are not in fact different but the same.

Wittgenstein appears later in Wollheim's book; at this stage he is little in evidence. 'It is plausible,' he writes, 'to assume that things are physical objects unless they very obviously aren't.'[2] Again I am puzzled. It is an assertion that has to me an odd air of willing itself to its conclusion by a kind of autosuggestion, by treating it as already arrived at. We are offered two phrases; Wollheim refers to 'what it is plausible to assume' and again to what things 'obviously are'. Certainly assumptions may be plausible and views obvious; except that the latter adjective is perhaps somewhat stronger, they might, I think, be taken as virtually synonymous. Wollheim's manoeuvre, it seems, is first to prise apart the two sides of the autology, and next, having done so, as it were, to use the leverage of the one to hoist up the other. For myself, I might add incidentally, I fail to find the assumption plausible at all. Why should material objects, chairs, trees and pieces of marble, have some privileged ontological status? Platitudinously, they are what they are, and are known in appropriate ways. They may indeed, as Strawson argues, have a primacy of a different sort; without these things we could never conceive of others. But that is a different sort of difference, providing no passage to reductionism.

But perhaps my criticisms pass Wollheim by. He seems to advance from the ontological options offered in the first part of his book to some sort of Wittgensteinian view at the end; the transition in question is what eludes me. I expect that I may have failed clearly to have followed it. I shall not pursue the issue however; as I indicated, my interest in what I call the presentational theory is, I think, rather different from his.

My concern is with the integrity of art, with the integrity of particular works as well as that of the concept itself. The point of presentational theory is, as I understand it, precisely this: it asserts, platitudinously, that works of art are what they are. But it serves, too, to compare them with other things; to register, on the one hand, their likeness to physical objects, say, stones or tables; on the other to propositions or theories. They are also of course unlike both; our con-

[2] Richard Wollheim, *Art and Its Objects* (New York, 1968), p. 3.

cern is with both likenesses and differences. The quasi-propositional character of much art is to Wollheim a main objection to the theory; for me, at least for my version of it, I take it to be a paramount advantage. Theories have a kind of autonomy and a kind of publicity too; when you and I discuss, say, the Quantum Theory, we are, it seems, considering the same object, in some sense a public object, then, and one that is unique of its kind. The same is true, I believe, of works of art. Theories, too, are irreducible to material things, even to types of material thing; classes of inscription, for instance. Of works of art, I suggest, the same holds. And further and more important, a point I shall have to return to, they belong to history. The history of thought is a mosaic where each piece is wedged in its place. The same holds for history of art. Theories too are called good or bad; they are intrinsically objects of assessment. And these merits or demerits are their own, and not alterable with their creator's intentions. In some sense, at least, the same is pretty obviously true of works of art. Yet another likeness: they invite interpretation, which can succeed or fail. It follows then that they are vulnerable to misinterpretation too—especially at the hands of those who ignore history. Some theorists use history, the history of thought or of art and some again political history, as a kind of Rorschach test, upon which to project their own preoccupations or fads. Each is malleable material to be manipulated; one can rebuild it, if not nearer the heart's desire, at least nearer one's own interests, or nearer those of one's own clique or culture. Old works are brought up to date. *Hamlet* to some Freudians is a study in the oedipus complex; the sculpture in the Medici Chapel was sometimes taken by Italian patriots of the period of the *Risorgimento* as having to do with the political dismemberment of fifteenth-century Italy.

Now the past is still of course a living past. It would be superfluous to illustrate the fact that artists use the work of their predecessors, which sometimes might have looked pretty remote, and is strangely transformed in the process. But that remains honest and open; it is plainly neither interpretation nor misinterpretation, but merely part of the normal creative process. Interpreters such as I have been speaking of, I mean those who give themselves leave to ignore history, are, one may suspect, often at bottom perhaps artists *manqués*, producing variations on a theme—a thing harmless in itself. Francis Bacon and other artists have done it explicitly and overtly. A philosopher similarly may use Kant or Aristotle, though translating what he uses into a different philosophical idiom. Cézanne set out to re-do Pousin 'd'après la nature'; one might similarly perhaps, concerning oneself with the conditions of any possible language, seek to re-do Kant after Wittgenstein. No sensible person would object, at least not in principle. All that would be obviously vicious would be to confuse the historical Kant, the philosopher of the eighteenth century, whose background was Leibniz and Wolff, with what later analytic thinkers educe from him. That confusion, however, would be gratuitous. Pater's *Mona Lisa* by contrast or Jones's oedipal Hamlet form, as it were, an indeterminate mode, neither fish nor fowl; though indeed, forgetting their professed status as criticism, one may still enjoy in the former the elegance of its laboured prose—though the cadences are a little weary—and even a kind of ingenuity in the other.

Let me briefly enlarge on the last point, adding a more specific example. There is a moment in *Henry IV, Part I* where the Prince has got rid of the Sheriff; 'certain men', the latter says, having been traced to the house after the robbery. And he adds:

> One of them is well known, my gracious lord,
> A gross fat man. (Act ii, sc. 4)

To which the Carrier briefly subjoins, 'As fat as butter'. Falstaff must have been easy to identify. And the Prince afterwards, having extricated himself with 'a true face and good conscience', observes—with that odd mixture of contempt and amusement, perhaps a kind of affection that characterises his attitude—'this oily rascal is known as well as Paul's'. Now Shakespeare in general, seeking appropriate epithets for Falstaff and his enormous bulk, seems positively to glory in hyperboles, in the extreme and gross preposterousness of his comparisons. For myself, with the reference to St Paul's, I could never help thinking of the great drum and dome that Wren was to build a hundred years later; perhaps a still happier image than the Early English Gothic of the contemporary building. The point is worth pausing on, I think. My dominant concern, I repeat, is simply the integrity of works of art. And I answer with Johnson that the old reading may not be better; it suffices that it is Shakespeare's. Johnson, it is true, was speaking of licentious emendation; but the questions raised by licentious interpretation would seem to be essentially the same. 'If phraseology is to be changed,' he writes, 'as words grow uncouth by disuse, or gross by vulgarity, the history of language will be lost; we shall no longer have the words of any author; and, as these alterations will often be unskillfully made, we shall in time have very little of his meaning.'[3] On behalf of interpreters it may be said that they at least leave the object intact; and subsequent generations may still dig it up again, extricate the ancient forms from among the rubble. Why they should on their

---

[3] Samuel Johnson, *Plays of William Shakespeare* (London, 1765), Note on Hamlet, Act iv, sc. 5, 84.

own principles is obscure; at least where, like Wollheim, they positively acclaim the grand liberty they allow themselves. If so, I find no difference between them and those eighteenth-century editors who rewrote Shakespeare to accord with their own superior taste—even if, by comparison, modern interpreters lacked the courage of their convictions, or perhaps only opportunity to implement them. For a few small changes would surely make *Hamlet* fit Jones's reading far more convincingly than the quarto or folio text fits it.

A work of art, I have said, belongs to history. Wollheim himself says the same, at least at one point in his argument. To appreciate particular works we need some understanding of their background, for the history of art raises problems—once again like the history of thought—which these works may precisely seek to solve. Now with that I would certainly agree; though as to the example that Wollheim uses to illustrate the point I have some doubts; namely of the steeple of St Martin-in-the-Fields. The facade is to be seen, Wollheim writes, 'as a solution to a problem which for fifty years exercised English architects; how to combine a temple facade or portico with the traditional English demand for a west tower'.[4] I see no trace of such a tradition.[5] But the general thesis remains unaffected.

So far my conclusion is this; works of art invite comparison, a rewarding comparison in many ways, with works of philosophy or science, which is one thing the presentational theory—if any such theory indeed exists—can be usefully seen as insisting on. Each can be spoken of as objects. We apprehend each in its own way, and each must be thought of accordingly. For such apprehension defines the concept. But the comparison it more obviously insists on is with objects of ordinary perception: trees, tables, teaspoons and the like. There is some sort of immediacy, we feel, in our awareness of so-called aesthetic qualities, say, the serenity of an early Renaissance facade or the dynamism and power of its Baroque counterpart; an immediacy that is naturally comparable, as I said, to our ordinary perception of shapes or colours. The point is a familiar one, and for present purposes can be taken for granted, though doubtless much more might be said. It is more relevant to note that this immediacy, however we regard it, need

[4] Op. cit., p. 62.
[5] A portico is very different from a temple front. The former presents no special problem. Gibbs himself had handled it wholly comfortably in his little chapel of St Peter's, Vere Street. The attempt to combine a steeple with a temple front is quite another matter, a temptation that was understandably strong. That can help to make Gibbs's failure intelligible; it could not possibly transform it into success. And, it seems, the pediment was anyway a feature Gibbs was never happy with. With no temple front, instead a semi-circular portico, in the west facade, it is the one inept feature marring the otherwise exquisite church of St Mary-le-Strand. And the podium-like ground floor of the Radcliffe Camera hardly does better.

do nothing to block further enquiry. We can still seek to explain or understand it. Now perception, naturally enough, has a physiological and psychological basis; an unremarkable fact, long supposed—by a familiar fallacy—to cast doubt on the status of its objects. I see a red apple in front of me; but the redness could not really be 'in' the apple, for the fact that I see it depends on the state of my eyes and my brain. Nor, I suppose, could two and two really equal four,—at least I have no reason to think so—for without a brain I would certainly never apprehend it. We do of course see things like apples, and their qualities are real qualities of those objects; the explicability of the fact does nothing to render it problematic. How could the discovery of an explanation be grounds for doubting the fact that it explains? The same holds of so-called aesthetic qualities, or again of those 'presentational objects' that theorists are supposed to believe in. In literary theory at least something like the latter notion does certainly occur. Now those who uphold the view, as far as I know, are in fact content to leave it there. As for such qualities, it is as though their mere 'perception' sufficed and no further explanation is called for; which may have helped to bring the theory into disrepute. One can in fact explain them, I believe; though the enterprise is one I shall not remark on at present. (I have elsewhere attempted to throw light on our quasi-immediate apprehension of what I call aesthetic form.)[6]

Those, of course, are *qualities*, not objects; and, we may observe, Wollheim himself believes in such qualities. He speaks explicitly for instance of representational and expressive qualities; which are presumably not to be 'perceived' quite as colours and shapes are perceived. And Beardsley and Sibley talk of qualities, so-called aesthetic or regional qualities, apprehended in their own special way. Yet neither, I believe, talks of objects; only *objects* are what Wollheim seems to quarrel with. I find the point a somewhat puzzling one; it can hardly be that the whole hot dispute is over the use of an adjective or a noun.

For another powerful exponent of the presentational theory, at least as I myself understand it, I mean to invoke the name of Collingwood. Wollheim of course puts him in the opposite camp; but, I find, the issue invites further scrutiny. It is complicated, for one thing, by Collingwood's metaphysic. Material things, as he sees it, are 'constructs', they are somehow put together out of sensa. And these sensa he thinks of as private. The passage from such private sensa say to public chairs and tables may be one that presents logical difficulties; but those are not our present concern. But allow it to be possible, and for public works of art the same holds. It is of course true that to perceive any

6 See Chapter 6.

qualities belonging to them we must bring to bear appropriate faculties. 'But,' Collingwood writes, 'this applies equally to colours.'[7] Let me put the point in a more realist terminology: works of art may be thought of as physical things apprehended imaginatively. I would not say that Collingwood never confuses the two relevant adjectives, namely 'imagery' and 'imaginative'; he does so in fact in the very passage I have quoted from. He sometimes indeed makes it look as if what he is speaking of were a species of private or imaginary object that could only exist 'in our heads'. But he certainly conceives of the artist as starting work, so to speak, with the senses, with what he calls sensa; and hence with a particular medium. And one great advantage of his view is precisely the stress it enables him to lay on the medium. The artist's gift is to see it imaginatively, in other words, grasping its inherent potentialities.

But that does not affect his basic thesis: art is the expression of emotion. Such is Collingwood's theory, which connects it with dreaming and daydreaming. The same connection had been noticed by psychoanalysts. Collingwood's contribution however, which he makes in the section called 'Imagination and Make-believe'[8]—a minor landmark in the history of aesthetics—is to see not only the likeness but the difference, which is broadly this: it is the difference between a disciplined and a self-indulgent use of imagination. Wollheim too stresses the distinction, but I cannot but think that he mishandles it. The difference for him is the difference between the privacy of day-dreaming and the public institution of art. But Collingwood had anticipated the point; day-dreaming can be publicly institutionalised too—a process, as he says, that has proved vastly profitable to those who exploit it.

I have sought so far to champion the so-called presentational theory; I have gone along with it as far as I can. But there remains another critic to be met, if not precisely of that theory—anyway, as we found, a somewhat elusive object—at least of a similar approach which sees the appreciation of art in terms of the perception of aesthetic qualities. Ruby Meager in an excellent article[9]—only marred by what seemed to me compulsive and distracting genuflections to the sage of Königsberg—put her finger on the relevant difference, aesthetically relevant, not merely metaphysically. I mean the difference between physical objects and works of art. The former we merely perceive, and perceive better with keener discrimination; the latter we inwardly respond to. Let me take an example: I do not know whether the

[7] *The Principles of Art* (Oxford, 1938), p. 150.
[8] Op. cit., ch. 8, section iv.
[9] 'Aesthetic concepts', *British Journal of Aesthetics* (1970) x, iv, pp. 303–22.

antechamber of the Laurentian Library brings my faculties into harmonious interplay. It hardly seems to. I find no liberation, no free
play, and certainly no reaching towards infinity. Yet it strangely
troubles, oppresses and fascinates me. Here Michelangelo indeed
makes me see, but also feel; and the two things are hardly to be
distinguished.

It may seem then that the theory breaks down. Yet we find in fact
that critical discourse circumvents the difficulty quite painlessly.
Critics both of literature and visual art are much concerned, doubtless
rightly concerned, with the responses of either readers or viewers; with
the difference, more especially, between right responses and wrong
ones. In other words they implicitly distinguish between a response
and its object; the latter is of course the work itself. It is at least a style
of discourse that seems to work, to accommodate whatever we need.
We can side-step ontological issues, which might possibly or profitably
be pursued further. But I shall not attempt the enterprise. My own interest in the presentational theory is, as I indicated, more limited; it is
confined to its usefulness in illuminating questions that belong more
properly or essentially to art, to its appreciation and understanding qua
art.

Now for such understanding and appreciation another issue is certainly central, one that I have already touched on. I mean that of right
interpretation which, I think, still calls for fuller treatment. Two people
who 'read' a work differently are likely to evaluate it differently;
and—the normal view, I think, and perhaps naïve one, which I none
the less mean to maintain—if one reading is right, the other, we
assume, must be wrong. Interpretations, we find in point of fact,
spawn freely in the writings of critics; they cover the true face of art, as
it were, with some distorting, translucent jelly. Understandable efforts
have been made to bring some sort of order into this chaos; to define
clear rules for right interpretation. But no general rules are to be
found; the enterprise, however tempting or promising, seems to me a
mistaken one. Works of theory, I have argued, like works of art, may
be seen as presentational objects. Now it seems that for the right interpretation of, say, Aristotle or Newton there exist no rules. Nor I believe
has anyone sought to formulate rules. At most there is the vacuous rule
that the best interpretation makes the best sense of them—always bearing in mind the simple but crucial qualification that I have insisted on.
These works are historical entities; interpretation must not violate
history. For the rest, they will vary indefinitely, and make sense in
ways that differ indefinitely. We can state no finite list of aesthetic requirements. One may stress the requirement of unity; it is one feature
that is very generally valued. Accordingly in Anthony Savile's account

of interpretation it figures prominently.[10] That doubtless is eminently plausible; yet it remains one feature only, one among others. Artists, I think, left to themselves, rather than perfecting unitary works, might be happier to tinker indefinitely; such is my own limited impression at least of painters' studios cluttered with bits and pieces, or poets' papers with fragments and odd lines. Yet such fragments surely may already possess aesthetic qualities, nor wholly defy interpretation. As to those 'whole objects' that Wollheim has also spoken of; unitary objects, I suppose; we owe them, I suspect, as much to the pressure of dealers and publishers as to any deep psychic needs explored by Klein. Not that I would discount other and more intimately relevant considerations; the connected concepts of unity and aesthetic form I mentioned that I myself have spoken of elsewhere.

There exists, I said, one right interpretation; ideally only one, I shall argue. The capacity to produce in every age some new unpredictable response has sometimes been ascribed to works of art; and in a way rightly, as we shall see. It has even been made their defining property; it is equated with the greatness of great art. Now if so, it is a mysterious property. Let me take an analogy: dexadrin produces excitement, alcohol intoxication and barbiturate sleep. Imagine the following properties as belonging to one and the same drug: in the eighteenth century it served to rouse excitement, in the nineteenth intoxication and in the twentieth it induces sleep. In some sense, at least, works of art are widely allowed to be mysterious. I cannot see that we illuminate one mystery by invoking another. And, pretty obviously, to get any further what we should need would be, first, to isolate this singular property, and then, if we could, go on to explain it and its curiously various manifestations. I find besides that the theory breaks down; it has already been falsified by the facts. Art is mysterious, certainly, and our powerful response to it is mysterious. It is natural enough then that critics should seek to explain it, and hardly less natural that they should often fail. They respond strongly, and seek to explain the fact. Their explanations—interpretations—often differ. But we must add this: we find in fact that it is not only masterpieces that invite an indefinite variety of interpretations; the same holds of minor works, too. 'This was sometime a paradox, but now the time gives it proof.' The academic industry has taken over. There exist nowadays not only emotional factors at work, leading people to explore what underlies acknowledged masterpieces or to project on them their own *idées fixes*. We find institutional pressures as well. And, as I say, minor works

---

[10] Cf. Anthony Savile, 'The place of intention in the concept of art', *Proceedings of the Aristotelian Society* (1968–9) 69, p. 116.

prove no less patient of the process in question than those of great masters.

I may perhaps seem to be hinting that the activity itself is illegitimate. I mean only that it is widely abused. But the term itself must not pass unexamined; it can be used to mean widely different things. Let me illustrate: I recall a lecture in which a distinguished English scholar set out explicitly to discuss the topic. He placed side by side, first, different interpretations of a novel of Conrad's *(Under Western Eyes)*, and secondly different interpretations—the same word was used—of certain primitive fables or myths. Now for most of us, I take it, Conrad's novel already makes sense; in one way then interpretation is superfluous. The latter case was radically different. I cannot recapitulate the fables in question; but precisely that sense was what one lacked. The narrated events, to people of our culture at least, seemed wholly pointless. In other words they cried out for interpretation; just that point was what one wanted to know. There are in brief at least two different ways in which art may admit of interpretation. A work that needs no interpretation in one sense, that achieves effect without interpretation, may invite it in another. We may ask how those effects are achieved. For instance, William Empson taught critics long ago to tease out ambiguities from poetry, and thereby helped to explain the ordinary reader's response. The process, clearly enough, also presupposed that response. Otherwise, using such methods, we would be interpreting nothing, and that requires very nice instruments.

Not that I doubt that experts exist by whom appropriate instruments have been perfected. For the rest, old works, for obvious reasons, can call for interpretation in a different and more radical sense. The same goes for obscure works; and the vogue of obscurity currently provides much employment for academics. Nor would I deny, even in explanatory criticism, that occasionally the two processes merge, that to highlight a given response, or rather to highlight what underlies it, can also be to vivify or reinforce it. And yet in a sense it remains true that successful works should need no interpretation, that that need is a measure of failure. Otherwise one must imagine the following: that a serious artist will consciously rely on critics to help him out; that he will be content to let the effect at which he aims turn on the lucky chance of finding a critic who gets it right. Now such works have of course been produced. But the practice, I believe, carried beyond a certain point would undermine the very conditions in which art as a meaningful institution can exist.

And here I must return to Wollheim. His rejection of the presentational theory goes along with a view of art as something in this way distinctive; it is and must be indefinitely reinterpretable. He denies—using examples from literature—that any line can be drawn between what he calls 'fact' and interpretation. Yet he himself needs the distinction. For he favours the innovations of interpreters; later ages, he argues, will always reveal to us old masterpieces in new ways. But then, one must ask, what is it that they are supposed to reinterpret? There must be something for such interpretation to work on, something contra-distinguished from interpretation if we are to speak at all of 'the same work' as reinterpreted. Besides it is as plainly a fact in Shakespeare's play that Othello is a Venetian general, or at least a general in service of the Venetian State, as that, in the University of London, Wollheim is Grote Professor of Mind and Logic. Considerations of essentially the same sort, *mutatis mutandis*, will serve in either case.

I have already mentioned Jones's oedipal Hamlet, as indeed Wollheim does too. He himself further favours a homosexual Iago; and I myself finally have suggested the possibility—I take it a pretty fanciful one—of reading a phrase in *Henry IV* as referring to the cathedral built by Wren. Now in each case, as I myself see it, the same simple objection is decisive; each reading is grossly ahistorical. Certainly, as regards Hamlet or Iago, an alternative view remains possible, if not very plausible, perhaps. Shakespeare himself, let us imagine, obscurely felt, merely felt, what he wrote was somehow right, and relied on his audience to feel the same—yet without either being able to say why. That was left to Freud, centuries later. This is however a possibility that I am happy enough to disregard; and I do so on Wollheim's own authority. For as to the interpretation he favours, it was, he supposes, 'not open to earlier generations to perceive'.[11] The phrase, perhaps, is not wholly unambiguous. It might be the very thing that I referred to, the unknown explanation underlying an actual response that was, as we are told, 'not open' to contemporaries. But the reading is an unnatural one; and besides Wollheim's other examples, and an epigram that he quotes from Valéry—the French love to philosophise in epigrams, this one being that 'A creator is one who makes others create'—would seem to leave the point in no doubt.

Now none of these interpretations is merely arbitrary. For each, it may be argued, not only fits but positively enhances the work; at least the passage in question. The rights and wrongs of these arguments do not concern me. (In fact I think it false in the cases of Hamlet and Iago, but true of the reference to St Paul's). And each age brings, we are told, new ideas, a new outlook, to alter the features of old masterpieces. It seems now however that we are back with our magic drug; for, we must ask, why only masterpieces? It would seem to be a mystery past

[11] Op. cit., p. 76.

fathoming. Why in that period should one man, namely Shakespeare, have produced so many works which repay this interesting process—undergoing, let us recall, transformations that he himself could never possibly have foreseen—while so many others, a sizeable body of anonymous hack dramatists, produced, as far as I know, none at all? We saw, indeed, that they are equally subject to reinterpretation. But here reinterpretation, it seems—and this is what I call arbitrary and mysterious—never serves to transform them into masterpieces.

Perhaps it is attributable to chance. Of the mystic of chance glorified by Arp (in a passage quoted by Andrew Forge in one of the lectures of the present series),[12] I shall say nothing—influential as it has proved amongst artists. I have no space to argue the issue, even if I thought it deserved it. But to remain with Wollheim: suppose a Freudian reading does indeed fit and enhance one character in the play, or one passage. What of others? We ought, it seems to me, to take account of what diligent research might be reasonably expected to reveal. There must be passages or features that would benefit no less say, by a Jungian reading, a Lévi-Straussian reading, a neo-Marxist reading and so on. Should we switch our reading from line to line? As to that possibility, I think Wollheim himself, with his interest in whole objects, will hardly welcome it. But then any preference will be arbitrary. Besides, countless further possibilities will always remain to be explored. Works of art prove creative indeed, and make other people create; Valéry is vindicated with a vengeance. One can go further; Wollheim is not, I hope, merely denying the possibility of history. Yet we not only interpret works of art—I previously mentioned the sculpture in the Medici Chapel—but also thinkers, say, Machiavelli, and again political figures, say Savonarola. Michaevelli and Savonarola have in fact both been seen as prophets of Italian unity. Now here, I presume, we have views that admit of historical assessment. But if so, there ought also to be the possibility of a historical approach to works of art. Wollheim then, even on his own terms, should surely distinguish between two equally possible viewpoints, two ways of regarding such works, either on the face of it being legitimate—or if not, the point emphatically calls for argument. And these are the historical and the ahistorical. But in fact, as we see, with the latter any work will break up, not only from age to age, which Wollheim welcomes, but even at any given moment, into an indefinite multiplicity. The argument argues art out of existence.

Now the concept of art, to repeat, and the meaningfulness of talking of given works, require a grasp of their historical context. And I think it

[12] Andrew Forge, 'Art/nature', *Royal Institute of Philosophy Lectures*, vol. 6 (London, 1973), pp. 228–41.

is in the ablest among the apologists of artistic modernism, Harold Rosenberg, that the views I oppose find their *reductio ad absurdum*. Among such apologists Rosenberg, along with other assets, enjoys the great advantage of a sense of humour; for what could be more out of place than solemnity over a species of art—or as he himself seems to see it, so to speak, of post-art, that is, a movement that has superseded art—that perhaps chiefly thrives on self-caricature? Only read the opening chapters of *The Anxious Object*, however, but imagine its emphasis slightly shifted. The author, it is hard not to feel, is in danger of dropping into ridicule, of seeing the whole scene as a gigantic farce. He notes, very accurately, our terrorised generation of critics; who, faced with works ten times more outrageous than any that shocked Dickens or Ruskin, dare not breathe the least murmur of protest. One may search the journals or the 'quality' weeklies: 'pretentious', which appears just now and then, is, I think, the boldest expression of condemnation you will find. Since their predecessors came so frightful a cropper over the Post-Impressionists and *The Waste Land* it is all changed. And in all seriousness the point may be worth dwelling on: it is hard to imagine any object, an object of any sort whatever, whose presence in an art gallery would move them to the mildest point of exclamation. True, they generally fail to take notice of attendants, who after all may have been sent there by Walter Rauschenberg; one is to see them, in Rosenberg's Pickwickian sense, as objects of art. Rosenberg sees too the compulsive novelty of the perpetual revolution with its effects on our artists themselves, and on dealers too who assiduously promote each new mutation. Yet none of this apparently disturbs him. In this climate serious art is supposed to germinate; which, to put it mildly, seems unlikely.

My own heretical views I have, I fear, already betrayed all too clearly. I take a good BBC serial, say *Z Cars* or *Softly, Softly*, to be doing, with unpretentious commitment, something at bottom far more serious than half those producers of artefacts who claim the prestige and, like Rosenberg, repudiate the tradition of the artist. But *Softly, Softly*, you may say, is mere entertainment, not art; which is probably true. But the line between art and entertainment is one I find harder to draw than some aesthetic theorists, who make it absolute—Collingwood for one. Besides, one may notice that Ben Jonson, similarly devoted to high ideals, was disdainful of the popular stage, which he had happily to write for none the less; and produced masterpieces like *Volpone* and *The Alchemist*. 'Our dungy earth alike / Feeds beast as man.' Such, it will be found, are the lowly conditions that have time and again manured the potentiality of art.

Rosenberg, I said, emphatically repudiates the tradition—em-

phatically if not very consistently. He has, I suspect, Hegelian longings
in him and remains a romantic at heart. What he tells us explicitly
however is that you kill the new art by looking at it in terms of the old.
The very concept is seen as misleading, whence my suggestion that we
should speak of it rather as post-art.

He quoted, in the preface to the 1970 edition of *The Tradition of The
New*, a comment of Mary McCarthy's made, apparently, when the
book first appeared. 'You cannot hang an event on the wall,' she
wrote, 'only a picture.' I have failed to find the original review; she
seems however, not uncharacteristically, to have put her finger on the
precise point. For, we gather, she went on to accuse Rosenberg of what
she called 'a weird contradiction'. Now as to Rosenberg, his first love
was Action Painting. The picture is what one hangs on the wall; the
event, then, is the action of painting it. That action expresses, for
Rosenberg, the anguish of the artist, perhaps also of the age, or both at
once.[13] For the *Zeitgeist*, along with other left-overs of romantic
aesthetics, make spectral appearances in his pages. As to that
troublesome spirit, uttering its ominous noises from the cellarage, like
the ghost in *Hamlet*—*hic et ubique*—one might have thought that serious
scholarship had long since exorcised it, long since laid it to rest. But the
point here is this: we have before us an object, the production of a
speculative event. Now either, the *ne plus ultra* of romanticism, you
think of the artist's spontaneous gesture as imprinting itself meaningfully on the canvas; or you look at the latter itself, the object as it
actually is. Rosenberg vacillates, I think: but his real wish, one
suspects, is indeed to look at the object—what else could one do, after
all?—yet, looking at it, to see an event: 'a weird contradiction' indeed.

My interest however is in his answer, which is as follows. It is, he
says, a contradiction only if,

> through the habit of looking back to other times, we forget the multiple
> existence which a painting now enjoys in separation from its physical
> body: its ghostly presence through reproduction in books and
> magazines that carries it *as picture* far from its durable being of paint
> and canvas; the intellectual character it takes on from interpretations
> irremovably tacked on to it by critics, art historians, psychiatrists,
> philosophers of culture . . . the power of transformation it wields over
> its own creator through the energy it accumulates in its passage
> through the social orbit.[14]

What puzzles me is how all that, a brilliant verbal barrage as it is, can
even seem to bear on the point at issue—at least to a man so evidently

[13] Harold Rosenberg, *The Tradition of the New* (London, 1970), p. 249.
[14] Ibid., pp. 10–11.

intelligent as Rosenberg—let alone to be a satisfactory answer. What, it seems, McCarthy complained of was the impossibility of responding to an event that is unavoidably inaccessible; to something not there to respond to. Rosenberg answers by referring us to others; events loosely connected with the first, but for his purposes, one would have thought, hardly relevant. Suppose as a patriotic Briton I glory in King Arthur's mighty deeds. But those deeds, I later learn, and even the king himself, are all very possibly mythical. In fact, I suspect, in most cases at least, the same holds for the fine frenzy of action painters. Well, I am told reassuringly, I can respond instead to the subsequent accumulation of legend—the only trouble being that a different response, antiquarian curiosity rather than fervid patriotism, might now seem more appropriate.

For the rest, those processes certainly occur; I mean the processes that Rosenberg speaks of. We can add others too, which belong to the passage of time. Pictures fade, statues get chipped. They also are photographed and reproduced, better or worse, and students often study only reproductions. It is true, too, that later developments, in art and elsewhere, may serve to obscure what preceded them. We can no longer see what contemporaries saw. None of this is likely to be disputed. But all I maintain, to repeat, is the possibility of historical scholarship, which remains an intelligible enterprise; it remains one, whether or not it can ever quite attain its goal; it may progressively approximate to it. And its goal, it would seem, is precisely to reverse the processes in question; to undo, so far as possible, the work of time. The historian of ideas strives to grasp, say, the original thought of Machiavelli, to see it as he himself saw it; and the same holds of the art of his contemporaries. Reviewers too persist in commenting on the quality of reproductions in art books, as though they took it to be important to get as near as possible to the original—a strange practice, nor, on Rosenberg's principles, easy to understand. His position, to repeat, amounts to this; the denial of the possibility of history. And that, incidentally, consistently carried through, leads to much larger consequences; it leads to general denial of the whole possibility of thought.

For the rest, my own heterodox view of the present condition of the arts will, I fear, be sufficiently plain. I shall not speculate as to how it came about. But as to what, speaking very broadly, it represents, I tentatively offer the following notion. What I think we see is some sort of general loss of confidence; which seems at least to tell us more than another somewhat similar concept sometimes appealed to; that of self-criticism. For instance it helps us to relate such seemingly disparate phenomena as the compulsion that drove architects, some fifty years ago, to strip all ornament from the face of their buildings—a phenomenon, I believe, unique in history—with those empty canvases of Rauschenberg which, in the lecture I mentioned previously, Forge spoke of; and again with the reduction of so much literature to a sort of confessional monotone—though sometimes, one must add, a confessional becomes more like a shriek, a shrill noise of self-vindication. Or take the modern dogma, introduced in the last generation but now very widely upheld, in at least visual art, of truth to the medium; it seems connected with an equally inhibiting dogma in the novel, namely the dogma that condemns telling in favour of showing. The object of each is the same; it seeks, I think, to cling to some failing plank. Indeed it is happily true, as to the latter, that novelists more recently appear to be widely in revolt against it; but modernism is a hard thing to keep pace with. Why is so much recent art, even qua art, paradoxical? From time to time some illusory formula releases a new burst of energy; it seems to open the way that was closed, to reveal the possibility of something that both is and isn't art. And a new art form survives as long as the illusion survives. Both more and less significant work in recent decades seems to me largely to answer to this pattern.

But suppose this conjecture is right: one must still ask what brought it about. I said I should not speculate. As to the forces that make and unmake cultures, that channel and swell human energies, that disperse and undermine them: of all this, if one wants succinct explanatory generalisations, they are plentifully available. But having wandered too far from my subject and doubtless given provocation enough, I shall leave the issue for others to pursue.

9

Goodman and the 'Naïve' View of Representation

To a complaint that his portrait of Gertrude Stein did not look like her, Picasso is said to have answered, 'No matter, it will'.[1]

I begin with this quotation from Goodman's brilliant book not only because it is amusing like so much else that he writes, but also because it is patently false—assuming, as we are plainly meant to, that he endorses what he quotes. At least, with the passage of some fifty years, the process shows no sign of getting under way. One may, I think, be legitimately suspicious in such cases; one may be suspicious of views that lend themselves to this sort of summing-up and score their rhetorical point precisely by flouting credulity (like Tertullian's famous dictum concerning the Trinity).

But perhaps we shall do better to proceed in more orderly style, to begin further back. 'To resemble' in ordinary daily speech—say I am talking of physical things—most often means not 'to be like' but 'to look like'. I am struck by some resemblance and remark on it: what I mean, then, on our normal presumption, will be a visual resemblance—which may be loose usage but is actual. Now philosophers who rightly watch linguistic points and are themselves careful to use words precisely also need to do so self-consciously. Otherwise they risk mistaking common sense for naïveté, hence reading in one way words that are meant in another; or rather, to speak more accurately, that would be so meant supposing common sense were not only, as it often is, sensible but also consciously articulate. That, I think, or something like it, has happened on the very first page of Goodman's book, where he speaks dismissively of 'the most naïve view of representation'—one, I suggest, that turns out, sympathetically looked at, to be a most sensible view. Of this view he gives the following rough formulation: 'A represents B if, and only if, it resembles B'; or again, as an alternative, 'to the extent that it resembles B'. This, evidently, is meant only as a first shot; on any terms, as he himself recognises, it stands in need of refinement. But, I think, as a first shot it does pretty well, at least as expressing the com-

[1] Nelson Goodman, *Languages of Art* (London, 1968), p. 33.

mon sense view—if you like, the naïve view. But then the word 're-semble' must be read 'naïvely', too, not sophisticatedly as I think Goodman reads it. (Later he seems unsure or inclined to vacillate; we find him writing of the possibility of an artist's copying how 'the object is *or looks*'.[2] But that hesitant disjunction, anyway forgotten at once, does little to help. Indeed, the rest of the paragraph, as we shall shortly see, proves pretty bewildering.)

Goodman devotes his first dozen pages or so to demolishing the view in question, 'the naïve view', a task he tackles with self-confidence and considerable zest. Self-confidence in philosophers often makes for en-joyable reading (examples spring to mind) yet assessed seriously, sure-ly, is a questionable virtue. A little brisk and determined good sense is unlikely to prove sufficient equipment to conjure away the obstinately intractable problems of this, our strange discipline. But then, surely, Goodman never thought so, or gave the impression of thinking so. In finding or setting himself problems, that is to say, he never gave the im-pression of underestimating them. I conclude, then, that he really thinks the 'resemblance' theory self-evidently foolish. And those who champion it are to be knocked out in round one and with a few quick jabs to the jaw. Hence, perhaps, something uncharacteristically cavalier in the conduct of his argument.

I do not mean to prejudge the substantial issue. Can such a theory ultimately stand, or stand without major qualification? I do not know, but it is more than I mean to argue for. I am sure of this, that it can stand in face of far more punishment than Goodman has so far delivered. More important, its basic approach is sound and relevant; the resemblance theorist, in other words, has his eye on the target, which I do not find self-evidently true of Goodman. The target, of course, is visual art and specifically pictorial representation (I use the word broadly to include sculpture, but not literature; and leave open any questions of its significant connection with representation of other sorts).

The first formulation, to repeat, is no more than that and can hardly be meant to be. Goodman accordingly seeks for ways of qualifying or amending it. But he treats the search summarily. His real view, which he is at no pains to disguise, is that no plausible qualification is available—though, strange as it seems, he himself offers one, and in the next breath; one which, in all essentials, does pretty well. But first we need to look at his objections: why, amended or otherwise, is the naïve view dismissed as untenable? Resemblance, unlike representa-tion, is a symmetrical relation, and also reflexive. A portrait of the Duke of Wellington represents and, according to 'the naïve view',

[2] Ibid., p. 7. My italics.

resembles him; if so, he also resembles the portrait. Since, obviously, he does not represent his own portrait, it follows resemblance by itself cannot furnish a sufficient condition of representation—a possible claim, I suppose, but a large one, which, as far as I know, no one ever made for it. Clearly it may still be a necessary condition. But let me take another point first. It is one that Goodman presently touches on, without highlighting; which, however, I find convenient to make explicit from the start. To talk of resemblance, and talk of it significantly, we need to talk specifically too. Otherwise anything will resemble anything. That is to say, we need to limit ourselves to some aspect either actually specified or understood. Now some such limitation is implicit in the amendment Goodman himself suggests to the first formulation quoted above; he suggests the further clause 'If A is a picture . . .'. 'Resemblance', we noted, in ordinary idiom, means resemblance in appearance. What concerns us, then, is only this: not what things are but how they look. Secondly, what concerns us are pictures, as Goodman's own suggestion implies. The two things go together; for pictures are made to be looked at—which, if nothing else, will serve to dispose of Goodman's first problem of asymmetry. The picture may resemble the Duke, and the Duke—quite symmetrically—the picture. The qualifying clause does the rest. Wellington doubtless was a fine figure of a man. But no one would literally assert that he was made to be looked at. Hence no absurdity arises. Suppose a fellow Londoner or a visitor to London should ask me what Wellington looked like. One might answer; 'Read the books, descriptions survive.' But that would sound oddly indirect. The best way to discover is by looking, which is also the simplest—not indeed at the Duke himself, whose features are no longer to be seen. Yet men may look again, if not on his like, on his likeness. Goya's great portrait in the National Gallery, being no mere description but a resemblance, an authentic image, outdoes any record in words.[3]

Our account of resemblance, however, is still insufficiently specific. I spoke of things made to be looked at. Our concern strictly speaking, however, need not be confined to what they were originally made for; what matters is not their initial purpose but their present role. Objects in principle might serve us as pictures and be looked at accordingly, regardless of their makers' intentions. Even of *objets trouvés* the same

---

[3] It must not be thought that this argument trades illegitimately on the use of the word 'likeness' for portrait, though that use doubtless has its significance. Here we have one prominent object and the background is neutral. But take, say, a seventeenth-century townscape, perhaps representing the Piazza San Marco in Venice. It is the whole picture surface, viewed appropriately, that resembles the whole of the scene—or, to be explicit, its appearance.

could be true. For the rest what we find is the same paradoxical situation.   Goodman himself seems to supply—substantially if not
exactly—the further specification the theory needs. Indeed for its principal assailant he would appear remarkably ready with the essentials of
its support. We began simply by imagining two objects each resembling the other. Now we find next that where the first is a picture—here
of course salvaging Goodman's own discarded suggestion—it does
more than resemble the second; it serves to represent it as well. Since
pictures, to repeat, are to be looked at, our interest is confined to
appearance; the resemblance is resemblance in appearance. And for
the next point: a copyist, Goodman shortly adds—in his terminology
'the copy theory' is merely another name for the resemblance theory (a
disastrous equation, but I waive this point for the present)—will not
copy any aspect at random: 'rather, we may suppose, the way the objects looks' (one notes the crucial concession made, it seems, unaware)
'to a normal observer at a proper distance . . . in a good light . . .'[4] I
shall shortly return to finish the quotation. So far it seems perfectly
unexceptionable. Common sense can have little to add. But one small
point we should notice for the sake of accuracy: the conditions, strictly,
need not be normal so long as they are known. For the rest I can find
nothing to object to. And as to the example I have been using, Goya,
one may suppose, did just that—or so the picture itself would suggest.

The same holds if we switch our attention from the relation of the
artist and sitter to that of picture and viewer; from Wellington and
Goya to the object in the gallery and oneself. The finished picture
plainly enough is also to be seen from an appropriate distance—a
point, incidentally, that we might have learnt from Hume. Hume, it is
true, has nothing to say about lighting, which he may have felt he could
safely take for granted. No resemblance theorist, as far as I know, has
ever advocated looking at works of art in total darkness; though a possible exercise of ingenuity would be to produce a work that required a
green light, or purple light, for its resemblance to its original to appear.

'*A* represents *B* if and only if *A* resembles *B*.' Such was the original
formula, which, with certain small qualifications, I suggest will now
yield pretty much what we need. First, *A* is made to be looked at, and
secondly, to be looked at on that account. To look at a picture qua picture is to look at it as the likeness of some original—which distinguishes
a picture from a replica, even the sort of exact replica that Goodman
likes to hold up to ridicule. For, as we saw, he identified 'resemblance
theory' with 'the copy theory', a very different creature, suppose it exists at all. Imagine some expert or enthusiast who makes a perfect

[4] Op. cit., p. 7.

model, say of Stevenson's Rocket or Puffing Billy. He might make it to be exhibited in a museum; hence make it, apparently, specifically to be looked at. Further *being*, by hypothesis, just like the original, it will also look like it. But it is not to be looked at on that account, or rather not merely on that account. Or suppose it should be; then, if so, it is a representation, or serves merely as a representation, not—what Goodman wants—as a replica. The upshot, given Goodman's premises, is not without its irony. Even 'copy' theorists are right in a way. For an exact replica, and precisely in virtue of its resemblance, its visual resemblance to the original, may serve in special circumstances as—perhaps more, perhaps less than a replica—a representation. To return to the Duke: it is evident, I suppose, that he was not made to be looked at—in the context we should perhaps say 'begotten'—in virtue of his future likeness to the portrait that Goya was to paint.

I have undertaken the defence of naïvete or, as I prefer to call it, common sense. I find for myself that I understand the notion of likeness, which I meet every day, rather better than the jargon word 'denotation'; at least in this logical setting—rather the lack of any setting—in which Goodman in his handling of the latter contrives to imprison it, one might say in the confinement of vacancy. You can suffocate in a vacuum no less effectively than in a tomb; excess of liberty and too little are alike. But as to his objection to his own excellent suggestion, namely the crucial clause: 'If *A* is a picture . . .' what he writes is as follows: 'if picture means "representation" it will not help'. Presumably it will be circular. But, he goes on, 'if we construe it broadly enough to cover all paintings' it will be 'wide of the mark in other ways'. Here I must confess to being lost, and I fear I must have missed the drift of the argument. 'All paintings', as against representations, would suggest, say, Mondrians, Pollocks and other such proliferating objects and entities. In fact what he goes on to discuss is precisely an old-style representation, a Constable picture of Marlborough Castle, so that what follows, however interesting in itself, seems unconnected with what went before.

It is well worth looking at on its own account, however. Constable's picture, Goodman writes, 'is more like any other picture than it is like the Castle, yet it represents the Castle not another picture . . . not even the closest copy'. This last point is evidently a nice one. I shall return to it. But as to the rest, our previous distinction seems to serve. The canvas is to be seen as a picture; hence what matters is its looking like the Castle—looking, not being, to repeat. We can rewrite Goodman's sentence accordingly: 'The picture *looks* more like any other picture than it *looks* like the Castle (as seen, of course, from the appropriate spot); yet it represents the Castle not another picture.'[5] Yet, perhaps, in a sense even that remains true. It depends on what resemblance is in question: for the notion of resemblance is one that functions differently, for instance, from identity. If *A* is identical with *B* and *B* with *C*, then *A* is identical with *C*; that is, the relation is transitive. The same fails to hold of resemblance. It depends on what features one attends to. Suppose *A* resembles *B*, say, in respect of shape, and *B* in respect of colour resembles *C*; no further conclusion ensues. The resemblance theorist as we meet him in Goodman, however, is confined to looking, or trying to look, with an innocent eye. Hence, unsurprisingly, he comes to grief.

To return to the copy: the case is undoubtedly more complex. At first sight the objection may look damaging and not only to Goodman's own target, the simple-minded dummy of a resemblance theorist he sets up to shy stones at. Our own emendation seems exposed to it too. For the copy, no less than the original, is made to be looked at: further to be looked at for this reason, for the sake of its resemblance to the original. Yet, I think, a significant difference remains. I do not speak of dealers and connoisseurs, I mean connoisseurs of copies and copyists. False teeth, to take an analogy, are made to serve as teeth, not as false teeth; in other words, they are false *faute de mieux*. What we value is, so to speak, their tooth-likeness, not their falseness. Yet, I said, the case presents some complexity. A copy, say, of the Titian portrait called 'An Englishman'—perhaps a real Englishman though unidentified—is valued for its resemblance to the original; that is, to the Titian, the artist being known, not to the sitter who is unknown. And of course there exist works of fancy; there need not be a real sitter at all. Yet the main point stills stands. The Titian, to be seen as a portrait, *eo ipso* is seen as a likeness, the likeness of an object real or possible, but anyway existing independently. Now the point to notice is this; precisely the same holds of the copy. We shall look at it, not as a copy, but rather as what it strives to be, a picture so to speak in its own right; (except, as before, for connoisseurs of copies qua copies, who perhaps interest themselves in comparing the skill of different copyists.) A portrait, and a representation of any sort, is seen as resembling something else, something existing independently or at least something possibly so existing.

Let me speak, at least briefly, of mirroring. Certainly it is a notion to be handled with caution. Our prime interest of course is in resemblance, and what chiefly seems to need underlining is the distinctness, the non-identity, of the two. Apparently there are real

---

[5] To be strictly accurate we should say 'Like the *view*' from the point where the artist stood; for the likeness is general or comprehensive, though the Castle may be its prominent feature.

dangers of confusing them, to which Goodman would seem to have succumbed. For Goodman, we find, slips to and fro between talk of 'resemblance' and 'the perfect copy'. Yet looking-glasses have something to teach us—quite apart from what they ordinarily show, to be acknowledged with complacency or otherwise, that visual aspect that we present to the world. Suppose, before Marlborough Castle, just where Constable set up his canvas, we should instead set up a looking-glass, though we face it the other way round; and a second before Wivenhoe Park. Now here we have four different objects—the objects of our present concern all, to repeat, being appearances. The first is the appearance in the one glass, the second in the other; and next we have either original, the two appearances of the Castle and the Park. Let me rewrite Goodman's dictum a second time. 'The appearance of the first mirror (roughly the mirror image) is more like any other such appearance (any other mirror image) than it is like the visual appearance of the Castle, yet it represents the Castle, not the second image.' I fear this awkward recasting spoils the confident ring and rhythm of Goodman's prose—but, it seems to me, not only his prose. To pursue the point further. There *are* things that look like each other. Representations may not in general be mirror images, yet even perfect resemblances exist; mirror images are perhaps a subclass of representations. The objects we in fact hang in galleries may not be precisely of this sort; but though they are not, yet in principle they might have been. The account is doubtless false, but not nonsense. In other words the mere notion can hardly be incoherent or logically absurd, as Goodman would seem to imply.

Yet, I said, the point is a risky one to overplay. Take two similar triangles: they *are* alike, and hence normally look alike. (Or, one may imagine, two dissimilar ones might look alike from an appropriate angle; but the former example will serve.) Now here plainly there is no question of mirroring; they look alike only in shape, not in size. Mirroring and visual resemblance are different things, if partly overlapping; it is the more reason for keeping them apart. But one other phenomenon remains, another sort of likeness and of look, which we need to take account of; something rather different and more elusive—or so one may feel. We find that the same noun, namely 'look', has a further use. Let me take an example. Two people emerge from the inner room who differ in age, build and colouring, perhaps also in sex; yet have in common—what immediately strikes us—the same look, a strange ghastly look, of sickened bewilderment. (Today, evidently, the Thing is visible in the inner room.) Or two landscapes that differ in detail may share a look of deep, mellow repose. I call the phenomenon an elusive one; yet I do not know that we ought to be

puzzled. We may be happier, which would doubtless be understandable, with things we can measure and check, can lay rulers against or
run fingers along. Yet such descriptions are surely intelligible. We
understand them and could hardly do without them—unless we are
merely to ignore a large class of perceptual phenomena. And these are
phenomena, as it happens, of special importance in visual art.

But so far I have said nothing of Goodman's main argument, or
what seems to be meant as his main argument. Resemblance theorists,
as Goodman conceives them, are committed to 'the innocent eye';
which he constantly assumes, though I find no grounds for it. I must
return to the quotation I began earlier. The question was, to recall,
what the 'copyist' is expected to copy; and, Goodman supposes, it will
be, not just any aspect, but

> the way the object looks to the normal eye, at a proper range, from a
> favourable angle, in good light, without instrumentation, unprejudiced
> by affection or animosity or interest, and unembellished by thought or
> interpretation. In short, the object is to be copied as seen under aseptic
> conditions by the free and innocent eye.[6]

This passage, I consider, is best taken slowly, notwithstanding the swift
pace of Goodman's prose. I even feel a certain need to pause for
breath. To look first at the form of the argument, seemingly meant, I
said, as the main argument. Plainly it is a *reductio ad absurdum*. And it
does certainly reach its end when we finally touch down amid absurdities, blatant absurdities, which, reasonably enough, Goodman relies
on our rejecting. Yet, let us note, it all began quietly enough. It began
with the artist at work, his vision being normal, as we should expect,
his subject set before him at a proper range, in good light. Recall
Goya's *Wellington*. In all that description there is no absurdity; it
merely answers to the historical facts—or so the finished picture suggests. But the story now rapidly changes. Did Goya paint Wellington
'without affection, animosity or interest'?—a patriotic Spaniard, also a
liberal, painting the successful commander of the British expeditionary
force in the Peninsula. It seems unlikely, absurd if you like. And what
comes next is quite plainly absurd, and plainly meant to be, namely an
artist who looks at his sitter quite without 'thought or interpretation'.
It is this time a conceptual absurdity. For perception in its nature involves thought, which I take to be knowable a priori. Last of all, sum-
ming up—'in short' is the phrase Goodman uses—the whole amalgam
is equated with 'the free and innocent eye'. One may feel, I said, some
need to pause for breath. Up till now we have had phrases in apposi-

[6] Op. cit., p. 7.

tion. In these matters the syntactical rule—and I use the word as philosophers rarely seem to, to mean common bona fide syntax—is that clauses in apposition are identified. They either are roughly equivalent or anyway serve to specify the same thing. Now suppose we read Goodman accordingly; we must identify normal vision in good light with the vision of the innocent eye—an absurdity certainly as gross as one could ask for. But who is supposed to be committed to it? If anyone, Goodman himself; not, certainly, the resemblance theorist. He himself appears then in the prepared seat where we had expected to see his victim. As to advocates of the innocent eye, they precisely contrast it with normal vision. And we shall find that any reasonably sophisticated resemblance theorist need have no truck with the former notion at all; all he needs is the common notion that Goodman began with, precisely that of normal vision.

To return to the argument, however, the innocent eye is a myth. So Goodman asserts and, I think, rightly. He appeals to the authority of E. H. Gombrich (though Gombrich, one may note, however much he may insist on the slogan that 'making precedes matching', never tells us that it eliminates matching. He remains too sensible merely to scratch out the latter notion.) But perhaps I lay myself open to the charge of celebrating too easy a triumph. Goodman, I may be told, cannot seriously mean, deliberately intend, the equation his syntax suggests—though I confess I see no other way of reading the passage. Anyway we can concede the possibility, for otherwise he has no argument at all. The innocent eye is an irrelevance, at least for present purposes; resemblance theory has no need and no use for it. As to his other objections to the theory, these, if I am right, tell only against so simplistic a form of it that no serious resemblance theorist need be worried by them. Suppose we ask ourselves how the Duke looked to Goya. The answer is ready to hand, at least barring freakish assumptions. It was roughly as the portrait looks to us. But we know it is so, and indeed know of visual resemblances in general—whence our normal ability to read pictures—in virtue not of our innocent eyes but rather our shared sophistication.

The process, one that begins pretty early in our culture at least, is eminently unmysterious; after all, we have all learnt to look at pictures. We have likewise learnt to look at people, a process that begins earlier still. Pictures, it is true, vary in kind; they make different demands on their viewers. Some assume more specialised equipment, familiarity with conventions or techniques. In looking at etchings, for instance, we do not complain of the absence of colour—though the example, perhaps, is a doubtful one. Colour is too easily dispensable. Say I see the Prime Minister on television, black-and-white television, and of course recognise her. That we still call it 'seeing' is significant. And pictorial conventions for the most part raise problems essentially similar. Denotation and reference are irrelevant. The case is merely this: we recognise known things in new guises—a pretty basic perceptual capacity. Without it—I mean wholly in default of it—there would hardly be such a thing as perception at all. Yet, of course, conventions can matter. But where they do, happily we can also allow for them. And so with habits and modes of perception. Artists aim in general, not at anyone, but at competent viewers. Yet that is perhaps to misrepresent the point. A certain minimum of competence is presupposed in the very existence and viability of such activities, in the mere concept of representation. Even the simplest picture, say a drawing in a children's book, needs to be read and admits of being misread.

Goodman, then, seems to me right in rejecting 'the innocent eye'. The precise form of his argument leaves me less comfortable. The eye, he writes, so far from being innocent 'selects, rejects, discriminates . . .' and so on.[7] (Goodman always has an adequate supply of verbs and adjectives.) Perception, I said, involves thought; and the point is a conceptual not an empirical one. But to speak of relevant empirical fields; psychologically and physiologically, a rather different matter, perception must certainly be based on other processes, without which it cannot occur. The eye, in Goodman—which may mean the brain, retina and optic nerve—selects and discriminates: selects, then, from pre-existing material, discriminates among available data. We are to contemplate two things, it would seem, both process and product. And in the latter the raw materials are metamorphosed. What emerges, as he sees it, I think, is a kind of amalgam. Yet those materials, those data, if no longer accessible in fact, are still recognised in principle; they retain an essential place in the theory. They must still, so to speak, be pre-envisaged for the story to be intelligible at all. What goes into the omelette can come out. Now, on these terms, why should that be unthinkable; or if so, what sort of impossibility is in question? As to facts, as to natural necessities (if Goodman will allow such a notion), we can certainly grant it. In the frying pan the ingredients are transformed, which is a process not to be put into reverse. Yet, to begin with, let me repeat, there were and must have been such ingredients, which Goodman cannot consistently deny. His whole style of talking commits him to it. 'The myth of the innocent eye and the absolute given are unholy accomplices.'[8] The apophthegm, of course, is his own and, I think, in form and content equally felicitous. Yet, as we see all too plainly, the apparition still troubles Goodman's thought; the

[7] Op. cit., p. 8.
[8] Ibid.

absolute given has reappeared for the innocent eye to stare back at. A different sort of exorcism would seem to be requisite. The myth otherwise will continue to haunt us, and miracles bear witness to its tomb.

Resemblance theory, if I am right, can stand against Goodman's utmost efforts so far. I have not said that it can stand against all-comers. Indeed my real suspicion is this: to deal with resemblance we need a different notion, that of seeing-as, which has figured much in recent discussion (though Goodman says nothing of it). I confess that I would rather do without it; it looks like a mere replica of what it is invoked to explain. But it may be that more can be said.[9] As to resemblance, it need not follow that it can merely be dropped and forgotten. We need it to fill another role, to provide foundations for a second concept that Goodman indeed takes account of but, I think, finds it no easy job to accommodate. I refer to that of realism or naturalism.

Let me briefly digress to discuss it. It would seem that his main inclination is merely to appeal to familiarity; a local representational tradition, familiar in a particular culture, is what members of the culture will call naturalistic. The approach, I shall seek to show, is riddled with difficulties; but the most obvious countermove is simply to compare theory with fact. Duccio or Picasso are nowadays quite as familiar to us as Vermeer, which, it seems, does nothing to make us call them equally naturalistic. But if not, it certainly gives us no reason for merely scrapping a useful and obvious distinction—one students of art find invaluable. Besides we read, too, in Goodman of 'rapid shifts',[10] of revolutions and departures from tradition that none the less earn acceptance. A tradition that departs from itself while remaining the same, departs incidently not gradually but abruptly—and perhaps, for why not, presently, like a subelectronic quantum, leaps back again—is a phenomenon I have difficulty in conceiving. The obvious question of course is 'shifts in what'? Not in familiar conventions; with the shift they precisely become unfamiliar. Nor again in tradition itself, unless tradition is to be defined, somewhat accommodatingly, as anything that either changes or remains the same. Nor lastly—the possibility that may have misled Goodman, for here, clearly, the thing happens—in representation or conventions of representation itself. For then these two notions, representation and naturalism, collapse into one, or at least any acceptable representational convention will *eo ipso* be naturalistic too, which is empirically false. And even suppose it in fact is true: it would still be a risky prediction that acceptance could

---

[9] Roughly, I would argue, the possibility of perception in general, of the distinction of veridical and non-veridical, presupposes the capacity to see aspects, to see the same things in different ways.

[10] Op. cit., p. 33.

never be gained for non-naturalistic conventions.

Goodman has one further argument, perhaps his most ingenious one; though one whose consequences may prove more embarrassing to himself than his antagonist. He draws attention to a salient feature of representation and is, I believe, the first writer to have done so, which he calls representation-as. The point in different cases, he tells us, may either be a trivial or a substantial one. Trivially all representation is representation-as. Take Goodman's example: you may represent Churchill as an infant, which he once was. Every picture must show something *as* something. But say a caricaturist depicts the adult Churchill as an infant: here you have non-trivial ('genuine' is Goodman's word) representation-as. Again you might show Churchill as a bulldog, which he not only was not but could not be. Some war posters, if I recall, showed him as a pilot, which he was not in fact though he might have been. It would, I suppose, still be a case of genuine representation-as.

Goodman both poses the problem and sets out what he sees as its solution. We can classify pictures in two ways: either simply as objects of a given sort, perhaps—though not necessarily, and the point is important—in terms of their non-symbolic features, say shape, size or dominant colour; or, alternatively, in terms of what they represent or, as Goodman would have it, denote. But, I said, the classification of the former sort need not exclude what would normally be thought representational features—which for Goodman, I presume, are still symbolic ones. Pictures need not be of real things. But, for Goodman, Titian's *Bacchus and Ariadne*, say, is not, as for most of us, a representation of two mythical beings (and, of course, a number more), of beings who never existed. It represents strictly nothing; or, more accurately, is not properly to be spoken of as representing at all. Yet we can still classify it, and in terms of its own intrinsic character. You have Bacchus pictures as you have bulldog or pilot pictures, which latter may or may not also denote Churchill. This is an unbreakable predicate; what we mean is strictly 'a bulldog picture', as we might say 'a square picture', not a picture representing a bulldog. 'Dogtooth moulding' is moulding of a certain distinctive pattern which we can recognise without referring to teeth.

I said that the point, though we grant its interest and importance, need create no trouble for resemblance theory. Clearly the same object can simultaneously look like more than one other, resemble both Churchill and a bulldog—probably in virtue of different features. And much the same goes for seeing-as; aspects are notoriously ambiguous. But, it may be asked, is not this simple answer over hasty? There seems to be a damaging objection. Goodman's account is devised to provide for a certain feature ascribable to representation-as, that the alternatives I have suggested omit, the feature being logical direction. One might argue as follows: it is one thing to represent Churchill as a bulldog, another to represent a bulldog as Churchill. The deficiency, if so, would be a serious one. But the reverse is true. Our account, certainly, makes no distinction, but for the best of possible reasons. There is none. The would-be objection, then, boomerangs on its proponents, and serves precisely to confirm the alternative view that it was aimed against. For if I am right, to repeat, the theory yields precisely what it ought to yield, no distinction where none in fact exists.

Let me take an example. We have in our philosophical household a much loved and very recognisable bulldog, which we call Fido, like all good philosophers. Now you do a drawing of Fido, which is quite unmistakeably Fido. But it is also unmistakably Churchill. Suppose we ask next whether the drawing represents Fido as Churchill or Churchill as Fido. The question is, as it should be, strictly unanswerable; I mean, as it should be on the resemblance theory, or a theory cast in terms of seeing-as, but not on Goodman's. As to the cartoonist's bulldog-Churchill, I dare say that the public at large, who recognise the defiant war leader, take the bulldog—perhaps wrongly—as merely generic.

For Goodman, I suggested, the point may prove trickier. A bulldog picture may represent Churchill; that presents no problem. But what of the case where the same object, here the same picture, represents not only two other further objects simultaneously but also either one as the other? There are of course ambiguous names. Occurring in a seventeenth-century history the name 'Churchill' might refer to the future victor of Blenheim or the future war leader of the 1940s. Or let us, to pursue possibilities, name our bulldog, not Fido, but Churchill. The name is already ambiguous; the drawing denotes Churchill as Churchill either way. But what is it to denote A or B, or simultaneously A as B and B as A? These seem to me words without meaning.

10

Art and Generality

In every work of art we find a kind of mystery; perhaps in some sense it is bound to remain so. Yet we need not make things more mysterious than they are. The philosophers whom I would accuse of that perversity are Stuart Hampshire in his 'Logic and appreciation' published long ago; and P. F. Strawson more recently and bleakly in an article called 'Aesthetic appraisal'.[1] Both belong, though with no very clear sign of appreciating the fact, to a tradition deriving ultimately from Kant—indeed Hampshire does speak expressly of 'disinterestedness' and Strawson disclaims originality—and stretching through Hegel, to Croce and ultimately Collingwood. It is Collingwood who makes the point most ultimately: in art what we see is unique, we know the individual qua individual. Works of art in *Speculum Mentis* were earlier described as 'monadic'. *The Principles of Art* spells out, indeed is almost built around, the contrast in question. In craft and technology we generalise, and generality is seen as essential to them; which contradistinguishes them from art. Already for Kant, of course, it served as a central principle that aesthetic judgments, value judgments, are not arrived at by any ordinary process of argument, specifically not by argument using determinate concepts. (One might also name Bergson, for whom, and for his many 'aesthete' followers, art cut through the network of intellection, to show us reality in itself. But Gombrich's work, one would have thought, has settled that.)

Some such theme, broadly speaking, is common to the two writers I have named among our contemporaries. Let me look at their articles in turn (though in fact my main interest is in Strawson's). But to begin with Hampshire: he characterises the 'aesthete' as follows: 'Precisely his refusal to generalise,' he tells us, 'would be the mark of his aestheticism' and again, 'A copy of a work of art is not necessarily or generally a work of art'. The second is a dictum, I think, that we hardly need dwell on. For one thing it has been tellingly criticised by Ruby

[1] Cf. Stuart Hampshire, 'Logic and appreciation' in *Aesthetics and Language*, ed. William Elton (Oxford, 1954), and P. F. Strawson, 'Aesthetic appraisal', *Oxford Review* (1966), reprinted in P. F. Strawson, *Freedom and Resentment* (London, 1974), pp. 178–88.

Meager.[2] But anyway Hampshire seems to be arguing in a vacuum. I know of no proponent nor yet critic of generalising who has interested himself in the reproduction *in toto* of single works. What has certainly interested both is the problematic possibility of generalisations, general rules or the like for guiding practice either in criticism or creation. (Strawson has more complex views within roughly this area; but they concern identification not copying.) And Hampshire's contention seems so tame. Qua philosopher, perhaps, one need not concern oneself with what is generally the case; though surely a perfect copy of a work of art *is* generally itself a work of art. But that the copy of a work of art is not necessarily a work of art seems too weak a position to be worth contesting; besides that the same holds very widely. A copy of right action is not necessarily a right action; unless one is to write into one's description of the mere action—a questionable move that would need arguing—the whole complexity of a perhaps indeterminate context.

Hampshire, as far as I can find, has two other main arguments to advance. The first is that art is, to use his own expression, gratuitous; it seems, one can opt out of aesthetics as one cannot, by contrast, of morals. He writes further that a critic can reject an artist's work 'without showing what he ought to have done in place of the work rejected'. True, a critic need not himself be a creative artist. What he cannot do is reject the work without giving reasons, nor dismiss it as bad or insignificant. Suppose he should; then *eo ipso* he ceases to be a critic. 'Gratuitous' would seem to carry two suggestions: you can like or dislike as you please, which is the first; and secondly, decisions are never forced from you. For art, as Hampshire sees it, serves no need, it is never a requisite to a further purpose; its creation and appreciation are things that we are not bound to engage in at all.

Now this seems in some sense to be true. One can in some sense conceive of a world, however wretchedly impoverished, with no pure science or mathematics, no kind of sport and no art. One cannot conceive of one with nothing at least substantially corresponding to morality. But nothing further of special interest as to the nature of moral and aesthetic judgments seems to follow.

You are, to repeat, not bound to play cricket; you are not bound to practise pure mathematics. It does not follow that the application of words such as 'good' or 'bad' or or of descriptions like 'an invalid proof' or 'a splendid catch' are a matter of gratuitous choice. That, I think, hardly needs further argument; perhaps I have ascribed views to Hampshire that he never in fact meant to maintain. If so, all we have is

[2] Cf. Ruby Meager, 'The uniqueness of a work of art', in *Collected Papers on Aesthetics*, ed. C. Barrett (Oxford, 1965), pp. 27, 32.

the second contention. What appears from it is, I think, this: that Hampshire himself contemplates his art largely, say, as a stroller round galleries, certainly not as a curator or a planner. The latter has unavoidably to decide, say, on the best possible placing for the Tiepolo—at the expense of the Canaletto, perhaps. The same problem faces, and far more urgently, other groups in whom we at least hope to find some reasonably strong aesthetic interest; I mean for instance planners and architects; indeed all of us so far as we care about the cities and neighbourhoods we live in. There stands at the top of Ludgate Hill an old building devoted to a dying cult, or so some would say; which might be pulled down to make room for a new chemical plant. How would Hampshire respond to the suggestion, or will he be content to opt out? That is an attitude, I think, simply not open to one; it is not open to a non-Christian who maintains aesthetic values, any more than to one who being, say; at once religious and philistine, sees St Paul's only as a church.

Circumstances can also arise, at least as the terms are commonly understood, where aesthetic considerations override moral ones. Hampshire's ascription to the latter of an unchallengeable precedence—for if moral considerations are in their nature compulsive and aesthetic ones never so, that surely follows—is only asserted, not argued for. Will he then endorse the work of the immortal Dr Bowdler, whose edition of Shakespeare for the best part of a century was in every home—the original, as we all know, being not wholly morally accept-able—or the draping of the nudes in Michelangelo's *Last Judgment*? Or take Bernini's figure of Charity in one of the papal tombs in St Peter's; whose breasts—protest who will, the Vatican will not budge—are still covered by metal-foil drapery. (Many Londoners, incidentally, still bitterly resent the destruction of an unpretentious—and hence, perhaps, all the more pleasing—Georgian square in the interest of culture, and at the hands of a great university; which some of its teachers, in this instance, were ashamed to belong to.)

True, there is a simple expedient to put all such examples out of court, the expedient being a logical ruling. Wherever 'aesthetic' con-siderations are thought of as overriding moral ones then *eo ipso* they are no longer aesthetic but themselves moral. But that is to trivialise the point. Hampshire seemed to be concerned with two distinct areas of in-terest, intuitively distinct and recognisable, if hard to define; namely, the aesthetic and the moral. About these he brought us interesting news: that the two could not ever come in conflict, or if they did—for I think that is what he implies—the latter must always take precedence. What we have now is a redefinition, or at best one among numerous possible definitions, which needs to be argued for; and, I think, an unhappy one. For it prevents me from saying, or saying at all simply or clearly, what I hold to be true and important, what the previous examples make clear: precisely that aesthetic considerations can on occasion override moral ones.

Hampshire's article, I said, was written long ago; his mature judgment might reject (though I am only guessing) his own more extreme early views. To turn instead to Strawson's more recent work: in which, one notes however, he still cites and quotes Hampshire approvingly. First, as to uniqueness, he uses the type-token distinction. It is the former alone, the type, that is unique; a perfect copy, for instance, a good draft from an etching, taken, that is, from the same plate, will count as the same work of art. What strikes him is the Kantian point; to judge a work we ourselves must 'enjoy' it. We do not formulate principles to argue from. One concern of Strawson's—a Kantian concern too, but now closer to Collingwood—is with the individual thing that confronts us; what matters is, it would seem, the individual in its sheer individuality. We indeed argue about art and discuss it, but our arguments are distinctive in kind. Hegel contrasts instruments with works of art, the former having a purpose external to them; Strawson argues on similar lines. Let us, at least for argument's sake, accept the fact-value distinction; in wide areas it works plausibly and usefully. A merely factual description of an instrument, of any sort of functional object, for example, of a manoeuvrable car, entails at least some provisional evaluation. Suppose it manoeuvrable; then so far it is good; and so too for 'fast', 'safe', and so on. Now these terms are purely descriptive, applied here to tools and instruments. Yet therein we are committed to commending them. There may still of course be counterweighing objections, the manoeuvrable car might be uncomfortable, even almost impossible to get in and out of. But the pattern of argument, a universalising argument, remains the same. And all this holds good comprehensively. Say that one doctor diagnoses a rare disease. A colleague shows him a similar case. The onus is now clearly on the first either, in spite of appearances, to bring to light relevant differences, or otherwise to say the same here. And this is a pattern of argument, in some sense a basic one, that covers science, history, morals, what you will; but, it seems, with one exception. It does not, for Strawson, cover art criticism or literary criticism.

Now certainly we argue about art. We describe a drawing as 'delicate', perhaps, or a massing of columns as 'powerful'; we speak of 'harmony', 'balance' or 'richness'. But such terms, at least normally, Strawson notes, are already evaluative; which is hardly to be disputed. If delicacy is already a merit, that all delicate works are, so far, good, would be rather a tautology than a generalisation. But the possibility

Strawson explicitly denies, and what one must find to refute him, is an unimpeachably neutral description, one cast not in terms themselves 'evaluative', which none the less implies some evaluation—at least a provisional evaluation. But suppose that is our task, on one reading at least, it is no very formidable one.

I say, 'on one reading'. For Strawson has contrasted aesthetic argument not with other sorts of argument generally but only with one; and that one, being of a distinctive kind, may form no safe basis for generalising. Instruments are defined by their functions; hence *pro tanto* certain describable features count as excellencies, which follows virtually deductively—perhaps strictly deductively. But can that be the whole issue? True, there is no strict deduction of aesthetic excellence, even prima facie excellence, from describable features of works of art; that, doubtless, will be readily granted. But now we are no nearer than ever to what it had seemed we were promised, some sort of *differentia* of works of art. The same is true very generally. Say we interpret an ancient document, a philosophical text, or again psychoanalytic or historical data. Now I think one interpretation the best, and give reasons for thinking so. I point to this feature and that, I say broadly, it makes better sense of it. But I make no claim that such reasons are deductive. Suppose, however, Strawson is denying that in art criticism there can be a passage of any sort, not merely a deductive one, from description to evaluation; that would be quite another matter.

To start with an example from literature: Don John in *Much Ado About Nothing*, we may say, is a mere stage villain, introduced wholly ad hoc. So far of course Strawson's view is unshaken. These are certainly non-neutral descriptions. Let us try, then, to reduce them to neutral ones. 'Ad hoc' at least presents no problem. Don John has no function in the play except to set in motion the intrigue; the villain's whole role is to play the villain. He is left unprovided with any motive. And previous villainies are hinted at with the very first words that introduce him. Shakespeare goes out of his way; 'Let me bid you welcome, my lord,' he makes Leonata say after his arm greeting of Don Pedro; 'being reconciled with the Prince your brother, I owe you all duty.' So much for Don John. And his wickedness once accomplished, he disappears. As in *Measure for Measure* the grotesquely named Pompey expresses it, 'I hope here be truths'; and truths are the same thing as facts (a point Strawson himself, at least implicitly, I think, has drawn our attention to). These are facts that are unimpeachably factual. What is plain is that they imply evaluations—evaluations, certainly, which might be overruled, outweighed by other considerations, as in our former examples; though here, I myself feel, they must stand. Don John is a mere *diabolus ex machina*.

My next example will be different in two ways. First it concerns architecture, not literature; secondly, though it certainly involves a value judgment, it leaves in doubt—at least as far as I shall take it—which way the scales are to be tipped. I wish to speak of mannerist architecture, specifically of the work of James Gibbs. For myself, given my own place of work, I could conveniently cite St Mary-le-Strand. But for Strawson, should he wish to verify my findings, the Radcliffe Camera will be nearer to hand. John Summerson has analysed the Radcliffe and noted the following features: it has a ribbed dome, indeed with prominent ribs, and a drum that is circled with coupled columns. But the ribs of the dome are ostentatiously unaligned with the latter, and they in turn stand in alternating intervals longer and shorter, yet with no obvious relation between them; not, for instance, one half of the other. Last (a point not noted by Summerson) to the pediments over the projections in the podium or base; once again they lack any regular relation to the rest. One of the coupled columns stands directly above the slope of pediments; the other beside it, nowhere in particular. All these are mere describable facts.

But what follows, one may ask, as to evaluation? Something certainly, but there still remains room for disagreement. The building is 'interesting' perhaps; or alternatively one might say 'incoherent'. (For myself, I would argue that the treatment of the podium is indeed perverse and indefensible. But I shall not try to argue it here.) A point that seems worth noting is this: we have a pattern that is typical not only of aesthetic but of moral argument; one illustrated by the familiar facetious declension, 'I am firm, you are obstinate, he is a pig-headed fool.' Certainly something of relevance follows; though we may differ as to 'interest' against 'incoherence' or 'mere perversity'. And one thing that conspicuously fails to follow is that discourse concerning works of art is to be typically contrasted with moral discourse (though, in fairness, that contention was made more of in Hampshire's discussion than Strawson's).

Strawson has, I think, two principal themes, distinct though connected themes: first, the possible passage in art-criticism from description to evaluation, secondly the possibility of generalisation; both of which he denies. As to the first, I have sought to refute him with counter-examples. It is time now to turn to the second. I described the two themes as connected. We pass from a given description to a favourable or unfavourable evaluation; that at least suggests the legitimacy, or anyway the prima facie legitimacy, supposing the same feature appears elsewhere, of drawing a similar inference. It suggests the possibility of generalising. But the point is one to be approached carefully; it is full of pitfalls. Art springs from genius, not skill; so Kant at least teaches. And his teaching, with variations, has been echoed since by scores of philosophers and critics. Further, of course, it has great plausibility. If artists at work obey rules or profit from obeying them, as craftsmen are said to, they will be no more at best than broad guiding rules. No work of art was ever made, as works of technology may have been, by the complex reapplication in new contexts of generalisations abstracted from old ones. But our concern is different; it is with criticism. And again, as to the status of generalisations: there do, I believe, exist generalisations which it is possible to state quite explicitly. I shall presently offer examples. But, short of such statement, we may still be able to recognise generalisation as implicit, as it were, embedded in the critical process; they may be so even though the generalisations actually framed are treated as only tentative or rough. (Both Strawson and Hampshire use the word 'general' and its cognates. 'Universal' might perhaps be more accurate; but for the present argument, I think, nothing turns on it.)

I spoke of the case of a doctor who, on the basis of symptoms, diagnoses a certain disease. And if so, he must be ready to generalise; shown similar symptoms in another case he either must accept the same diagnosis or else point to relevant differences. The same, I suggest, applies here, though most examples may in fact be more complex. Take the presence of a motiveless villain, inserted solely to meet the need of the plot. I have treated it as a fault in *Much Ado*. And if so, it is the same elsewhere; the argument must admit of being generalised. I dare say it applies to scores of melodramas, a genre of which I am largely ignorant. It plausibly applies to 'the Arragonian brethren' in *The Duchess of Malfi*; whose lack of obvious motive has troubled critics. Now ought we to say the same of Regan in *King Lear*?—for she too is motivelessly villainous. The fact is one that Shakespeare makes Lear puzzle over, and sanely enough in his very madness: 'Then let them anatomise Regan and see what breeds about her heart. Is there any cause in nature makes these hard hearts?' Instead of a psychological puzzle we have something more like a cosmic mystery. I shall return to the point. For the present let me stress this: we implicitly recognise the legitimacy of the move—and therewith the pattern of argument—even in seeking grounds to reject it; hence to exculpate *King Lear* from similar criticism. I shall shortly argue that we may. To that end, one must appeal to relevant differences; and to do so is to imply that the argument, in principle at least, admits of being generalised.

Some summary assertions are unavoidable. Of course literature and everything that surrounds it are not easily reduced to simple terms. A play like *Much Ado* requires a motive. But to say 'like *Much Ado*' is already, however loosely, to generalise; so is it, etymology may remind

us, to speak cautiously of genres or kinds. But where in a literary work
the very absence of motive is made an issue of, that cannot count
against it as a fault. So far so good; but that alone will hardly meet our
needs. Shakespeare has had to work through two and a half acts to
reach the point where Lear's question comes naturally, only echoing
what we ourselves were half ready to formulate. There remain three
further differences to notice: the first of which fits Strawson's account
(and I would have to probe it much deeper, at far greater length than I
have space for to be able to say otherwise). But the latter two, though
dramatically less important, support mine. To knock down a
generalisation, which is what Strawson offers us—a higher-level
generalisation about the possibility of others—a single weak counter-
example would suffice. Regan, unlike Don John, is a character vividly
'realised'; she is certainly no common stage villainess. She has in fact, I
would venture, a peculiar mean vileness, being at once vicious and
mean-spirited, hardly equalled in literature. This is the first point I
spoke of—and I do not claim in value-free language. But for the others:
take Regan as we see her at the start, or rather hear her, for her first
speech is at once sycophantic and hypocritical. Now, certainly it is well
enough motivated; she is after her slice of the cake—the cake in question, of course, being the land of Britain. All this is surely unproblematic; but having seen her given to viciousness (which the rest of
the same scene serves to confirm), the motiveless viciousness that
follows will find us already half-prepared. 'Hypocritical' and
'sycophantic', you may say, are by no means neutral, value-free terms;
which is true. But the values are moral not aesthetic; they apply to
Regan, not to Shakespeare or his work. In contrast, on first meeting
with Don John, that is on first meeting him alone or with his own
followers and cronies, let us note what we find him engaged in; he is
seeking gratuitous occasions for mischief. At least he is sad and sullen
for no obvious reason; but perks up as soon as Conrad, who knows his
master, it seems, produces a promising suggestion. Secondly, returning to Regan, her very place in the play, hence her character, is largely
fixed by the fairy-tale background; we know how the story must go.
The one good, youngest daughter, we see at once, will be contrasted
with her two wicked sisters. And here again you have mere matter of
fact; the first a neutral description of the opening scene; the second
may be a trifle more recondite but none the less a matter of fact concerning popular cultural history. These facts in themselves in large
measure would suffice to differentiate Regan from Don John. True, I
granted one main point to Strawson; the immediate strong impact of
Regan's character, which it would be a formidable critical undertaking
to seek to explain in 'neutral' terms. Yet think that away; the rest

stands. Our judgment of Don John would prima facie admit of being generalised; and, even though they stood alone, the two features I have dwelt on would go some way to defeating the generalisation. To repeat, then: given what we said in the first case we must either grant the likeness and say the same, or else alternatively find the relevant differences. I accept the challenge, as one must, in literary criticism no less than in other fields that I cited. But the course I have taken is the latter.

Roughly we may say this: suppose a feature I have pointed to as a fault in one work appears as an excellence in another, or merely neutral. Suppose, secondly, the Hampshire–Strawson position acceptable. There would be no reason why I should see the situation as in any way problematic or other than normal. It would call for no particular comment or response.

Let me temporarily interrupt the argument—it will perhaps be no real interruption—to speak directly of the views of Meager in the article I have referred to. As I said, it contains detailed and, I think, damaging criticism of Hampshire. Yet, if I read her rightly, she never seriously considers the possibility of rejecting the whole approach, one may call it, an anti-generalist approach. We are still to have criticism without generality; for she writes:

> Aesthetic appraisal may take the form of noticing in a particular work those features that render it effective or ineffective most strikingly, but their value will be attributed to them only in the context of the particular work considered; only, therefore, in a context where all the other features present are relevantly present, making the work the work it is.[3]

That is certainly on the face of it convincing. But how far is it a position to contend over? That turns largely, I think, on the force given to the inconspicuous adverb 'only'. For military or economic measures, clearly enough, and much else of the same sort, might rightly be praised 'in the context'—perhaps even 'only in the context'—of the particular situation they were designed for; which would hardly be taken as showing the impossibility of generalising in matters of military strategy or economics.

I have no wish merely to multiply examples; and I have offered a number already. But for the present point, to handle in the concrete what Meager seems to imply, I still need one more. It is an example I have also used elsewhere. In writing of the excellence of aesthetic form I compared the domes of St Peter's in the Vatican and Wren's St

---

[3] Ibid., p. 39.

Paul's.[4] Indeed I was careful to say that my general analysis neither stood nor fell by the concrete application I gave it; which was just as well. For most of what I wrote of St Paul's was grotesquely misconceived. But one point, I still think, was sound. I dwelt on the importance of the lantern. The lantern of Wren's dome, unlike Michelangelo's, and unlike his own of the Great Model, does not echo the drum as one might expect; instead of a circular colonnade the lantern he built was rectangular. One difference is plain; the new form was relatively stable. Circles revolve; angles by contrast are fixed (though even as to the drum, Wren had slowed the movement by filling in the gap between each fourth column). This stability has a manifold significance 'in the context', to use Meager's phrase, of the building as a whole. Wren's building is reposeful in its grandeur; I described it in contrast to Michelangelo's, as 'earth-bound and self-sufficient'.[5] Further its ground-plan is angular; he had had, under pressure, to revert to the traditional English cathedral form; that is, with first nave and aisles, and secondly a transept at right-angles.

Now as to generalisations: for one such I need only repeat what I have just written. Circular forms revolve, a rectangle is relatively stable. A further generalisation: any prominent central feature of a building will reinforce whatever it echoes; for instance, the main body and its ground-plan. As to more complex considerations giving significance to Wren's lantern, its significantly differentiated form and its contribution to the felt stability, the reposefulness of the building as a whole, I must refer to my original article. They too, it will, I think, be found, admit of being generalised. To speak broadly of this prominent feature, then: 'its value is attributed to it only in the context of the work considered'. But that is true, too, only in virtue of a whole multiplicity of specific generalisations.

I suggested that Strawson has two theses, indeed perhaps three, whose connection is less than wholly clear. I spoke first of the derivation which he thinks impossible of value-judgments from neutral descriptions. And I have spoken, too, of generalisation. But that is bound up with obscurer doctrines concerning the uniqueness of works of art. One sort of uniqueness is accommodated—and rendered unproblematic in the process—by the use of the type-token distinction. But something, for Strawson, remains. A work of art, so he tells us, is defined—we might, I think, rather say 'identified'—by the totality of its aesthetically relevant features. So far I have no wish to take issue with him. But the contrast to instruments is puzzling; the issues it raises are very mixed. An instrument is, if not identified, at least

[4] Cf. above, Chapter 6.
[5] See above, p. 99.

evaluated, by the totality of its instrumentally relevant features. But next comes a difference. Another instrument *ceteris paribus* that achieved the same performance by different means, say, a differently constructed although equally manoeuvrable car, must be counted as equally good. By contrast we have no notion, or only the vaguest notion, of what it might mean for a work of art 'to achieve the same effect' by different means. As to that difference, Strawson nowhere directly states it, but it may underline his other sayings. What he explicitly tells us is this: though of course we often describe works of art, yet so to describe a work as to take account of whatever contributes to its value, is a 'task' that proves strictly impossible. To 'describe' *Paradise Lost*, for example, one might say, 'It begins, "Of Man's first disobedience. . . ." and goes on till one gets to, "Through Eden took their solitary way." ' But, of course, that would be not to describe but to recite it. It would be, as Meager has argued (using the same example), to produce, in her terminology, simply another 'manifestation' of the same work; to speak more roughly for simplicity's sake, another token of the type.[6] Yet Strawson's point is still an important one. We can, as I said, give little or no meaning in talk of art to the notion of producing the same effect by different means. Art serves no end external to itself; so Hegel emphatically held. Now given no external end, there is no room for alternative means. Works of art, then, in this way are unlike instruments. But this issue, this difference, is one that we need sharply to distinguish from what Strawson connects it with, the impossibility of adequate description—adequate in the sense that I specified. Its explanation is totally different. The concrete complexity of art—a theme I shall presently return to—is what I find relevant to the latter; but meanwhile I must leave the point on one side.

To return to the theme of imitation, and the possibility of learning by imitation. A good imitation, we may grant, though the new work resembles the old, still cannot ensure what we want. It will resemble it in specifiable ways, but may still not resemble it in value. Yet something must be said on the other side. The whole history of art will bear witness to it. Successes are invariably imitated; new effects, wherever they appear, are copied again and again. Take another example from architecture: the rustication of the ground-floor of a building, or the first stage, giving it solidity and weight, in contrast to the elegance (ashlar with pilasters or half-columns) of the piano nobile; which Bramante was probably the first to use. (The Palazzo Medici and other Florentine palaces have deeper rustication on the ground floor, but no contrast.) Now its subsequent constant recurrence, along with scores of similar instances, is surely a thing that needs accounting

[6] Op. cit., p. 36.

for; and the Kant–Croce–Strawson approach would seem to leave it an impenetrable mystery. Granted, there remains a 'tu quoque'. Imitation is often mechanical; what genius originally created uninspired mediocrity can copy. Hence Kant's teaching cited above; that art springs from genius—genius, that is, opposed to skill; and Hampshire's approach echoes Kant's. I shall return to the argument directly. But suppose I had no answer to offer; that would not help Strawson or Hampshire. The first point still stands and needs answering. Bramante's new motif was reused by half the major classical architects after him; by Palladio, by Wren (at least in unexecuted drawings), by Gabriel. Now a 'tu quoque' argument serves well forensically, but no more. However it shakes your opponent's stance, it does nothing to substantiate your own. And Strawson's, we see, and that of all the philosophers he follows, for all the great roll-call of names, is badly in need of substantiation.

But as to the objection itself: one preliminary point to observe is—outside the discussion of literature—the extreme inarticulateness of criticism. Criticism of architecture, for instance, in general is historical and scholarly, and elsewhere impressionist. The latter does for aesthetic effects—except for a simple point here and there: the lowness of Bernini's colonnade at St Peter's, we learn for instance, helps to compensate for the too broad facade. But that is hardly the sort of thing to take you far. The scholarship concerns influences, rules or standards of the period, or the practical problems of building. And in painting it thrives on iconography. But of course our failure up to now cannot entail that success is impossible. And literary criticism points the way. Shakespeare's contemporaries knew his greatness; yet Johnson has little more to tell us, though hailing him as outdoing Greece and Rome, than that he joined 'nature' with 'art'. These are regions where powerful responses are only slowly and with difficulty made articulate.

To return now to the previous argument: let us forget about art, at least momentarily, and think instead, say, of landslides and earthquakes. (I shall speak shortly of political crises.) Certainly such a phenomenon, say a given landslide, is never exactly reproducible, reproducible in its full actuality. Rather, where we seek to explain them, factors taken one by one are reproduced in laboratory conditions. True, technology emerges in the process; at last we build aeroplanes and spaceships. We have, I think, in noticing the point, given Hampshire a better argument than his own. As to his own difficulty over generalisation, the truth we extracted will suffice—the truth he himself seems to grope for. Slight differences can change the whole picture. That cannot make it impossible to generalise; conversely, it holds widely of generalisation. What remains unanswered, however, is why creativity in art has no use for the methods of technology. Other architects may learn from Bramante; other poets from Dante or Dryden. But the manner of their learning is different; for here there is no isolating of established laws—to be recombined in new works later realised.

We have been taught by the romantics, especially Coleridge—whether or not drawing on German sources—to think of art as 'organic', not mechanical. Yet the distinction is profoundly unclear. Let an organism be other than a mystery, or let it, conversely, be explicable at all, what other form is explanation to take? I assume that 'mechanical explanation' will be one that invokes rules or principles; those in their nature are universal. I have illustrated their working, I hope, sufficiently. Yet Coleridge's immense influence makes one pause. One course may be to ask ourselves again what we in fact mean by 'organic'? Now part of the answer is surely this: works are described as 'organic' in so far as their parts interact—parts, features, qualities or so on. 'Organic *form*' is expressive of content. Now in works of art, it would seem, these things not only interact, but do so with more than usual intensity. But the point to be noticed is this: they still need not do so other than 'mechanically'. For each action of one on another must surely be governed by law—which, being a law, is universal. The difference, I believe, lies in this; the extent and the multiple complexity of such interaction in works of art.

But not merely that: indeed, the word 'complexity' may not be altogether happy. It suggests a multiciplicity of parts, parts that may remain fixed or determinate, systematically arranged and perhaps rearranged. Mathematics concerns just such items, as well as readily handling them in technology; fixed items, as well of course as continua. But what confronts in works of art is rather different. Indeed we identify parts or elements; some salient aspect remains fixed. Yet we often find their aesthetic character radically modified as they 'move' from one context to another. Now such modifications, one may expect, admit of no easy mathematical handling. Not that we need think them merely arbitrary, or think them explicable—if explicable at all—only on some wholly new principle, hitherto unknown, unexpounded. They still surely obey laws—'mechanical' laws, if we choose to say so. Yet it is such interaction, the modification in new contexts of the aspect each feature presents, that defeats analysis; that prevents our reducing aesthetic effects to principles that might subsequently be systematically reapplied. Artists copy isolated effects with uncertain, not infrequent success. Copyists make replicas of whole works. What we cannot do, by reason of their complexity and their distinctive kind of complexity, is dismantle and subsequently reconstitute them.

In fact Dryden anticipated Kant; a century earlier he said much the same thing:

> A pretty task, and so I told the fool
> Who needs must undertake to please by rule.[7]

Doubtless great art does more than 'please'—an error Kant (barring the sublime) shares with Dryden. But the main point can certainly stand. Perception, too, offers an analogy; intuitive perception in some people is wonderfully certain and fine. Their less intuitive companions see nothing; they perhaps ask to be shown what the other sees. And of course there is no answer to give. It is something we all know in some degree. We see what we see, we cannot analyse it. Nor can we state a body of rules, or none of any practical use, that govern the sort of intuition I speak of. We none the less implicitly postulate them; we use the idea regulatively in criticism. For just that was what our examples revealed. Some feature, in this work, is an excellence; elsewhere it is neutral or even damaging. In that case we proceed here as elsewhere; we look for some relevant difference, and often, it proves, with success. Unless such differences are governed by law, explicable by law, the whole process could only be idle.

In fact works of art defeat analysis. But criticism presupposes in principle the possibility of a task that in practice it cannot complete. What we do characteristically is to pick on some salient strands; we pick them out against a background that we take for granted. At any point we can be challenged, and in response seek to open up more; to articulate further distinctions. But there still stands behind it a whole continent.

Two brief points remain to be dealt with. First, none of this is peculiar to art-criticism. Take, for instance, political analysis: wise statesmen may learn from their predecessors, but no *statesman* was ever a copyist. Richelieu, if anyone, should have known: 'No one is more dangerous in a state than those who set out to rule kingdoms by maxims to be met with in books.' Now will Strawson assign to 'political situations', to crises, negotiations or the like some singular quality of *uniqueness*? Secondly, what given hard matter is impossible—beyond a certain level of complexity—may be eminently possible elsewhere. Hence of course the recurrence of motifs; say, Bramante's handling of the ground-floor and piano nobile. An unspecific rule is still a rule: 'Combine a rusticated first stage . . . etc.' Besides we can progres-

---

[7] Epilogue to *Aureng-Zebe*. In fact there lies behind the point a whole renaissance and even classical tradition.

sively specify it; though, to repeat, we reach a point where mere complexity inevitably defeats us. (Nor, incidentally, could we calculate in mathematics, or attain to calculations of much difficulty, given too unwieldy a notation.) On one issue we have already found Strawson echoing Hegel. What he needs here, it would seem, is another Hegelian doctrine: a point comes where mere difference in quantity, dialectically transmuted, assumes the character of a difference in quality.

But that raises another issue. I must defend myself against a possible objection, at least an *ad hominem* objection. I have in fact spoken elsewhere, in the article I referred to above, in different terms; a work of art, I wrote there, is an artefact; one specifically made to be contemplated, to be seen, read, listened to, and so on, and to repay appropriate contemplation. ('Appropriate' of course carries no special weight. The word is not meant to mark out some sort of contemplation as distinctively aesthetic; it means only appropriate to the work, a cathedral, say, as distinct from a salt cellar.) But how are these two accounts to be related? They surely go naturally together. A work of art has a peculiar richness—a theme central to my argument. Now doubtless it might be intricate yet bad. But that those qualities that reward contemplation—vivid expressiveness, finely varied yet unitary form and the like—should arise from or depend on just such complexity, is surely a thing to be expected. Hence the 'aesthetes' were wrong, I mean those who set art in a world apart. Art belongs to our ordinary world and criticism follows ordinary logic. It manifests no special individuality except, to repeat, as the product of that interplay, and specifically of the intensity of interplay among factors of the sort I have instanced; which makes possible its manifesting those qualities that reward our intensive contemplation.[8]

[8] I have often written elsewhere (e.g. in 'Virtue and reason', *Proceedings of the Aristotelian Society Supplementary Volume* 48 (1974), pp. 56–7) of what John Wisdom calls 'reflective argument', a distinctive thing, which may not admit of being generalised. I do not retract that. But such argument appears not only in aesthetics but very generally. I should like to add that in general I have benefited, or sought to benefit, from the criticisms of Roger Scruton.

11

Scruton on Art and Imagination

> Well then, the promised hour is come at last,
> The present age of wit exceeds the past.

To start with appropriate praise of a work one intends to find fault with is almost a matter of routine. 'I would not give time to criticising Professor Mugwump unless his work seemed to me to deserve criticism': so runs the predictable formula. I am hence the more anxious that my praises of Roger Scruton's book[1] should not pass as mere formalities. Aesthetics has too few such works to boast of for us to treat them undervaluingly. I admire in it not only breadth and rigour, though these are abundantly in evidence, but above all its centrality. It is a book for philosophers, of course. But a philosopher may find himself approached by some student of the arts, a critic, historian or the like, whose interest has led him towards theory; prepared, further, for the kind of distinctively hard intellectual work that any serious philosophising must involve. Now, to repeat, Scruton does philosophise; but his philosophising centres on issues that all students of the arts are bound to care about. I can think of no work more recent than E. H. Gombrich's masterpiece *Art and Illusion* which evoked eagerness from specialists in both disciplines alike. And Gombrich with all his brilliance yet suffered—as Richard Wollheim brought out in his masterly analysis[2]—from a certain central methodological unsureness, an unsureness of aim (that article too, incidently, is an exception to the rule I began with; Wollheim's praise is as obviously wholehearted as his criticism is searching). Scruton writes explicitly as a philosopher, and with no doubt of the sort of illumination he sees philosophy as able to bring to the phenomena, and to anyone seriously concerned with them; to the study and appreciation of art.

I must begin with some brief exposition. But brevity, I suppose, is forgivable. Readers of *The British Journal of Aesthetics* will probably be

---

[1] Roger Scruton, *Art and Imagination* (London, 1974).
[2] Cf. Richard Wollheim, 'Reflections on "Art and Illusion" ', in *On Art and the Mind* (London, 1973), pp. 261–89.

familiar with the original. I mean specially to focus on Scruton's central views: namely his account of imagination, of distinctively aesthetic imagination and again of the 'descriptivist' doctrine of aesthetic qualities; one whose inadequacy—in approaching his own objective—he first sees it as necessary to establish. All this, as I see it, is material of wholly general interest; which, incidentally, is to make a claim for it beyond Scruton's own. His avowed purpose is to develop an aesthetic compatible with Wittgenstein's doctrine of the character—the 'grammar' rather—of private experience. He accepts as a starting-point and without discussion the cogency of that body or drift of thought, inconclusive hints and manoeuvres, part divergent, part overlapping, and incidentally for some time now riddled with unanswered criticism, known under the rubric 'the private-language argument'. What of those who remain unconvinced? He says only this:

> It will be not without interest, even to a philosopher who imagines that all experience is in part at least irredeemably 'private', to see how far the public and observable aspects of aesthetic experience can be described.[3]

'Irredeemably' is, of course, question-begging. Experience is private, no doubt, but not irredeemably—if that means what it seems to mean, namely that I can know nothing of yours. One need not treat Wittgenstein, for all his greatness, as the first philosopher to have noticed the existence of the so-called problem of 'other minds', nor the only one to have attempted some solution to it.

To proceed, then, without more ado: preliminaries being disposed of, Scruton begins his central exposition of his own views—I think unfortunately—with the stock example of the sadness of sad music; unfortunately because his earlier talk has been of 'aspects', for instance the 'duck' and 'rabbit' aspects of Wittgenstein's 'duck-rabbit'. Why link things, a reader is bound to ask, on the face of it so strikingly dissimilar? Hence one's initial reaction is not unlikely to be one of incredulity. Scruton, of course, has his reasons; but there are several hard chapters to work through before those become plain. 'Seeing-as' is the prototype of his imagination, at least of imaginative vision; and the same approach, it will ultimately prove, can accommodate the initial example. But meanwhile one must take it on trust.

Aspects, we learn, are not 'properties', at least not in Scruton's usage, which proves to be pretty much the common usage. We ascribe them to objects, no doubt, but not as we ascribe colour, weight or the

[3] Op. cit., p. 12.

like. What is yellow cannot also be red, and it is true that a cricket ball is red. Hence, of course, that it is yellow must be false. So, too, the same thing, the same living animal, cannot be both a duck and a rabbit: it is plain that the two-sortal universals, no less than non-sortals, are incompatible. Hence the contrast with aspects: clearly enough the same figure—the whole point of the example—can exhibit incompatible aspects. Scruton's moral is this: we are speaking here of a perceiver's response, not of a quality he finds in the object. Incompatible responses can alternate: I see it now as the one thing and now as the other. And that is a true account of my experience. But the object and its qualities are unchanged; an ascription to it of incompatible qualities would, of course, necessarily be false. And here already, let us note, we are on something like Kantian ground: 'the judgment of taste is aesthetic'. Its apparent character is like that of sense-perception. In reality perception of an object so acts on the mind of the perceiver as to give rise to an appropriate response. It was some time ago that I myself used the following example: I imagined a mechanically efficient assistant editor who sorts comic pictures; he goes through them by the score and can be relied on to back a winner almost infallibly. Yet the job is for him mere routine; he has done it for years, and always under pressure of the clock. He scans and takes in the point of the best of them, the most comical, without the least glimmer of a smile. You have a judgment and *ex hypothesi* a sound judgment, but nothing like an aesthetic response.[4]

Yet Scruton, a kind of subjectivist, is hardly more a relativist than Kant himself. There are appropriate and inappropriate responses. One's 'judgment' admits of vindication, an attempt that may presumably fail but may also succeed. None the less the subjectivism stands. Aesthetic utterance, in the ideal central case, cannot count strictly speaking as assertion; it ascribes no sort of qualities to an object. What it does is express a response; the response, ideally, of an observer appropriately placed—his faculties active, his mind trained—to the work itself. Its status elsewhere seems less clearly worked out. In the course of discursive enquiry I speak, say, of the achievement of the Carracci, of the distinctive features or qualities of their work. I express no immediate response. The utterance must, I think, be akin to a hypothetical; it makes known, not necessarily how I feel now or respond now, but what my response would be or presumptively be suppose those ideal conditions were met. As to the sort of justification such responses admit of; that point is one I shall return to.

Now imagination does not deal in truth or falsity, or need not. It is licensed to go beyond belief; its utterance is other than assertion—a

4 See above, p. 29.

doubtful formulation, I shall argue. (One of Scruton's own examples
goes as follows: I believe you to be in fact deeply afflicted yet fail to
'see' the affliction, to see it 'written' in your face. Next, surely, I might
bring imagination to bear and watch before my eyes your aspect
change. Imagination goes no inch beyond belief. And other qualifications will shortly follow.) But to proceed: the expression of such experience, to repeat, makes no claim to truth. Scruton insists only on
this: these responses, subjective as they may be, are still quite as much
cognitive as emotional. In the familiar concept of supposition or
hypothesis he finds a useful starting-point; these certainly are exercises
of the intellect yet not ones that pin us down to belief. Scruton speaks
here of 'unasserted thought'; and thence proceeds to an exploration of
'imagination', of the ramifying complexity of expressions that
apparently centre on that one notion: we have 'mental image',
'imaginary', 'imaginative', 'mere imagination' and so on. The last
pejorative phrase, it seems to me; a point he perhaps insufficiently
brings out, stands somewhat apart from the rest. Nor is *belief*, I suggest,
quite the concept he needs to fit the pattern; nor even that of 'going
beyond'. A notion like *fact* might do better. Yet even so someone may
fairly object that imaginative theorising establishes facts, it alters our
view of the facts; and in doing so it alters our beliefs. Strictly, then,
what imagination goes beyond, where we may speak of 'going
beyond', are the facts as accepted at a given time. But take a historian
like Namier who transforms our understanding of eighteenth-century
British politics; it would surely sound odd to say that he went beyond
the facts, or even the known facts. Perhaps, rather, he saw deeper into
them. (To indulge for a moment in enlarging on my own ideas rather
than Scruton's: our very rationality itself is something essentially
imaginative. And belief is always founded on imagination; very
obviously if our concern is with advanced theory; no less certainly, as
Kant rightly held, in the exercise of ordinary perception.) Scruton's
next point: though here we may go beyond belief, the process need be
no random or arbitrary one. Imagination, he writes, is a rational
activity—which of course is clearly true of imaginative theorising.

But it is true of literature, too, and art generally. Flaubert, for
instance, did not merely spin fantasies like daydreams; rather he

> set himself to imagine what it would be like for someone of a vain
> romantic disposition to be married to a country doctor in provincial
> France, he did not tell a story about the likely consequences of such a
> marriage. He chose the details of his story in the light of what he
> thought to be most revealing and expressive of the provincial state of
> mind, whether or not such details were in any way likely to occur.[5]

5 Scruton, op. cit., p. 99.

Significance or quality beyond 'the given', the facts as accepted here
and now, or understood here and now, is what we admire as
imaginative.

But, naturally enough, here as elsewhere, evaluation needs justifying. And Scruton's account of this process, the justifying of our
responses to works of art, implicitly links it, it seems to me, with what
he writes later on another theme; the *differentia* of aesthetic experience.
All art simply as art, it will probably be conceded, is more or less
imaginative; but the converse fails to hold. Not all imagination is
aesthetic. In a rough formula commonly used—I am myself among
those who have done so—art is something that we value for its own
sake; we gaze, and we merely go on gazing. We concern ourselves with
no end it might subserve. But then the same holds of objects of many
sorts; think of other things men seemingly like to look at. Take pin-ups
or, generally, pictures in glossy journals of the kind displayed prominently in bookstalls; there, too, the same formula seems to fit. True,
what is looked at here and now, though something merely to be looked
at and no more, may yet belong in a context, have meaning in virtue of
other things, of the normal pursuit of other ends. But as to that just the
same is true of works of art. The two would still be normally thought to
differ; we distinguish aesthetic from mere erotic interest. Examples
could easily be multiplied; certain objects serve owners as status symbols and are contemplated with self-regarding complacency. Our
aesthetic interest in an object, in Scruton's formula—not, I think, a
wholly satisfactory formula—is 'founded on the thought of the object'.[6]
The drive underlying that formula becomes clearer on our returning to
the question as to how such responses are justified. Let the object be the
facade of a Baroque church: I admire it and invite others to do so too.
And further I argue the point, the style of such discourse being, surely,
familiar enough: I draw attention, say, to the massing of the columns,
bunched powerfully, generating energy; perhaps, further, progressively stepped forward, hence growing, as it were, towards a climax.
Two such groups face each other across the entrance. The energy that
they generate serves next to heighten the felt tension of that visible gap,
for they stand at some distance apart—the mere situation de facto—
yet are drawn together simultaneously by the dynamism of 'visible'
force. (This 'force' is not force proper, of course; any more than the
'movement' of lines, say the sweep of a curving entablature, is movement.) I may note, further, the nice handling of detail, in virtue of
which, it may be, energy runs no risk of degenerating, as it is apt to,
say, in Edwardian Baroque (for all the newest swing of fashion) into
loudness or mere crudity. In brief, I can justify my response here

6 Op. cit., p. 148.

precisely in redescribing the object (the example is my own and not Scruton's, but in the same spirit, I think). One who truly understands the redescription in doing so appreciates the response; and *ceteris paribus* he shares it. And thus the formula 'for its own sake', too often used glibly, is given substance. This response is no arbitrary thing but is founded on aspects of the object; they determine our vision, our view of it. Being revealed, they reward contemplation. We not only feel, we understand; and, redescribing it, we manifest our understanding. That supposes, you may say, a highly articulate onlooker. Inarticulateness is surely the rule, for otherwise we should all of us be art critics, and good critics too. But still the point of principle remains important; we can all grope towards and recognise articulateness. And the thing remains possible theoretically. The point is the contrast with mere sensation, which may also be enjoyed for its own sake. But sensations barely alter with description; to enjoy them we need only feel them. Understanding plays no part in the process, or only a minimal part. Or take the appreciation of instruments; that certainly implies understanding. But to appreciate them sheerly as instruments—though such appreciation, one should add, may easily pass into something else, something at least quasi-aesthetic—one does not merely rest in redescription of the object, or a fuller perception of it. One's thoughts pass beyond to its use; in that sense one judges it externally. That contrasts with aesthetic appreciation; understanding and response are one thing. To appreciate an object aesthetically is no more than to see it appropriately, where the seeing is itself a response.

To come back to the example we began with: in hearing music as sad we are not ascribing sadness to the music, far less to the musician who composed it. We do no more than hear it appropriately; hear it, that is, in a way that admits of being justified by redescription; which others may be then brought to share. In a full-blown aesthetic response such claims are explicitly present; elsewhere they are present in embryo. It is also, then, a normative response. Scruton's view is explicitly Kantian; we demand universal agreement or seek it at least. For he is, compared to Kant, somewhat tentative. Actual agreement, of course, actual universal agreement, is not something we seriously expect. And that 'demand' is less demanding, it would seem, than its counterpart in ethical judgment, which Scruton thinks of in similar terms. But this much seems true: we see art and speak of it—as *mutatis mutandis*, Scruton might have said, we see philosophy too—only under or in virtue of some such notion; the notion of an ideal beyond our reach, that would command universal assent; a response here ideally to be recognised as a fully appropriate response.

This is, of course, no more than a sketch. Yet I hope it will suffice for my purpose; it at least outlines Scruton's central themes, including those I myself see as problematic. My main doubts will follow immediately. But first, rather trivially perhaps: the duck-rabbit, with its alternative readings, each alike being equally legitimate so that no question arises of any choice between them, is perhaps a tendentious example to fill the role for which it is designed: namely, to lead in a theory that will finally end by suggesting—suggesting at least as an ideal—the appropriateness of some single response. Scruton, I dare say, would insist that it is still what I called it, a response; it is an imaginative vision of the object, hence something in whose nature it lies to go beyond assertable fact. I myself would connect it with judgment, undeterred by the ambiguous duck-rabbit where either reading is equally acceptable. (For the complex issues raised by designedly ambiguous works of art, I have no space at present.) But allow that we are to talk of response: one might, of course, ask a response to what? Not to the art object qua art object. Such objects assume their aesthetic character in virtue of that very response. It must be, then, to the physical object (say where architecture or sculpture is in question) but as viewed in the relevant way. And that is to view it aesthetically, to view it, in the old formula, for its own sake. Viewing it so, we respond to it; rather, view and response are one thing. And the latter admits of being justified in ways such as those I have indicated. We justify it in the terms of the thing itself, in re-characterising, redescribing the object.

One great strength of Scruton's account is its recognising and seeking to do justice to a crucial point for understanding in this field—the ambiguous autonomy of art. The twin dangers are what we might call 'externalism', some sort of utilitarianism, and 'aestheticism'. By aestheticism here I mean mere aestheticism; art, wholly divorced from other things, might be valued for its 'significant form'—assuming the phrase to be itself significant—and set in a world of its own. In contrast, at the other extreme, it is valued for what it subserves; say as soul-building or therapy or as otherwise subordinated to some ambitious, if vague, functional project. As to Scruton, the objects of his 'unasserted thoughts' though contemplated and valued for their own sake, get all their significance from the world of things external to art; from the real world of ambition and fear, tenderness and tedium, of alarm clocks and atom bombs. Yet even this finely held balance must ultimately lead us, I fear, to too radical a divorce of these two realms; it must cut off the objects of imagination, imagination however richly and significantly imaginative, from 'reality'—the objects of belief.

I may be forgiven, I hope, for reusing examples I have made use of before: I need perhaps have little fear that readers of *The British Journal* will have all my own more esoteric writing at their fingertips. Scruton writes specifically of art. He might agree with Gombrich, perhaps, that our aesthetic response to natural things is anterior to, not consequent on, our response to art. Man learnt to look at the land as first of all artists had taught him to look at 'landscape'. Now that is an important half-truth but the reality is more complex, I suspect. The process in fact goes both ways (a point Wollheim illuminatingly explores).[7] The aesthetic has multiple roots. In attempting a few lines back to describe one sort of non-aesthetic appreciation—a technician's appreciation of an instrument, a fine instrument nicely fitted for its purpose—I found that I involuntarily paused. I was in fact forced, in expounding Scruton's views or attempting to expound them, to enter qualifications which do not appear in the original—qualifications of some significance, I think. And as to one sort of example, I quite avoided it, anticipating the trouble it would involve me in; I mean games, games of skill that is to say, which a spectator bringing understanding to bear may appreciate for their own sake. Most, doubtless, want their own side to win; some roaring football fans, it would seem, having spent the first part of their day in the nearest pub, want little else; they care about little else. But, of course, the discriminating spectator enjoys all the subtleties of the game; he appreciates power, skill and purpose in either team or any player wherever it appears. Say Clive Lloyd, with a stupendous command, steps forward and drives through the covers. The ball might be barely overpitched so that sheer footwork turned it into a half-volley. Now suppose one is watching on television; 'That's worth seeing again', says the commentator with relish that is un-mistakably aesthetic. And a replay accordingly follows. Appreciation is of 'visible' mastery, a quasi-aesthetic appreciation which yet takes us no inch beyond the fact. That mastery was both 'visible' and actual, at once fact and aesthetic appearance.

Now turn to the facade of the building. It expresses power, say, authority and energy; all of which is now 'merely' imaginative. The stones have real properties, no doubt, shape, hardness, and even causal properties. The columns, it may be, are functionally designed to take relevant thrusts. But our theme is aesthetic response. Contrary to current dogma, or recent dogma, the role actual function plays here is at best secondary and largely obscure. Appearance is what matters in art; power is generated in my previous example—I in fact had in mind Longhi's SS. Vincenzo ed Anastasio in Rome—by the visual effect I described, the massing of columns about the entrance; which serves, to the best of my knowledge, no functional purpose whatever. It is clear that this second example fits comfortably into Scruton's account; we

[7] Cf. Richard Wollheim, *Art and Its Objects* (New York, 1968), p. 88. Cf. also p. 83.

are here in the world of imagination. My difficulty, however, is this: it is, first, an account I have no wish merely to scrap. Where it works, in my judgment, it works admirably. Yet examples of the first sort remain and we need some more comprehensive perspective to cover and relate both at once.

Examples from literature are harder, for literature is art at one remove. Communication is the first function of language. To make the point persuasive, besides, one has no choice but to quote at some length; the point being, of course, that 'belief', the truth of the thesis advanced or at the very least its plausible truth, is intrinsic to the 'literary' effect. Take Boswell's *Life of Johnson* or Burke's *Reflections on the Revolution in France*, works reckoned as belonging to literature. Yet the truth about Johnson, his true image; the truth about the French Revolution and its hideous significance as Burke saw it—such truth was what both authors pre-eminently aimed at. And to realise that truth for their readers they draw on all imaginative resources; and they do so because they are bound to, because no other method will serve.

I said I would have to quote at some length. Perhaps a couple of paragraphs will suffice:

> To proportion the eagerness of contest to its importance seems a task too hard for human wisdom. The pride of wit has kept ages busy in the discussion of useless questions, and the pride of power has destroyed armies to gain or keep unprofitable possessions.
>
> Not many years have passed since the cruelties of war were filling the world with terror and sorrow; rage was at last appeased, or strength exhausted, and to the harassed nations peace restored with its pleasures and benefits. Of this state all felt the happiness, and all implored the continuance; but what continuance of happiness can be expected, when the whole system of *European* empire can be in danger of a new concussion, by the contention of a few spots of earth, which, in the deserts of the ocean, had almost escaped notice, and which, if they had not happened to make a sea-mark, had perhaps never had a name.[8]

This, a piece of occasional writing, the opening of a political pamphlet, I would claim unhesitatingly to be literature. Now ask me to divorce these two factors, its literary quality from its 'content', the insight it serves to embody, the truth it makes real to the imagination. That raises the huge issues that I must side-step. But one thing is immediately clear: that literary quality itself is largely depleted in the process.

Meager has repeatedly in conversation accused me of conflating two different things, and things that are essentially different; namely truth

[8] *Thoughts on the late transactions respecting the Falkland Islands*, in *The Works of Samuel Johnson* (London, 1797), vol. 10, p. 34.

itself and mere vividness. Think of sheer fantasy vividly presented or even gross misrepresentation of fact; these inasmuch as the issue is a purely literary one, lay equal claim to a reader's appreciation. That itself contains, plainly enough, much truth. But the issues involved here are complex. Take Burke's *Reflections*, for instance: I myself, perhaps, read it more sympathetically than readers, more numerous nowadays, of the intellectually fashionable left. Believers in ideal social systems, in all-curative political remedies, seem still to be strikingly numerous. I am, none the less, I imagine, as far as most readers from wishing to endorse every sentence. But endorsement and rejection are extremes. Burke's very errors contain insight, or do so more often than not; and what he writes, however wrong, is never silly. Suppose it were, one's response would differ radically—a response which is literary, too, not merely intellectual and political. One might indeed subsequently sift it, rephrasing the theoretical theses, factual generalisations and the like; one may assess this or that doctrine as true or false, say, or profound or superficial, independently of its literary expression. But that is not how one reads it at first, how one responds to it at first. So, too, I think, Christians may legitimately complain that 'the Bible to be read as literature' is simply no longer the Bible. But much has been written, of course, of the issues we are touching on here, of the possibility of literary appreciation of writers whose attitudes we condemn, whose views we reject. I urge only this: one's response, whatever fullness it may achieve, can never be the same as the response of either a reader persuaded as he reads or a reader who wants no persuading.

These theses need pulling together. But I have one more example to offer before I can seek (as I see it) to set them in their proper relation. And one other point requires brief treatment. I return first to Scruton's treatment of two themes—themes which, as I previously suggested, it is proper and natural to link. He writes of our aesthetic responses and the sort of justification they admit of; he writes further, giving substance to a familiar formula, of art as something valued for its own sake. I am happier with the second than with the first; here I find myself reacting ambiguously. Unimpeachable as far as it goes, it still leaves a certain odd dissatisfaction. One redescribes and merely redescribes; a process in which, incidentally, some philosophers have seen their whole task. Philosophy, as I see it, must probe deeper. Indeed, Scruton's account as it stands is, I think, not easily to be faulted. And intuitively it may be evident enough; to describe *eo ipso* is to justify. But can we be content to rest here, to rest with intuitive evidence, where our theory aspires to be philosophical? Besides, there are two other things to take into account, other responses we claim to justify and justify in similar ways. Now these, one may reasonably expect, will throw light on our own present theme, namely our strictly aesthetic response to works of art. Take ordinary emotions for a start, fear, for example, or admiration. I might redescribe a harmless looking object, or one that someone else sees as harmless, to justify a different response. Or nearer still, take our previous example, Lloyd's masterly off-drive; it combines sheer power, immense power and energy—running, it seems, through every muscle of that black sinuous form—with exact control, technique or expertise. Full appreciation here, as often indeed in aesthetic appreciation—say, of the product of a particular school or period—presupposes some grasp of technique. There is the bat-lift, the body behind the line of flight and the front foot to the pitch of the ball. The expert takes notice of that; but he sees, too, much more. We imagined, to recall, a good length ball, not one overpitched. Hence there is aggression in the immediate response, aggression being combined with superb confidence. For to venture such a shot at all implies total confidence; it takes for granted perfect speed and control in executing barely possible movements. And here I parenthetically pause. A batsman's business is to stay in and score runs; either primarily to stay in or to score fast according to what the situation demands. And here we can speak wholly generally: beneath aesthetic attitudes lies the non-aesthetic, broadly speaking the 'practical'. A cricketer might appreciate Lloyd's shot and all the relevant qualities it implies, with no hint of aesthetic concern.

What, however, may begin to emerge is how mere redescription serves to justify. To enforce the point let me add a last example. It is, as I said, one I have used before.[9] King Lear, returning from hunting, finds the Duke of Kent disguised as a poor man waiting in his hall, and asks him who he is and what he wants. 'A man, Sir,' Kent answers (not uncharacteristically), 'What wouldst thou with us?' 'Service.' The dialogue proceeds:

Lear: Who would'st thou serve?
Kent: You.
Lear: Dost thou know me, fellow?
Kent: No, Sir, but you have that in your countenance that I would fain call master.
Lear: What's that?
Kent: Authority. (Act i, sc. 4, 24–30)

Now 'authority' implies fitness to command. What Kent sees or pretends to see—rather, sees in good earnest, subtly changing play-

9 Above, p. 107.

acting to earnest—is simply a man to be obeyed; which is so far a straight practical judgment. It as yet implies nothing bordering on the aesthetic; or does the unostentatious preposition 'in' carry some hint of it? We pause momentarily over the strangeness of a 'countenance', a man's face or bearing,[10] that has authority 'in' it, 'visible' like an ordinary quality. But explicitly what Kent offers is a judgment. His concern is with truth not appearance; yet with truth as made good in appearance. What we have here is a simple judgment, assertion; not, certainly, Scruton's 'unasserted thought'. But secondly this: to describe Kent's response to what he sees we nowadays might appeal to 'intuition', a word whose main function is negative. We assert what we see, perhaps confidently; but beyond that we apply a sort of closure. We offer no argument or evidence and have none to offer. And that is the commonest of attitudes; we constantly respond and judge intuitively. But suppose none the less, the question being pressed I abandon that negative stance; I must get you to see it as I see it, or at least I attempt to. How can one attempt it at all? My former example from cricket, deliberately developed more fully, may suggest, I think, the form of an answer. And formally it strikingly resembles what we found Scruton saying of art: we justify our response by redescription.

We come next, or we ought to come next, to our proper concern, to the 'authority' whose presence we feel, for our earlier example will serve, in the facade of a Baroque church in Rome. No practical question arises. There is strictly no judgment at all; or if there is, we must borrow Scruton's phrase and describe it as 'unasserted judgment'. We have passed from the practical, the partly practical, to the realm of the wholly imaginative. I said that that ought to come next; but first a brief lemma is called for. There was one word I threw in too casually; much turns on the adjective 'intuitive'.

Intuitive judgment is holistic. Explicitly spelt out it has two terms, and further a relation between them: from the premise we infer the conclusion. Now imagine a judgment like Kent's, that is like it in content but laid out in articulate form. We first face a physical thing, an object of ordinary perception; we pass next to an object of thought. We infer, what we could never perceive, the abstract quality of fitness to command. (Expressive things are expressive of qualities as often as of emotion or oftener; though emotion so fixates philosophical attention.) More follows, however. In fact we find two judgments in one and a yet further object of thought. We have, generally, for obvious reasons, a pro-attitude to fitness to command; and we sometimes confront figures

[10] 'Countenance' in Shakespeare often means 'bearing'; but it also means 'face' (see above, p. 107, n.6). Here it might equally be either, but I treat it as referring to his face.

that have 'in' them not authority but rather visible weaknesses and hesitancy. I spoke of two judgments in one: there is something both present and good or sometimes both present and bad. You might have the one without the other. But look back to works of art or our response to works of art, which of course the present discussion is meant to throw light on; it is something pre-eminently evaluative. The term 'ugly' is, like 'beautiful', an aesthetic one. To repeat, then, two judgments combine, two essentially separable judgments: one existential, one evaluative. Return now to what Shakespeare portrays; all this is given at once. Kent's response, as I said, is holistic. And objects of judgment reappear, assuming the character of qualities—the 'tertiary qualities' of theory—informing the object we began with, the thing we immediately see. They appear 'in' or hover over the object, not quite like ordinary qualities.

We see a facade as authoritative; which already includes an element of 'seeing as'. The central place in all such response of that one supremely expressive object, the human body—one might add, the body and face—has been dwelt on by Wollheim, surely rightly.[11] Take even the words 'facade' and 'face'; their cognate etymology is no accident. Yet we contrast the metaphorical with the literal; a person, appropriately placed, exhibits fitness or unfitness to command; there you have, not appearance, but the thing itself. You may, if you wish, when words like 'authority' are attributed to structures made of stone—very properly if not very helpfully—speak of 'metaphor'. Words and phrases as they occur in discourse permit or prohibit certain inferences, invite certain questions and so on. Now used metaphorically they differ; they are shorn of some part of that context, of the logic that ordinarily belongs to them. 'His legs bestrid the ocean, his rear'd arm Crested the world.' Which particular ocean? We are not to ask, nor seek to draw a line at some distance that the angle in question might subtend. Nor again may we imagine a Baroque church assuming command in a crisis and showing or failing to show the energy or effectiveness in authority the facade, one might say, makes us feel.

Certainly imagination is essential; Scruton, I believe, is wholly right. We first see the facade as a face and we see next the would-be face as authoritative. To justify our vision we redescribe, set the object in this light or that, give prominence to appropriate features; we proceed in fact essentially similarly (granted that technical considerations are bound to differ) as we would if the judgment were a straightforward, practical one. And now, at length, I can locate more precisely that dissatisfaction I earlier registered with a seemingly impeccable

---

[11] Op. cit., p. 28.

analysis. It left me, so to speak, in mid-air. But now we can build on surer ground, on ground that is solid and familiar; for the aesthetic is parasitic on the practical.

I began with straight, practical judgment, though specifically intuitive too. Now we find that that account must be qualified to cover art, for with works of art as often as not no real judgment is in question. I used to meet the point too glibly, perhaps; I spoke simply of a 'quasi judgment'—and have been, incidentally, taken to task for the phrase.[12] One might speak instead, perhaps, of 'pretence judgment'. But pretence is a matter of behaviour and, further, is voluntary. To pretend to be in pain when one is not is simply to behave as though one were. (Indeed we may and should bear in mind 'method' acting and the species of 'inward' pretence, the voluntary imagining of experience it is said to involve; or of charlatans who do best, it seems, by entering into and living their roles. But the core of the problem remains.) There are, however, as Scruton points out, thoughts we do no more than entertain. A pedant might possibly quarrel with his formula 'unasserted thought'; for what strictly is asserted or unasserted is not the thought itself but its expression; as current philosophical logic has it, we assert sentences. I myself prefer to speak, with ordinary usage, of statements or things people say. But the point is a merely terminological one; and thought will of course include judgment. So I can avail myself of Scruton's own account.

But the reader may naturally ask: How can I fall back on his views, having spent so much energy in finding fault with them? I answer that here I find none; I see Scruton's treatment of imagination as wholly admirable. It is a major contribution to aesthetic thinking. Yet it stands, I feel, in too splendid isolation. Further, we evaluate or appraise works of art; it lies in the nature of such responses to be describable as positive or negative. At least they range between these extremes, they range on the relevant scale (the position after all might be neutral). Now that feature is conceptually necessary; an adequate theory must account for it. We admire, I said, fitness to command, or 'authority' as we see it in a facade; we react negatively to limpness or weakness. Thus the practical illuminates the aesthetic; that 'ugly' is, no less than 'beautiful', a term of aesthetic appraisal is nothing accidental or arbitrary. That is indeed its whole role, its *raison d'être*; which requires to be recognised and understood. Our judgments are positive or negative; of 'unasserted judgment' the same holds. But we also respond and all-but-aesthetically, perhaps fully so sometimes, where the judgment retains its normal force; which needs to be accounted for too. We do so in fact. But let us suppose we never did. The concept in ques-

[12] In correspondence by F. E. Sparshott.

tion, that is Scruton's concept of unasserted thought as invoked in aesthetics, would still need relating to others, need to be seen in its context, so to speak, and thus rendered more fully intelligible. Scruton, to repeat, leaves it isolated.

A last word on the phenomenon of 'seeing-as'; the grounds of my quarrel with Scruton, so far as I quarrel with him, remain the same. For as to what he positively says, I have no fault to find with it; I complain of its disconnection from other things. Imagination is cut off from 'reality'. Yet as Scruton himself is well aware, it is thanks to imaginative vision (intellectual or sometimes literally visual), it is, to repeat, thanks to creativity of imagination that we deepen our grasp of reality; we come to see it more truly as it is. We extend understanding or belief, not merely go beyond them in thought, the free play of imaginative thought. Take any utterance in English, which I, an English speaker, hear accordingly. I hear it as meaningful, not mere sound; nor even sound—like an interpretable sign or symbols—as a vehicle or carrier of meaning. If I tried, I should be simply unable to. A foreigner will hear speech, even English, but perhaps will hear nothing of the meaning. Last, an animal, an undomesticated animal, might hear it as sound and no more. Here one recalls Godfrey Vesey's formula, namely that all seeing is seeing-as; it is not one I would wholly endorse. He himself might no longer fully endorse it: I do not know. None the less it contains an important truth. What we see and quite literally see depends on our equipment of concepts. We see a metal disc as a coin; or, in other words, we simply see a coin. The aspect, what the object is 'seen-as', cannot, as it were, be divorced from it (as though there were first of all some 'pure' object) and referred to the observer's response. Yet it is just that that Scruton seems committed to, and more too: he connects the point with his Kantian leanings. We do not strictly see beauty, we respond. We see *things* that set up a response; and that response is identified with seeing-as. Now that will sometimes undoubtedly be a fair account; we see faces in clouds and the like, which is simply imaginative play. But a sentry may point to a shape; he sees it, he whispers, as a crouching figure. His concern as he utters the words is, very clearly, with truth or falsity; and further—since the hearer's interest, as against an optician's, is unlikely to be in his comrade's mere visual experience—a truth about the object, not himself.

Kant rightly stresses felt response, and Scruton, no less rightly, seeing-as. The two in some cases may be identified. To return to what I said of Clive Lloyd; his fielding once won him a formal accolade, the judges according the adjective 'spectacular'. The same might be said of his batting. Consider a batsman who scores no less effectively yet with little of that 'visible' mastery; he lacks the would-be quality we spoke of, animating or informing his very movements. Or consider the example I began with, recalled to service from what I wrote twenty years ago; I mean the sub-editor we imagined, who judges and judges soundly but feels nothing. There is feeling in the response as well as seeing. There comes a quick stir of admiration, or the vehemence of something like contempt, accompanying appropriate judgment. Here Scruton's account, I suggest, however much he speaks of our 'response', has failed to do justice to the phenomena. It certainly covers what we see; it fails adequately to cover what we feel.

One final point must be dealt with, or rather must be set on one side. Scruton, in the course of his subtle analysis of imagination, comes on what he mistakes for an objection. There is a sensuous feature that it is difficult to attribute to 'seeing-as'—the feature of vividness or intensity.[13] Happily he extricates himself at once from his own self-created, would-be problem. Aspects may, he notes, strike us; they may stand out. We found the power, the authority of the facade; something vividly, 'visibly' there. The very stones, so it seems, gather energy. Now first comes non-aesthetic perception; one sees simply a doorway and columns. But merely to see them, let us note, is to see them under the appropriate aspect. But next comes our enhanced aesthetic vision; this vivification of what we see is a further and different phenomenon. One might naturally go on to ask how such a thing is possible at all. Here, qua philosopher, I fall silent; the problem is rather one for an art critic. The answer must be: 'In many ways.' Critics analyse and explore them case by case. But the two roles need not be exclusive. For the form such an enquiry might typically take, a brief indication at least, I can refer once again to Scruton's work. He has a splendid short passage on Dryden, the analysis of a couple of lines, which illustrates the process in question.[14] For a poet generates an energy in his words, a heightened expressiveness, no less than an architect in stone—in entablature, volutes, columns, pediment. Art, truly, is something we experience and the quality of experience is what matters to us. But the notion of seeing-as, central as it certainly is, proves inadequate to the load Scruton rests on it; seeing-as must be intensified in works of art.

[13] Op. cit., p. 111.
[14] Op. cit., p. 185.

12

Leavis and Literary Criticism

Philosophers almost by profession are minders of other people's business, that is their intellectual business; which, though a necessary trade, is not always a popular one. So Socrates found long ago. Discretion may therefore seem called for, and still more so in writing of F. R. Leavis. Leavis is, so to speak, a hot subject; and not only so in himself, hence to be taken up with caution, but a cause of heat in other men. Nor is that all; other, harder obstacles remain. It would seem that Leavis explicitly shuts the door on any philosophical approach. Philosophers, broadly speaking, deal in abstractions (even those who profess not to). Leavis wrote long ago, at the start of *Revaluation*, 'No treatment of poetry can be worth much that does not keep very close to the concrete'.[1] That ruling, which might debar my whole enterprise, I can take instead as raising immediately its main theme.

My concern is the cause of rationality, both the concept and its critical exercise, which of course involves logic and logical rigour, and further, where necesary, abstraction. In Leavis's eyes it seems that such concepts or the commitment to them threatens whatever he most values; not only the study of literature but something else larger too; something that informs literature but also is nourished by it. He tells us of 'something that can't be discussed or taken account of in terms of what can be measured, averaged or defined . . .'[2] For Leavis himself this negative verdict will be bound up intrinsically with his own constructive and creative work on literature. And I happily concede the word 'creative'. The passage I quoted comes from a singularly fine late essay, the piece on 'Eliot's Classical Standing'. But for me the two things are at most simply distinct; and more often, I shall seek to show, even his best criticism is much weakened by everything it excludes. Larger issues lie behind. Suppose we should play for a moment at naming two men but for whom—more than any others—Western culture

[1] p. 2.
[2] F. R. and Q. D. Leavis, *Lectures in America* (London, 1974), p. 51. It is true that the emphasis here falls, rather tendentiously perhaps, on measuring and averaging. But they are run together with *defining*. All this is clearly of a piece with his general hostility to abstract thinking, which we have met and shall meet again, and to theory, which will concern us soon. It is a pretty comprehensive repudiation.

could barely exist. One would surprise nobody by the names of Plato and Aristotle. Plato's dialectic, in any fair sample of the mature dialogues, represents for me everything that Leavis, even at his best, signally lacks. Leavis's focus, the whole drive of his polemic, amounts to the repudiation of what—with legitimate plagiarism—I shall call the great tradition; the tradition of intellectual rigour and criticism, of closely questioning reason, which makes one half of our cultural heritage, and which literary criticism disastrously impoverishes itself by turning its back on. And, we may suppose, Plato and Aristotle, or Abelard or Bishop Butler, were not advocates of the technological Benthamite ethos.

How much does Leavis repudiate? His remarks on the point are apt to be brief, their tone marked with a certain sharpness. But in a passage written relatively early in reply to René Wellek we find a rather fuller and cooler statement. I shall quote at some length.

> Philosophy, we say, is 'abstract' . . . and poetry 'concrete'. Words in poetry invite us, not to 'think about' and judge but to 'feel into' or 'become'—to realise a complex experience that is given in the words. They demand, not merely a full-bodied response, but a completer responsiveness—a kind of responsiveness that is incompatible with the judicial, one-eye-on-the-standard approach suggested by Dr Wellek's phrase: 'your "norm" with which you measure every poet'. The critic—the reader of poetry—is indeed concerned with evaluation, but to figure him as measuring with a norm which he brings to the object and applies from the outside is to misrepresent the process. The critic's aim, first, is to realise as sensitively and completely as possible this or that which claims his attention; and a certain value is implicit in the realising. As he matures in experience of the new thing he asks, explicitly and implicitly: 'Where does this come? How does it stand in relation to . . . ? How relatively important does it seem?' And the organisation into which it settles as a constituent in becoming 'placed' is an organisation of similarly 'placed' things, things that have found their bearings with regard to one another, and not in a theoretical system or a system determined by abstract considerations.[3]

Here, I said, we have something more like an explicit statement than we shall easily find elsewhere. We need, then, to examine it with some care.

Leavis writes of the experience of poetry, the kind of response it invites; of a sort of concern with norms or standards that seems to him harmful; of 'theoretical systems' of which the same is true; lastly, by

[3] 'Literary criticism and philosophy', in F. R. Leavis, *The Common Pursuit* (London, 1952), p. 213.

contrast, of something called an 'organisation' whose emergence he welcomes.

First for the right response to poetry, the 'realising of complex experience'. (For the present I by-pass the distinction, which I find obscure, between a 'full-bodied response' and a 'completer responsiveness'. Nothing in what immediately follows seems to turn on it.) By and large we may still ask who is supposed to deny it. That 'one-eye-on-the-standard approach' ascribed to Wellek—whether rightly I do not ask—could equally plausibly be thought incompatible with either. But what follows generally? Abstract and concrete are obviously contrasted, that is, in logic; it will not follow that they are incompatible in the practical process of inquiry. The reverse is true; they should be seen as complementary.

But one other point first: what counts as an adequate response to relevant material here or elsewhere—or any sort of adequate grasp—will vary from one field of inquiry to another. Electronics are different from literature. You still need, in appropriate terms, a grasp of the concrete material, which is something that abstract inquiry does not exclude but presupposes. Even the most thorough-going mathematiciser will rightly believe, if not indeed in *keeping* close to the concrete—that is, always—at least in remaining anchored there.

As to working with one eye on the standard: we may grant the point at once. It is harmless. There are certainly dangers in premature concern with evaluation, or excessive and anxious concern, which is true wholly generally. Leavis may want no truck with standards. But he himself explicitly raises questions of relative importance; he concerns himself with the placing of particular works in a larger, emergent organisation. The same dangers meet us here. Pursued wisely, such questions are acceptable and indeed essential; misguidedly pressed they may be equally damaging. Precisely the wrong moral to draw would be 'Do not judge, do not abstract'; the right one, 'Do not judge prematurely' or 'Respond first and theorise afterwards'. (In science one might say, 'Observe first and theorise afterwards'. But that would be to oversimplify.) It is plain, then, that where Leavis writes that poetry invites us '*not* to "think about" and judge *but* to "feel into" . . .' [my italics] he is working with a misleading dichotomy, with false alternatives. To repeat, he might more plausibly have written 'First feel into, then think'.

So far we find nothing that any protagonist of 'theory' need jib at. Here are merely preconditions of sound theorising. The study of literature doubtless differs from other sorts of inquiry. But in Leavis's treatment of it no difference appears. Hence everything must turn on the obscure, barely more than implicit, distinction with which the paragraph ends; here 'theory' is unfavourably contrasted with something else called an 'organisation'. This being so, one may perhaps be forgiven for finding his statement of the issue condensed, the key terms obscure. What further hints can be gathered? An organisation would seem progressively to emerge; it emerges in the course of inquiry. But we find that 'abstract considerations' rather 'determine'—the verb suggesting rigidity, insensitiveness. Similarly 'standards' were 'applied from the outside'. Leavis's picture of theorising—a rather paranoid picture, perhaps—is insinuated, not argued. Indeed, were it not for his admirable positive depiction of an 'organisation', not as static but emerging, one might have supposed him merely oblivious to the ordinary process of creative thought, its mutual feed-back of abstract and concrete. But that, we infer, is unknown not to thinkers generally, only to that tribe labelled 'theorists'. And we get no further: the distinction is left there, with no sort of substantiation or support. This whole plausible, muddled paragraph contains in its way hard lessons for those who undervalue logical rigour.

To theorise quite generally is first of all to question. Let us try. Does no element of theorising, then, enter into a Leavis-type 'organisation'? Or suppose we seek to conceive the process itself; I mean the process of analytical and theoretical thinking, a degree less 'abstractly' (at least in what seems to be the sense of that favourite word 'abstract' in Leavis's own critical writings, suggesting something dim and remote). May not his approach at least involve presuppositions?—which in other hands, those of critics trained in abstract thinking, might be less likely to pass unexamined. For ordinary intellectual analysis is the core of all abstract thinking, indeed of all theoretical inquiry, and is something that Leavis's less friendly critics will probably think his own ideas might with benefit be exposed to.

To get further we must seek, however summarily, to achieve some sort of view of the real thing. It must still be schematic of course, yet not wholly empty perhaps. Abstraction, which, I said, is part of all inquiry, may be usefully seen as involving two aspects. They are these: we grapple initially with the immediacy of concrete impressions, with things in the mass. We analyse, we discriminate, we compare—and that is already to abstract. Distinctive qualities, likenesses, features of all sorts, are isolated and picked out. For the second aspect, it appears in different forms, we may, and often do, frame generalisations, laws and rules, which are also called abstract. But those I mean to by-pass. They raise intricate problems that do not concern us here. What is certain is this, that all inquiry involves, not only the closer discrimination of concrete things, but some opposite movement too; a movement towards wider perspectives (which may or may not involve rules or laws). Leavis's own talk of 'organisation' will equally illustrate it. We press outwards, but return, too, and return, we may hope, with a deepened response; which holds of the study of literature, and holds indeed generally. (The basic difference we sought, incidentally, might spring partly from a different direction of concern or main concern. One can either study concrete things for the sake of theorising, or else move further afield for the sake of a deepened grasp of the concrete.)

Now the process possesses its own dynamic. It always points further. To see them better we step back from concrete particulars; but then we return to them too. Next, further again, we go behind even those first procedures, which as yet were relatively concrete procedures. We now grow more radically self-critical; they themselves now appear within our lens; our own practice in turn must submit to scrutiny. It is here, strangely, that Leavis calls a halt; we meet his ban on abstraction and theory. Yet how is a general body of thought to be examined otherwise, or a method of criticism? How is it ever to be scrutinised, ever assessed, without using the common tools of abstract thinking? Consider as an analogy a court of law where we find, probably, much attention given to procedure. Hearsay evidence, perhaps, is always inadmissible, while testimony as to character is allowed in some cases but not others. Now the business of the court is of course with justice; its function is to establish liability or guilt, which it does well or badly. Hence the very same interest leads us further; it forces us, rather. For as to those legal practices themselves, we need not only to use but to evaluate them; are they themselves conducive to justice? Now, how should we start? Hardly, I think, with a general prohibition on logical precision and abstract statement; which would make it impossible even to hold these things up for examination, to formulate the points at issue in explicit terms.

In fact, as we constantly find, Leavis himself works with abstractions. Someone concerned, as he is, with large questions of the relations of literature to morality and literature to society must inevitably work with abstractions. All he does is to avert his eyes; in other words he works with them uncritically. Now those issues, and Leavis's handling of them, are what I must turn to. Leavis's concern with morality, I suppose—morality in its widest sense; in other words, the human and moral concerns that inform his criticism and his whole view of literature—are what his name is chiefly associated with. It is this we must look closer at.

He is no straightforward didacticist. Moral values that give significance to literature are not things inculcated by precept. A poem, he tells us, enacts its moral; an appreciative reader re-enacts it and is, it appears, modified in the process profoundly and permanently. But the point here is this: poetry works through its rhythm, its imagery, through all poetic powers, and it is they that embody the enactment; and fiction similarly through the presentation of character, situation and so forth; by everything that makes literature more than discursive prose and gives it imaginative reality.

Such, broadly, are the views we must scrutinise. I shall offer no further apology for dealing in abstractions or using the techniques of abstract argument. Shortly indeed I shall be looking in some detail at examples of Leavis's critical practice. I find it useful, however, to single out certain main issues first. The issue, to repeat, concerns the relationship of morality to literature; a relationship whose reality and importance I certainly am not disposed to question. Few critics nowadays would question—and here our deep debt to Leavis is not in dispute—that the quality of moral insight found, say, in the novels of George Eliot and Jane Austen is relevant to their literary excellence. But to grant that is, for Leavis, to grant very little. So far we have no reason for denying that much else may be relevant too; or, if in some works their literary quality reflects the moral qualities they embody, quite different things may fill the same role elsewhere.

The question is, broadly, do these alone matter or, so to speak, matter essentially? Certainly literature must be itself, a thing distinct from morality. But the thesis would seem to be this, that even its properly literary value can only essentially rest on or reflect non-literary or broadly moral value. Let me attempt to construct an argument; not indeed an argument of Leavis's own, who does not construct arguments. But as to those other possibilities I spoke of, certainly he seems to reject them; values of form, for example, which he sees as trivial or worthless, divorced from any human or moral concern such form might embody.[4] If so, it is a large step to take. But let us proceed. It is granted, at least in certain cases, that literary values underlie moral values. Now morality matters, of course. Hence, we may infer, literature matters, too, being—let us say—*bound up with morality*. And elsewhere presumably, as in the case I mentioned where the connection fails, it ceases to matter.

The argument is invalid, no doubt. Good batting matters, for example: it matters to the outcome of the game. But what of a spectator's appreciation, let it be thoroughly informed, discriminating appreciation, which is similarly 'bound up with' good batting? It might be welcome for all sorts of reasons. But, so far, merely on these terms, it does not follow that it matters at all. We need first a clear grasp of

[4] See, for instance, 'Lawrence scholarship and Lawrence', in *Anna Karenina and Other Essays* (London, 1967), p. 195.

these concepts, and I deliberately state the issue in general terms. It is one thing to see and appreciate, even though with aspiration, with zeal, another to be modified in consequence, modified in oneself. We may value and aspire, but in vain. The Devil gazes on goodness and remains evil: 'Sees and mourns his loss'. But suppose this granted: literature might remain a special case. It is something such that, entering into it imaginatively, we are assimilated to those objects that we respond to. (And Leavis may hint at the notion with phrases like 'feel into' and 'become'.) Indeed we may. The thing is possible. But is there any reason to think that it happens?

Literature does of course often influence people, and sometimes dramatically. So much is commonplace. It may certainly modify one's *outlook*; occasionally it may also work more deeply. It acts variably and unpredictably, I suppose; nor need the appreciative reading of good literature be always more efficacious than of bad. All these are mere impressions, you may say. But in these areas what else can one appeal to? Yet it would seem that for Leavis at this point everything is at stake; and here we must be bold and explicit. Moral values can underwrite literary values—the premise that morality matters can directly lend value to literature—only on these terms: so far as the reading of novels or poetry tends to make bad men good or good men better. Otherwise—for think again of the spectator at a cricket match—you may have all sorts of connection but none to the purpose.

I have, I repeat, on the substantial issue offered only impressions. We are faced with large, dubious speculation. I have not sought to settle it. The onus of argument surely lies on its proponents.

Literally, of course, one cannot become a novel or poem. But one may doubtless come to possess in oneself something of the moral qualities it embodies. How widely does it happen in fact? That remains as doubtful as ever. For a phrase such as 'feel into' might seem apt—simply as a happy evocation of certain vivid responses to literature. Or we might indeed momentarily 'identify' with it, but only momentarily. If I were to speak again for my own impressions I should answer that moral character, malformed or imperfectly formed character, is singularly resistant to change.

But for my main argument I have already said as much as I need. For imagine the project seriously embarked on. Indeed it is hard enough to conceive. But this much is plain: to settle it, even make progress towards settling it, first you must frame the issue abstractly, in general terms. Two extensive social phenomena are to be correlated. They must first be distinguished, then, be separately marked and identified—we need to specify the relation we seek as well as both terms to be related—for the issue even to be meaningfully considered. And, I must still insist, it is this or this sort of thing that is at issue. Literary people, used to handling their own material in their own way, will not like a discussion that requires them to contemplate a question akin to that, say, of the connection between cigarette-smoking and lung cancer. But, as Socrates likes to remind his hearers, one must follow where the argument leads. Or, if there is something wrong with the argument, that must be shown. My own view is that a certain discomfort is indeed justified; there is something wrong. But the trouble lies in a general approach to literature among whose unexamined presuppositions we find questions such as these.

So the substantial, factual issue remains. I said that I hardly know what a serious exploration of it would be like; perhaps any existing techniques, sociological or psychological techniques, are too crude. But there must be some technique; unless we are to accept such a hypothesis on the sole ground that we have no notion of how to go in search of evidence for or against it.

It is time to turn to Leavis's critical practice, in which it seems to me impossible not to feel at work everywhere the influence of an unspoken or unformulated theory. In the essay called ' "Thought" and Emotional Quality'[5] Leavis developed a contrast between two prima facie rather similar poems, Lawrence's *Piano* and Tennyson's *Tears, Idle Tears*:

Piano

Softly, in the dusk, a woman is singing to me;
Taking me back down the vista of years, till I see
A child sitting under the piano, in the boom of the tingling strings
And pressing the small, poised feet of a mother who smiles as she sings.

In spite of myself, the insidious mastery of song
Betrays me back, till the heart of me weeps to belong
To the old Sunday evenings at home, with winter outside
And hymns in the cosy parlour, the tinkling piano our guide.

So now it is vain for the singer to burst into clamour
With the great black piano appassionato. The glamour   /
Of childish days is upon me, my manhood is cast
Down in the flood of remembrance, I weep like a child for the past.

Tears, Idle Tears

Tears, idle tears, I know not what they mean,
Tears from the depth of some divine despair
Rise in the heart, and gather to the eyes,
In looking on the happy Autumn-fields,
And thinking of the days that are no more.

[5] *Scrutiny* 13 (1945–6).

Fresh as the first beam glittering on a sail,
That brings our friends up from the underworld,
Sad as the last which reddens over one
That sinks with all we love below the verge;
So sad, so fresh, the days that are no more.

Ah, sad and strange as in dark summer dawns
The earliest pipe of half-awaken'd birds
To dying ears, when unto dying eyes
The casement slowly grows a glimmering square;
So sad, so strange, the days that are no more.

Dear as remember'd kisses after death,
And sweet as those by hopeless fancy feign'd
On lips that are for others; deep as love,
Deep as first love, and wild with all regret;
O Death in Life, the days that are no more.

Now Leavis's explicit concern here is with 'the point of literary criticism', with the problem of standards, related at once to what he calls 'emotional hygiene and moral value'.[6] On these grounds he will find Tennyson's poem, or at least habitual indulgence in the habit of mind that it offers, 'something to deplore'.[7] Hard to find as general statements may be, the broad commitment I have been ascribing to Leavis seems indeed to be his. But to proceed in due order, both poems, he begins by conceding, at first sight look pretty 'emotional'. Indeed *Piano*, with its 'vista of years', 'the glamour of childish days', and so on, might not only be thought emotional but dismissed as cluttered with banal phrases. But look deeper, first as to *Piano*: Leavis in fact contrasts its real complexity with 'the sweetly plangent flow' of *Tears, Idle Tears*. He writes (referring to the poems respectively as (a) and (b)):

When we examine this effect of complexity we find it is associated with the *stating* manner that, in spite of the dangerous emotional swell, distinguishes (a) from (b). And when we examine this effect of statement we find that it goes with a particularity to which (b) offers no counterpart. For the banalities instanced do not represent everything in the poem; the 'vista of years' leads back to something sharply seen—a very specific situation that stands there in its own right . . . The child is 'sitting under the piano, in the boom of the tingling strings' and 'pressing the small poised feet' of its mother. . . . The actuality of the remembered situation is unbeglamouring, becoming more so in the second stanza, with the 'hymns' and the 'tinkling

6 Ibid., p. 45.
7 Ibid., p. 59.

piano'. Something is, we see, held and presented in this poem, and the presenting involves an *attitude towards*, an element of disinterested valuation. For all the swell of emotion the critical mind has its part in the whole; the constatation is at the same time in some measure a placing. That is, sensibility in the poem doesn't work in complete divorce from intelligence; feeling is not divorced from thinking: however the key terms are to be defined, these propositions at any rate have a clear enough meaning in this context. . . .

We note further that in the ordinary sentimental poeticality inspired by the 'insidious mastery of song' it would not be 'vain'; the poet would be swept away on the flood. . . . It is a remarkable poet who, conveying the 'insidious mastery' and the 'flood' so potently, at the same time fixes and presents with such specificity the situation he sharply distinguishes from the immediate.[8]

First let me stress the obvious; it would be absurd to belittle the quality of such criticism. Yet something seems half to emerge beyond the critic's intent, something that troubles me too. Leavis never shared Eliot's uncomfortable attitude to emotion, emotion proper; one basically of fear and hostility. (Eliot even introduces a verbal non-difference between what he calls 'feeling' and 'emotion', chiefly, it would seem, so as to keep the latter at a still safer distance.) Yet, unless I am wrong, even in Leavis we find something not quite unrelated. Emotion to be acceptable must be 'placed', apparently set at arm's length. We are to adopt an *'attitude towards'* emotion, which requires 'elements of disinterested evaluation'.

I return to my larger question concerning theorising and its relation to practice. It is just false that one can write of 'thought' and 'emotional quality' and merely assume that for the purpose we know well enough what emotion is, not interesting oneself in 'how the key terms are to be defined'. The general point becomes clearer if one looks at particular emotions. Hobbes, for example, has these definitions: 'Aversion, with the opinion of hurt from the object, *fear*; the same, with the hope of avoiding that hurt by resistance, *courage*'.[9] I note the word 'opinion', that is, precisely, *thought*; and broadly similar definitions appear in Aristotle.

Emotion as such stands in no need of distancing to achieve right evaluation. It is already evaluation: for instance, pity of what, rightly or wrongly, we see as pitiable; or fear, as involving, we found, an opinion, again right or wrong, of the likelihood of hurt from its object.

[8] Ibid., p. 57. Italics in original.

[9] *Leviathan*, ch. 6. The definition of courage, even if one recognises it as an emotion or passion in Hobbes's phrase, is plainly faulty; for it implies that courage entails confidence.

As a very rough formula one may call emotion energised thought; and the power of poetry, among much else, is power precisely to energise the expression of thought.

Leavis's discussion of *Piano* seems concerned less with emotion *simpliciter* than with something very different, specifically sentimental or at least potentially sentimental emotion; his praise is of the power with which it presents it, making us feel its tug, while at the same time resisting it. But what of the alternative, that surely arises?—I mean emotions that, quite simply, do not call for resistance; like pity of things truly pitiable. The last is, so to speak, emotion proper, straight, unsentimental emotion whose proper place in poetry, therefore—and this is the crux—never gets discussed at all. We hear only of 'dangerous emotional swell'.[10]

Let us speak of emotion then. What we ask of it is the following: first, its fitness or unfitness to its objects (an example of the latter being fear, say, of mice, creatures unlikely in fact to be very hurtful); and secondly, important in literature, its mere authenticity or genuineness; lastly, here too, the conviction with which it is realised or conveyed—a question not unconnected with its genuineness—in other words, the conviction with which the energy that I spoke of makes itself felt.

I am old-fashioned enough in real life, I confess, to prefer people who sometimes exercise self-restraint; who are, if you like, inauthentic; who sometimes choose to behave inauthentically where authentic behaviour, the behaviour of course of imperfect human agents, would be cruel or vicious. But literature is different; here the issue of authenticity is indeed paramount. All these are things we value in literature; hence for critics they all equally raise legitimate questions. For instance, Milton's God as presented in *Paradise Lost* seems to me no very appropriate object for those emotions that the poem directs on him. But they are much harder than what Leavis has drawn attention to in *Piano*—roughly a firm control of what is also powerfully felt, the tug of sentimentality—to represent as available for beneficial or harmful re-creation in the reader.

To return to our contrasted poems. As to *Tears, Idle Tears*, Leavis himself discriminately allows it 'a highly personal distinction'; and I, not to press excessive claims, would concede a touch of something akin to sentimentality (though our current cult of literary toughness, it may be worth recalling, if obvious, is only sentimentality written backwards). Leavis writes:

[10] Is this fair? For Leavis varies his examples. In an earlier and lengthier version of the present paper I looked at others too. But what he objects to in Wordsworth's *Calais Beach* still seems to be akin to sentimentality; or at the very least it remains true that the notions at issue need clarifying. F. R. Leavis, 'Imagery and movement: notes in the analysis of poetry', *Scrutiny* 13 (1945), pp. 125–30.

Complexity, we can see at once when we pass on, is not a marked characteristic of Tennyson's poem, which is what at first reading its movement seemed to indicate. It moves simply forward with a sweetly plangent flow, without check, cross-tension or any qualifying element. To give it the reading it asks for is to flow with it, acquiescing in a complete and simple immersion: there is no attitude towards the experience except one of complaisance; we are to be wholly in it and of it. We note, too, the complete absence of anything like the particularity of (a): there is nothing that gives the effect of an object, or substantial independent existence. The particularity of 'the happy Autumn-fields', 'the first beam glittering on a sail', and the casement that 'slowly fades [*sic*] a glimmering square', and so on, is only speciously of the kind in question. No new definitions or directions of feeling derive from these suggestions of imagery, which seem to be wholly *of* the current of vague emotion that determines them. We note that the strong effect of particularity produced by (a) is conditioned by the complexity—by the play of contrast and tension; but (b) seems to offer a uniform emotional fluid . . .[11]

Here I am first moved irrelevantly to protest—irrelevantly to my own proper argument—that something, merely at the critical level and on Leavis's own terms, seems to have gone wrong. Tennyson's exactness of eye and ear have long since been a critical truism. Now the line 'The earliest pipe of half-awaken'd birds', and above all that eminently characteristic word 'pipe', seems to me admirably to bear witness to it. And similarly with other touches: Leavis, I am inclined to suspect, having been misled by the absence of that 'distancing' that alone reassures him in the presence of overt emotion (one notices the strange misquotation). The evocation of the dying man at dawn, dawn with its still-sleepy, first stirrings of life—having in front of it a whole summer's day, and then again night and again day—does anything but merge into a smooth undifferentiated emotional flow or invite a stock response.

But my own proper business lies elsewhere. I mean merely to raise certain questions; not, turning critic in my own person, to attempt to answer them. What matters is that such questions exist. In *Tears, Idle Tears* what I myself am chiefly impressed by is precisely, in the final stanza, the gathering of energy and passion, the power of emotion, the greater from the rebound of the preceding hush and strangeness; which may count, perhaps, as the very singleness of emotional flood that Leavis explicitly deplores. But is that power really to be found there, and if so, is it also—like fear, say, not of mice but of mass slaughter by nuclear weapons—an emotion objectively justifiable? I must confine myself to raising the question, which Leavis's methods provide no

[11] *Scrutiny* 13 (1945–6), p. 59.

place for. But for the former, besides the point just mentioned, that is, the sudden and strange shift in tone, I note the rhythms, assonances, alliterations, all that presumably make up what Leavis rightly, if not very consistently, calls Tennyson's 'highly personal distinction'. (I say 'not very consistently': for if poetic quality precisely consists in qualities of other sorts, qualities of mind and sensibility, embodied and re-enacted, how then, we are bound to ask, can what is highly distinctive as poetry be at the same time, emotionally, something to deplore?[12]) I had best perhaps state directly my own impression that the whole passage I have quoted on the Tennyson, though marked by the same qualities of prose, the same telling condensed vividness of phrase and epithet, is far inferior to the corresponding piece on Lawrence. Leavis, I think, looked for and failed to find those 'checks and cross-tensions' that, for him, indicate moral maturity; and, I suppose, admit of psychologically hygienic re-enactment by readers. But the issues are complex as, I hope, appeared from my brief glance at the concept of emotion and the different questions it raises in practice. And just because here the emotion offered is in a sense emotion at one remove, and the question of sentimentality does properly arise, a firm handling of these distinctions is the more necessary.

It is time to return to finish my initial and avowedly abstract argument. But I shall append a single final example, and it will be of poetry the conviction of whose emotional power goes far beyond Tennyson's. It represents feelings notably wrong or vicious, even hideous, expressed with incomparable power; its power, in our purely literary estimation, outweighing the evil that it imports. I refer to the great speech in Act 4 of *Timon of Athens*, where Timon addresses Alcibiades. And I ask the reader to imagine the following: that this fragment alone has survived, that we are even ignorant as to whether it presents dramatic utterance or that of the poet in his own person. The supposition, you may say, is objectionable; it is Timon, not Shakespeare, who speaks, and in a context that makes all the difference. Much difference certainly; but since what I ask plainly remains imaginable, the experiment may still be instructive.

> Tim. Warr'st thou 'gainst Athens?
> Alcib. Ay, Timon, and have cause.
> . . .
> Tim. . . .
>   Put up thy gold. Go on. Here's gold. Go on.
>   Be as a planetary plague, when Jove
>   Will o'er some high-viced city hang his poison

[12] We should say boldly, I think, that the poem is best taken not as, it seems, the poet himself expressly and consciously took it; as referring to the personal, not the historical past.

In the sick air. Let not thy sword skip one.
Pity not honour'd age for his white beard:
He is an usurer. Strike me the counterfeit matron:
It is her habit only that is honest,
Herself's a bawd. Let not the virgin's cheek
Make soft thy trenchant sword: for those milk-paps,
That through the window-bars bore at men's eyes,
Are not within the leaf of pity writ,
But set down horrible traitors. Spare not the babe
Whose dimpled smiles from fools exhaust their mercy:
Think it a bastard, whom the oracle
Hath doubtfully pronounc'd thy throat shall cut,
And mince it sans remorse. Swear against objects.
Put armour on thine ears and on thine eyes
Whose proof nor yells of mothers, maids, nor babes,
Nor sight of priests in holy vestments bleeding
Shall pierce a jot. There's gold to pay thy soldiers.
Make large confusion; and, thy fury spent,
Confounded be thyself! Speak not, be gone.
Alcib. Hast thou gold yet? I'll take the gold thou giv'st me,
Not all thy counsel. (Act iv, sc. 3)

This, you recall, was to be the sole surviving fragment of an unknown poet, the rest of whose work was wholly lost (though I have in fact broken my own rule by quoting a bit of dialogue, too). But I now ask, if so, what should we say: that the poet was mad? Perhaps. He seems mad, with a particularly horrific, Hitlerian sort of madness; but none the less, we would surely have to add, he wrote poetry as great as any in the language. We might class it with the current extremes of literature of cruelty and the absurd, but with this difference; the latter, by comparison, seem like mere shrieks, violent gestures. But here is the substance, the thing itself.

With this I reach the last step in my argument. I said at the start that literary work may certainly embody moral values. It may rightly be valued itself on that account. But to grant that gives us no ground for denying that other works may also be valued, and no less rightly, for quite different reasons. This is suggested by abstract considerations which have been my concern throughout. We cannot merely keep close to the concrete. But I have nowhere denied that we must start with it, nor yet that we must constantly return to it. Abstract findings in a certain sense admit of testing in the concrete. My own present findings pass the test; they are confirmed by our experience of literature. For the passage I quoted from *Timon* hardly recommends itself as embodying moral values, far less as communicating them to readers.[13]

[13.]I am indebted to the criticisms of a former student, D. Wood-Stotesbury.

13

Philosophy and Literature

I. Literature as Prophecy: Sartre's Nausea

'About things that really matter we can't communicate; we have at best ceremony and courtesy.' I offer this dictum as a thing that needs saying, as something being widely believed or assumed. I mean less to endorse than explore it.

I shall distinguish between philosophers and prophets; also, a partly overlapping and connected distinction, between practitioners of logic and persuasion.[1] Of the former, examples will be Aristotle, Descartes, and G. E. Moore; of the latter, Pascal, Kierkegaard, and Nietzsche. The two enterprises still share common ground or rather, more accurately, they dispute it. For both sorts of thinker lay claim to truth and seek to induce conviction in readers; hence both, whether overtly or implicitly, are bound to be controversial and polemical. We are met with views that conflict and compete. Thus as to the nature of the mind, it is impossible that Descartes and Hume should be equally in the right; nor as to the significance of Christianity both Pascal and Nietzsche. Where the two enterprises precisely differ is of course in their method or style. Philosophers, as I use the term, set store by rigour and precision; they proceed characteristically by such methods as deduction and analysis. Alternatives are defined and eliminated, or the reader is manoeuvred from some starting point to conclusions he is bound to accept by a series of definite steps, for both the premises and the intervening steps are meant to be seen as self-evident. The latter is the method explicitly championed by Descartes. But as for the writers I call prophets, their methods are harder to characterise or to describe by one general term. Like philosophers, to repeat, they seak conviction; but in other ways they rather resemble poets or imaginative novelists. They seek chiefly, one may say, to reveal; to force on us some sort of vision or point of view which will change for us the aspect of objects.

[1] If this more or less slang use of 'prophet' that I have adopted and, as it were, warranted, calls for apology, I can only say that I have failed to find any better term. Some of my 'prophets' are simply moralists, and in one aspect most of them rhetoricians. But neither term suffices.

Of course what I have sketched here are ideal types. Most prophets, perhaps all of them, make occasional use of argument; all philosophers necessarily use 'persuasion' (in the sense I have given the word). The broad difference still seems tolerably plain. But secondly among novelists, too, one may distinguish two sorts: there are those who are, at least relatively speaking, 'pure novelists', for example, Stendhal or Fielding, and those in whose hands we see the novel become equally a vehicle of prophecy, for example, Dostoyevsky or Lawrence. (I speak for convenience of novelists: of dramatists and poets the same holds.) Every novelist doubtless has his own values and views which embody themselves in his work; these, implicitly at least, he seeks to validate. Indeed I have known critics for whom it would seem that they do nothing else; a novel—or good novel, at least so far as we are to count it as good—serves to show us things, to show and to substantiate that significant vision. Different novels differ, of course; but they present aspects on this view that merely diverge, rather than conflict. The inference would appear to be this, that all harmonise within some greater unity. It seems that Hegel should be living at this hour, for literary criticism has need of him. In some such vast, all-embracing system, with a similarly elastic dialectic, too (as it will need to be), all these partial views will be unified and contained. But meanwhile, if you say so, you live on faith. And here it is not something I mean to argue. To me it seems plain that one can admire literature, and admire it legitimately as literature, while dissenting from the standpoint it presents. Indeed, you need a pretty deep indoctrination in English critical thought of the present century before you lose touch with the ordinary reader's notion of ugly feelings or false views well expressed. And one would think it a truism that novelists, indeed artists in general, if sometimes they stand in genuine conflict, more often merely co-exist peacefully: their enterprise is certainly not, like that of theorists, explicitly competitive, so that where one wins his opponents lose—a respect in which logicians resemble footballers. And, though the rules remain more elusive, the same goes for prophets.

With these broad distinctions sketched out, I can turn to my imme-diate project—which, I fear, may be thought an ambitious one. My concern is with a species of criticism which, as yet, I think, barely exists—a conception, then, that I hope to play midwife to. As to literature, we know how to talk of it; we evaluate it and discuss rival evaluations. Of course we differ and will continue to; but there at least exists an on-going enterprise, so that we are reduced neither to silence nor mere noise. But how does the case stand with prophecy? One pic-tures possible rival responses: 'My God!' you exclaim, 'the man's got something. I see it now, it's true. It makes sense.' And I, perhaps, differing—not to disfigure the present page with four letter words—comment briefly 'Lord, what tripe!' If so, the case stands as indicated; unless we are content to leave things with no more than a contest of raised voices, a whole mode of discourse awaits birth. The most I can offer are pointers, which also will need illustration. My chief example will be Sartre's *Nausea*. But I mean first to speak briefly of another work, one which as I see it serves to vindicate, and with maximal clarity, the possibility of the enterprise I have embarked upon. I mean Plato's *Phaedo*, a work which, in philosophical material, is singularly rich; but also singularly unpersuasive in its upshot (at least I have never met anyone persuaded by it), that is as regards the main conclusion it seeks to demonstrate. But Plato of course has two aspects; he is a literary artist of genius, as well as a philosopher of genius. Now let the *Phaedo* be considered in the former light, I myself would regard it as his masterpiece.

I can make my main point very briefly. I mean to concentrate solely on one passage. Socrates has concluded his argument, or seems to have concluded it, to prove the immortality of the soul; and the young men are all quiet, until Cebes and Simmias are heard whispering. In the circumstances they are naturally reluctant to speak their suspicions aloud. They suspect that the argument is fallacious, and Socrates will go to his death armed only with the power of illusion. Here Plato deploys his finest art. He makes Socrates address them first, gently drawing them out. And so they are brought to state their objections, and state them in full; and as they speak Phaedo himself and the rest sit and listen bewildered and dismayed. The splendid edifice of argumentation whose gradual erection they had watched seems to vanish like a mirage, to collapse before their eyes. Socrates of course will shortly answer, and answer quietly and courteously, with calm assurance. Plato's metaphor here is of a general, cool and confident, rallying his forces in the face of a sudden reverse. But another short passage comes first. The business of a philosophical enquiry is temporarily interrupted and we read:

> I happened to be sitting close by him on the stool at the right of the couch; so that he was quite a bit higher than I was. Now he put his hand on my head and gathered all my hair in a ball on the nape of my neck—he always loved to play with my hair—and then he said, 'Tomorrow, Phaedo, I dare say, you'll have all this lovely hair of yours shaven off.'
> 'I expect so, Socrates,' I answered,
> 'You won't, though, if you take my advice.'
> 'I don't understand.'
> 'Today,' replied Socrates, 'Let it be today. If this argument of ours

is finished and done for, if it can't be revived again, you and I, we'll both shave our heads.'[2]

At this point I shall interrupt myself, too. Johnson in a well-known passage relates how Addison on his deathbed sent for the young and profligate Earl of Warwick that 'he might see how a Christian can die.' Now Plato wrote the *Phaedo*, one may say, with a purpose that is visibly parallel: he meant to show us how a philosopher can die. In one sense he succeeds triumphantly. Plato's Socrates with his charm and quiet humour—his last words, we recall, as he waits for the hemlock to work, are a sly joke—with that still lively curiosity undiminished and matter-of-fact courage at the last; it all lives in the imagination unforgettably. Literary heroes, and real ones, too, may have faced death more heroically; but perhaps no death in literature more vividly impresses itself on the mind.

But this is to speak of the man. Recall the crucial passage that I have quoted. What the man himself speaks of is his argument; and more, the fate of the two are vividly and dramatically identified. I for myself regretfully find it necessary to separate them. As to the argument, much as we may find it of philosophical interest, there is one thing we emphatically fail to find: a conclusion convincingly demonstrated. Now philosophy is on trial in the *Phaedo*. But at the crisis it is poetry that interposes, and the figure of Socrates as Plato draws it carries that conviction that in this instance his logic lacks. I spoke, and spoke advisedly, of poetry. Plato's own deep distrust of that deceitful and marvellous art is nowhere more dramatically vindicated—dramatically and perhaps ironically, too.

But Plato, no doubt, is a special case. He exhibits the rare example of a prophet who uses prophecy to vindicate logic, which prophets more often seek to overthrow. And it is to this latter class that Sartre belongs—at least Sartre the author of *Nausea*. My method, then, in discussing the *Phaedo* will hardly admit of being generalised. Yet one thing I hope to exhibit is the use of a similar manoeuvre, one might say, a displacement of objects. Sartre is capable, like Plato, of using his great powers of imaginative presentation to misdirect his reader's attention. It is plain in general, however, that I shall need a more explicit methodology—though, let me add at once, the procedures I propose are in fact nothing remarkable or recondite.

Indeed logic and prophecy still run parallel. Consider the traditional tests of the acceptability of logical maxims, which I for my part would

---

[2] *Phaedo* 89b. My concern here being literary, not philosophical, I have taken the liberty (with the kind help of Richard Sorabji, who however must bear no responsibility for it) of freely re-rendering the passage from the standard translation.

happily endorse. Two conjoint requirements are self-evidence and consensus. Something evident must be evident to everyone, or at least to the generality of thinking people, those intelligent enough to understand (or failing understanding, candid enough to acknowledge it: you can never wholly exclude cranks and fanatics). We require, next, mutual consistency among maxims that are otherwise acceptable, and of course internal consistency. Where a maxim is internally inconsistent it is condemned out of hand. But now what of prophets and prophecy? Here we deal not with maxims, succinct statements taken in isolation, but rather with some outlook or wider vision: a thing, in however favourable circumstances, hardly to be characterised as self-evident. It may still be felt compelling, more or less widely compelling. Indeed conflicts are bound to remain. Here we look, if not for general assent, yet for something not wholly dissimilar, extensive credibility. Next as to consistency, a logical thing: I take its imaginative equivalent to be coherence. We require internal coherence in works of prophecy; and indeed the same holds of literature. Here the two sorts of criticism coincide. But I fear that the final parallel falls out less tidily. We found that logical maxims, to be finally acceptable, must not only be acceptable in themselves but also be consistent with each other. The same cannot possibly hold of the varieties of overall vision that prophets offer: they stand in inevitable conflict.[3] Yet, I would suggest, some sort of analogue still remains. We turn away from the particular work before us not only to the work of other prophets but to human experience in general; to experience both as we ourselves know it and as imaginative writers, novelists and poets, make it better known. The picture was convincing before, perhaps, so long as it exclusively absorbed us; it may or may not look the same once we set it against a wide background.

One other consideration remains, and here finally the analogy fails. Prophecy, it would seem, pre-eminently convinces us by its tone; the fact is obscure but undeniable. We hear a voice, the mere accent of command, that makes others sound trivial or flawed; and literature impresses us similarly. It is a point indeed made much of by one prophet, lately popular, one who in fact contrived to trivialise by generalising it. Yet here it holds uncontestably, indeed is almost a definition of tone: the medium and the message become one.

I turn at last, armed with this rough equipment, to the particular work of prophecy I promised to speak of in more detail. But one problem I mean to disregard. Sartre, an irreligious writer, shares prob-

---

[3] The same goes for philosophies, of course. But ideally we can agree at least on axioms. Anyway, I offer the parallel, which nothing else turns on, merely as a way of getting to grips with the relevant issues.

lems that characteristically face religious writers. He is a prophet, he has a vision to convey, but in his case a vision that, as it were, is invertedly a mystical one. He must use language to point beyond language, to convey what he sees as the deeper truth that language itself only disguises. As with Bergson who probably influenced him, with Bradley, and one may perhaps add Nietzsche; intellect that, so to speak, blows the whistle and starts the game, must serve finally to discredit itself. Of this endeavour, in its more traditional role, T. S. Eliot has written compellingly and movingly:

> Words move, music moves
> Only in time; but that which is only living
> Can only die. Words, after speech, reach
> Into the silence. (*Burnt Norton*, 5)

But this problem, I said, I propose to bypass. I refer to it because it links with another and one that is much more peculiarly Sartre's. Something of a barrier for English readers, or most English readers, I suspect, is presented by the French intellectual's *ex officio* detestation of bourgeoisdom. In Sartre, however, it is more. In his readers he relies on the stock attitude; for himself it is quite plainly intense and personal, an anger and hatred, obscurely born, that co-engenders itself confusedly with much else, indeed with what seems to be his central message. I find here a deep incoherence, one that lies at the heart of the novel. I said that he rejects intellectuality and the very notion of namable objects. But it is as if the bourgeois of Bouville, the bourgeois in their smugness and self-assurance, are responsible for the universal lie; I mean the lie whereby tree trunks are misdescribed as 'tree trunks' or that makes us expect people to remain roughly as they are, rather than turning at any moment into centipedes—or some sort of more complicated monster.

Bouville, Sartre tells us, is 'very French'. I cannot help being reminded of E. M. Forster; for whom, of course, the imaginary town of his own special antipathy, Sawston, is typically English. It stands for all stuffiness and human emptiness, the denial of spontaneous life. Yet Forster, within the English tradition and feeling its force, was later driven—if not wholly successfully—to seek to pass beyond that narrow stance, to understand the class whose outlook he disliked.[4] This ethos of comprehensive understanding is not something whose weight Sartre ever dreamt of or feels. He remains fiercely partisan to the last. That, I myself see, with what might be called, paradoxically, an insular preju-

---

[4] The qualification was meant to apply to *Howards End*. About *A Passage to India* I have no similar reservations.

dice, as a pretty damaging limitation. But the main issue that concerns me is different. We end with a dead level of meaninglessness which repudiates all values alike—indeed more than values, as we see. Even the scientific ideal sometimes aimed at of so-called neutral or value-free description is equally excluded by Sartre's vision, at least here. (In *Being and Nothingness*, if I understand it rightly, the programme embraced is a more modest one.) But we reach it through much angry polemic which, even if negatively (it makes no difference), is saturated with values through and through. This argument perhaps invites a simple answer. If we allow, as I suggested, that intellect and even language may transcend themselves, why may not evaluation do the same? To this objection, clearly a formally sound one, I must for the present postpone my answer, which will concern incoherence of tone. Here, I suggested, literary criticism and the assessment of prophecy coincide.

I spoke of a dead level of meaninglessness, or rather a live palpitation, and of meaninglessness felt as disgust—as disgust itself, or alternatively as disgusting. The ambiguity is Sartre's, not mine. But of course there is one grand exception, the traditional romantic exception—though here made in its presentation and colouring to seem as unromantic as the case allows—the timeless perfection of art. Art purges the dross of contingency; for Sartre or Roquentin, his alter ego, as equally for Yeats, the 'last romantic'; not here the starlit dome of Hagia Sofia, but a jazz tune with a sentimental refrain (whose provenance, perhaps, gives Sartre the same sort of reassurance that he tells us the ladies of Bouville get from the statue of Impétraz.)

But as for the antibourgeois satire, we find it mainly concentrated in two splendid set pieces, though differing greatly in scale and tone. For the first is not far from high farce—in a writer of a slightly different temperament it might have been high-spirited farce—the second brilliantly and elaborately intellectual. The first is the Sunday morning parade, the puppet show of the rue Tournebride, the other the scene in the picture gallery. The technique of the former is external; here people are reduced to their clothes. The grand bourgeois of Bouville hold the stage as they go through their hat-liftings and salutations, their brief, elegant social rituals. The moral here hardly needs pointing. Bourgeois values turn realities to class symbols; they dehumanise whatever they touch. It is in my judgment at least too near a caricature to be taken wholly seriously, as for instance one takes seriously Jane Austen's satire in *Northanger Abbey*—though that, too, merely qua satire is bound to simplify—in the depiction of Isabella and John Thorpe. Yet even the possible comparison to Jane Austen suggests that something has gone decidedly wrong; especially a comparison, let us note, to the lightest of her novels—for she, unlike Sartre, quite clearly invokes the tradition, employs its satirical conventions, which flatten objects and narrow our vision; though they do so of course for good reasons. But how can writing of this sort find a place in a novel of horror and meaninglessness; a novel that asks us to face the final agony of the existential predicament? We looked for truth, the very nerve and marrow of truth, not convention, and we find the stylisation of an established literary form.

The second of the episodes I spoke of is something decidedly more substantial, which I wish I had space to do justice to. Indeed it strikes me with a similar note of discord, at least a kind of discrepancy. For Sartre has forgotten his usual style. Things are what they are here, they are described accordingly, though with singular insight; in an idiom, one might say, that is recognisably and straightforwardly novelistic. And to get at the object that concerns him, the meaning he finds in the pictures, no other method is possible. So both matter and manner are transformed. He forgets all the frenetic horror-laden tone and vision that so worked to erode the familiar substance of things. We have instead the natural manner not only of a very sane observer but of course a highly intelligent and sophisticated one. One other small aberration may be forgiven him. He commits, like almost all novelists who use visual art, what might conveniently be labelled 'the literary fallacy': he finds depths of meaning in these pictures that no artist who ever lived could have given them. It is none the less true that his painters—there are two of them named Bordurin and Renaudas—emerge from his account as something hardly less than men of genius. And Roquentin himself—in his changed mood, that is—treats them both with considerable respect. One might register in passing the remark that a society that supported this artistic culture could hardly have been quite so hollow a thing as it has been made to sound, especially in the previous episode.

But let me turn back to my central concern which once again is the deflation of bourgeoisdom. Here the enemy is taken with a different seriousness. The bourgeois as he appears at his most formidable in the portrait, the work of Renaudas, of Rémy Parrottin, 'Professor at the École of Medicine at Paris'. Here Roquentin pauses. Parrottin, to repeat, no Sunday puppet, is a man not so easily to be written off. One Dr Wakefield has spoken of him: 'a great man', he called him, a brilliant man, the inspiration of his students—but also, and more to the purpose, the saviour of young souls from socialism. That process, the spiritual rekneading, as worked in the hands of this master, is one that Sartre goes on to describe. He does so with much zest, with much subtlety, a description at once satirical and realistic, that is eminently effective. And yet even so, it would seem, he remains dissatisfied. Roquentin says he can look at Rémy Parrottin. 'I wasn't afraid . . .' he records, 'I returned his smile and left him.'[5] Yet the novelist does not leave him. What comes next is the portrait of his brother, Jean Parrottin, a bureaucrat and administrator, a man 'possessed with the simplicity of an idea. Nothing was left of him but bones, dead flesh and Pure Privilege'.[6] The thesis or vision—for the two things are the same—is once again developed brilliantly. But a certain tell-tale phrase comes before: ' "That's funny," I thought, "he looks like Rémy Parrotin." I turned towards the Master: examining him in the light of this resemblance, I suddenly saw something arid and desolate appear in his gentle face: the family resemblance'.[7] I must omit the two following paragraphs and go on at once to quote the final deflation of 'the great man'.

> Parrottin put up a good fight. But, all of a sudden, the light in his eyes went out, the picture grew dim.
> What was left? Blind eyes, a mouth as thin as a dead snake, and cheeks. The pale, round cheeks of a child: they spread out over the canvas. The employees of the S.A.B. had never stayed for long enough in Parrottin's office. When they went in, they came up against that terrible gaze, as against a wall. The cheeks, white and flabby, were sheltered behind it. How long had it taken his wife to notice them? Two years? Five years? One day, I imagine, as her husband was sleeping beside her, with a ray of moonlight caressing his nose, or else as he was laboriously digesting, in the heat of the day, stretched out in an armchair, with his eyes half-closed and a puddle of sunlight on his chin, she had ventured to look him in the face: all this flesh had appeared to her without any defence, bloated, slavering, vaguely obscene. From that day on, Madame Parrottin had probably taken command.[8]

I myself feel, faced with writing like this, that Sartre has missed his vocation. Sartre the satirist, in my judgment, far outmatches the philosopher, and the satirical novelist no less the novelist of anguished private vision (and also incidentally those larger developments that followed later). I would gladly give some half dozen not-black not-chestnut-tree-roots for a few more figures like those of Rémy and Jean Parrottin. But for the present point: let us recall what Roquentin first notices, that tell-tale family likeness. Rémy Parrottin it seems, to be finally deflated, must be merged with the ultimate hollowness, behind visible arrogance, of his brother. In much the same way, we found

[5] *Nausea*, translated by R. Baldick (Harmondsworth, 1965), p. 129.
[6] Ibid., pp. 129–30.
[7] Ibid., p. 129.
[8] Ibid., pp. 130–6.

earlier in Plato, the philosopher was equated with his philosophy, the fate of his argument with his own fate.

All this, whether acceptable or otherwise, must sound simply like the language of literary criticism; and yet, I shall argue, it may also be more. I promised to attempt a new thing, a sort of critical discourse that could discuss literature but discuss it as prophecy. The issue is undoubtedly a complex one. Here certainly,, where tone is in question, the two nearly meet and coincide. For here of course my concern has been with tone; the whole tone of the episode in the gallery, I have argued, falls apart from the rest of the novel. But that fact closely links with another. 'Theoretical' questions arise, too—'theoretical' for want of a better word. For what are we shown? That the bourgeois Jean Parrottin is a living lie; it is that reality that his picture reveals, and the miraculous brush of the artist Renaudas betrays the nothingness behind the facade. And it is through him that the whole bourgeois world is made finally to confess its bad faith. That famous Sartrean phrase, 'bad faith', never appears, I believe, before *Being and Nothingness*, the book in which Sartre denies the objective status of all moral value—the notion of moral value itself, so it seems, a bourgeois lie—while self-confidently writing, in doing so, a negative evaluation into its very name.[9] A naive critic is therefore left to ask, 'What is there bad in bad faith?' Or on what terms can Sartre blame anyone for preferring it to what seems to be the only alternative he offers; which to be sure is truth and 'freedom', but with it inescapable anguish. Perhaps, with no knowable values to guide us, mere nature will assume its authority.

I mentioned some while back a possible objection that suggests itself: if intellect can be used to transcend itself, why cannot the same hold of evaluation? But look again at the passages I have discussed, at the whole episode in the gallery. The style, as I said, puts it apart: it belongs to the satirical tradition, and traditional satire, of course, took its stance upon positive values and hence denounced hypocrisy or vice. Now it may be that the process I spoke of is indeed possible (I do not know), that it is possible to make an evaluation that transcends evaluation. That is emphatically not what we find here. I wish I had space to spare to quote yet another passage, describing this time a portrait by Bordurin, who found himself faced with the problem of painting a diminutive sitter—a five-foot, shrill-voiced champion of the forces of 'order', and hence a champion of bourgeoisdom, one who must be, therefore, carefully set among small objects, a footstool and a low armchair, that run no risk of diminishing his stature. Sartre's cruel, bitter

---

[9] If this itself is bad faith, then it has at least the merit Sartre denies to the serious-minded bourgeoisie of being transparently so.

fun—of course blatantly partisan—succeeds splendidly. But it is what it is, partisan fun. What we cannot do is leap straight from this into the *Néant*, into the desperate world of existential anguish. The fault of vision and of tone here at least do indeed reflect and echo each other. Sartre, to repeat my initial charge, runs together his hatred of bourgeoisdom, a political and social stance, and only intelligible in such terms, with that radical 'philosophical' fear and horror that springs from a quite different source: his rejection of all intelligibility, the repudiation of intellect itself.[10]

To return to my own wider themes: all this falls under the heading of coherence. I shall now turn to other considerations, for I sought to list several as relevant. For the remainder, however, I must content myself with brief notes. To speak first of the famous epiphany in the park, or anti-epiphany perhaps, which is the passage which most critics chiefly concentrate on. One question is how one should take it: whether as a novelist's vivid depiction, a subjective depiction, of a singular if not

[10] It may be objected that the anti-bourgeois polemic here is balanced by the latter anti-humanist polemic in the scene with the autodidact, which—take it formally—is doubtless true. Yet imaginatively the two differ radically. The latter is given none of the calm and solid objectivity, the intellectual control, of the scene in the gallery. Rather, it seems part of the onset of Roquentin's illness—if you like, the dawning of his revelation. Waves of blind anger sweep over him, the fierce diatribe seems subjective, part of the anger; and it ends with his abrupt, somnambulist self-ostracism. He leaves the restaurant, things spinning about him, the others seeing him in his own fantasy—the recurrent Sartrean image of a kind of crab. Make what you will of all this. There is here, certainly, no incoherence of tone, and as I say, a very different effect on the imagination.

Indeed problems still remain. A. D. Nuttall has urged (in discussion) that this incoherence in tone, as I have called it, reduces to straight logical incoherence. For the one episode uses or presupposes the stability of ordinary descriptive language, the acceptability of ordinary categories, while what follows explicitly denies it. That, I think, was the point, which may be true. Let me offer a two-line defence so that if one breaks the other may still stand. I use *Nausea* only for illustration; my concern is with prophecy in general. And in general the point seems to hold. We are shown, say, some prospect of life and shown it in a particular light, perhaps benign amusement or again contemptuous amusement. Now imagine the obtrusion of some object to which attitudes of other sorts seems appropriate: pity, for instance, or horror, anyway not amusement. In the discussion of literature such themes are familiar; we have incoherence or potential incoherence, which a writer's presentation of the material, softening or transforming it, may yet make us see differently. All this belongs, broadly, to what John Wisdom calls 'reflection', but not in the narrow sense to logic. And of prophecy, too, the same holds.

As to Sartre: suppose that the present discrepancy, or what I see as such, is indeed a fundamentally logical one. It need not follow that the difficulty was imaginatively insuperable. Sartre may fail; I think he does. We cannot say a priori that he was bound to fail. Think of Whitman's magnificent bravado in face of a similar predicament: 'Do I contradict myself? /Very well then, I contradict myself. /I am large, I contain multitudes.' Sartre's tone, of course, could never be Whitman's. It suffices that the thing is not impossible. Our immediate sense of incoherence may or may not reflect faulty logic. Even so, the concept of tone and its role in prophecy raise issues which I do not claim to have sifted to the bottom.

pathological mental state, or rather as a revelation of reality. For
Roquentin, of course, it is the latter, and presumably for Sartre
himself—in this stage in his development at least. In discussing logical
maxims, I spoke of self-evidence and consensus; and I spoke too of
analogous considerations applying to prophecy. Revelation, I said,
must not only be compelling but widely experienced as compelling.
Many writers deal in mystic revelation. I think of Tolstoy, of Wordsworth, of T. S. Eliot, and the sort of experience they describe and
celebrate. Pathological conditions are things merely to be explained—explained, if at all, by psychologists. For the founder of
psychoanalysis, religious experience in general called only for
psychological explanation, and similarly aesthetic experience. That
issue is not one I shall pursue. At least some form of such experience
seems to be common or recurrent, a possession, one might say, of
humanity. But here the case differs. A man looking at a seat in a tram
tells us with agonised seriousness that he might just as properly call it a
dead donkey—and presently, another possibility, a bleeding belly. I do
now feel, and with considerable confidence, as many other commentators have felt, that it is time to refer to the psychologist. One might
notice that Sartre himself asks the question: ' "Did I dream it up, that
huge presence? . . . I hated," he says, "that ignoble jelly" '.[11]

Disgust is desire joined with horror. The phrases quoted above
closely follow an angry description of a woman in a restaurant nar-
cissistically engaged in enjoying the softness and fullness of her own
breasts. The conjunction will hardly seem to need commenting on, at
least to those familiar with the discipline I referred to. But metaphysical
speculations are perhaps more in order here, in a forum devoted to
philosophy and literature.

Roquentin's last, horrific revelation is the contingency of things that
are 'there'; his own existence and that of the chestnut tree, all these
things are merely contingent.[12] But most of us learned that from
Hume, that all existential statements are contingent, and learned it in
our first year as undergraduates. Sartre, I have heard it maintained, is
quite consciously echoing Hume, as earlier he echoed Descartes. The
analogy, I fear, will hardly hold. Certainly he plays with the *cogito*.
What he never does is, say, having doubted his own reality, end an
agonised passage of spiritual scrutiny with the dazzling discovery, 'I
doubt, therefore I exist.' You cannot make a climax out of a truism.
Similarly for my own merely contingent existence or Sartre's, since

[11] *Nausea*, p. 192.

[12] By contrast, it seems, a mathematical figure, a circle, 'does not exist', and qua
abstraction, that is, having no specific dimensions, is presumably 'necessary': its whole
character fixed by its definition.

neither of us is God, the sole claimant with anything like plausible pretensions to the status of a necessary being, 'a being whose essence involves existence'. Hence for a philosopher in the British tradition, whose training has been in that tradition, a suitable response is hard to find. But for a continental rationalist the case may be different. I speak here of rationalism not as a theory concerning bases of knowledge but rather as a metaphysic or ontology. There is, one may say, a kind of megalomania of rationalism. It is the picture of the beauty of an intelligible universe, intelligible in every detail, each in its necessary place, such as Spinoza and Leibniz could still believe in. To come, then, on things that simply *are*, brute facts, as we normally call them, the contingency of the actual, and come on them from that rationalist background, might indeed be an experience to arouse dismay. But the real roots of Sartre's horror, I remain convinced, are both more personal and personally profound.

My third test remains to be applied; as to that process, I can do no more than point to its possibility. A vision of things, to stand up, must stand against others that conflict with it. The best I can offer is vague. We can ask any prophet or his followers to survey wider ranges of experience: 'Can you look at this, and again this, and still say the things you said before?' Writers whose range is already wide, who enter deeply into various experiences, have clearly less to fear from the process. The case, it seems to me, differs here. We can set Sartre—the Sartre of *Nausea* to which, perhaps unfairly, I confine myself—beside Tolstoy or Chaucer or Dante and try what emerges from the comparison. Here the special mode of this novel becomes relevant. Its method, it is worth noticing, is that of a fictional diary. The effect is enclosing, hence hypnotic; but its vision, of course, narrows correspondingly. It serves literature well, prophecy badly; for it forces us powerfully to identify with a certain unusual mental state—in fact, I suggested, a pathological one. It discourages, unless we deliberately disengage ourselves and step back, any survey that would place it in perspective.

These sketchy observations, I hope, suffice to indicate the sort of procedure I see as appropriate, I mean appropriate to literature taken as prophecy. I have of course attempted nothing by way of a general assessment or coverage of the novel: especially I have said nothing of the scene between Roquentin and Anny—the most humanly moving in the book, perhaps the most humanly moving Sartre has written.

In my initial comparison of the two modes I noticed one consideration that stands apart, that seems to belong exclusively to the former. Philosophy excludes questions of tone in proportion as it approximates to pure logic. Conversely they gain in prominence in proportion as it approximates to literature. Suppose we praise prophecy simply for its tone, its tone not its truth. It would seem that we are treating it as 'pure literature'—doubtless none-too-happy a phrase. For literature, too, for instance fiction, as I noted at the start, embodies its own vision, its own values, which it seeks to substantiate. Yet a difference remains. It is to treat a prophet less than fully seriously to read him 'as literature'. I recall Auden's 'Hermetic Decalogue':

> Thou shalt not be on friendly terms
> With guys in advertising firms,
>   Nor speak with such
> As read the Bible for its prose,
> Nor, above all, make love to those
>   Who wash too much.[13]

Values have changed since the forties, and in reaction the virtues of soap and water may make themselves more forcibly felt. As to the rest I must confess, for myself, to having often read Kierkegaard for his prose or as much as survives in translation (and it seems to do surprisingly well). Yet the problem after all is a complex one; the Arnoldian truism is still partly true. The quality of his prose is often—not always let me stress—something inseparable from the quality of his insight. And one who rejects Kierkegaard's 'message' may still marvel at the richness of his insight, as well as delighting in his wit.

Or is tone by itself a test of truth? The answer must emphatically be negative, despite Matthew Arnold's famous dictum—so often and, it seems to me, uncritically repeated. But whatever else tone may signify or fail to signify, its power over the mind and imagination remain undeniable and vast. Nor need this surprise us. In a thousand daily situations these are the things we must go by; in trivial or crucial decisions, it is a man's manner, the sound of his voice, that affect us, in which we find something that reassures or disquiets us. Appearances are notoriously deceptive yet remain indispensable. And after all, intuitive people can amaze us by how much they rightly read from what seems like a mere absence of evidence. So here, too, we listen to tone. And we would be foolish, I suppose, either wholly to discount or wholly trust it. To reverse the story: 'Suspicion,' writes Halifax. 'is rather a virtue than a fault, as long as it doth like a dog that watcheth and doth not bite. . . . A wise man will keep his suspicions muzzled, but he will keep them awake.' So *mutatis mutandis* of reliance on sensitivity to tone.

---

[13] 'Under which lyre', in *Nones* (New York, 1951), p. 70. Auden's distinction between Ariel-dominated and Prospero-dominated poetry is relevant too. Cf. 'Robert Frost', in *The Dyer's Hand* (New York, 1962).

A last point is relevant, too. Let me turn back to 'pure' philosophers. We judge them and their followers, and assess and compare their respective merits, we recognise, say, the greatness of Kant and Aristotle, without necessarily accepting their doctrines. And so too with prophets. We spoke of Kierkegaard. Now think by way of contrast of a novelist like George Eliot or a philosopher like Cook Wilson: Sartre and Kierkegaard, deeply and widely as they differ, may seem still to belong to the same breed. Both veer towards intensities and extremes; a hostile critic might call either frenetic. Both love paradox and choose, as it were, to live in paradox, challenging us with its breath-taking stance. To take *Fear and Trembling* alone by way of a fair comparison to *Nausea*: in Kierkegaard such extremism is still compatible with what, in my judgment, we fail to find in Sartre's novel, the range of awareness, of human possibilities suggested. He distinguishes himself from Nietzsche, in my ears at least, by his mastery of tone. The voice of Nietzsche, with its ever-growing shrillness and stridency, which the more it cries 'Life!, Life!', sounds to me more and more like the precise opposite; tone here, I believe, does truly reflect something more, a vision increasingly distorted. Yet, I may be told, that is easily said. How can one make this distinction or know when tone may or may not be taken as indicative of more? These are questions that need further inquiry.

I have discussed no prophet with whom I sympathise or sympathise deeply and widely; which, I fear, may have given my own remarks too predominantly negative a tone. Let me end, then, by merely naming two of my own favourites, whom I wish I had space to defend, which will also be to come clean as to my basic commitments or attitudes. First, Johnson, especially the *Lives of the Poets*: Johnson wise and deeply pessimistic. And also Thomas Love Peacock as he appears in *Nightmare Abbey*; Peacock wise yet cheerful—capable, rather than horror, of cheerfulness in face of odd contingencies. *Nightmare Abbey* might be taken as an interesting study of how much may be worked and how much touched on within a small canvas. But his main difference with Sartre is still the obvious one: Peacock takes his absurdities with relish.[14]

II. Some Notes on 'Acting it out' and 'Being in it up to the nose'
by William Righter

Iris Murdoch remarks that *Nausea* is Sartre's 'most densely

[14] I have benefited—partly, I fear, only as helping me to the sharper definition of differences—from discussing my themes with Barbara Hardy and Mr and Mrs Bernard Howells.

philosophical novel',[15] meaning the 'most' I suppose as a comparative. Yet the very term 'philosophical novel' is one we have come to use with a touch of irony, or at least with that distancing appropriate for something that seems to have forced itself upon us, presenting us with the awkward feeling that the category is necessary while its contents are somehow dubious. Of course several things might be meant by a 'philosophical novel'. There is the narrative in which philosophical ideas are mentioned and discussed, and it is this weak sense of 'philosophical' that you might find in those novels that concern themselves with debating the great issues of the day, say in several novels of Huxley, in *Les Thibault* or even perhaps in *Les Chemins de la Liberté*. There are also those works in which our interest in a character's own growth and change is inseparable from those general ideas about himself and the world around him that seem essential to his character or form of life. Levin in *Anna Karenina* must confront the problems of the Russian soil, the peasants that work on it, the implications of being himself, the starry heavens, but in a way that concerns us far more with the posture of a self-questioning agent than with the substance of the questions asked, even if the posture of the agent derives its point from the feeling that they have a substance. Finally, there are perhaps works which present an experience that seems somehow to have 'philosophical' implications, to display some quality or aspect of life that has a general importance for the whole of it.

These are rough categories, and in particular cases are perhaps not always that distinct. But they do serve to separate out works like *Nausea* where the 'philosophical' interest is contained less in the actual talk about such matters of general importance than in the directness with which some significant experience is conveyed. This would, on the surface at least, seem to be the exact point where the language of an imaginative work did not simply contain an imitation of a conventional sort of philosophical argument, but was working in its own right, giving a kind of 'presentational immediacy' to something which nothing other than its own powers could convey—something untouchable by a conceptual or analytic language, yet of the greatest importance in that world with which such other languages also deal.

Of course when we say 'philosophical' it is with another kind of uneasiness as well. For we are habituated to a sense of the word in Anglo-Saxon academic philosophy in which it could have no other character than one which is conceptual and analytic. Imaginative and analytic have always seemed to have quite separate lives, with what David Pole calls prophecy filling an ambiguous and somewhat suspect middle ground. And it is this uneasiness that informs some remarks of

15 Iris Murdoch, *Sartre: Romantic Rationalist* (Cambridge, 1953), ch. 1.

Mary Warnock in a review of Ricoeur's work on Freud:[16] 'The romantic attraction towards Nietzsche, and towards Existentialism, springs from the fact that in these philosophers human feelings are as important as human knowledge; that man's attitude to the world, and not merely his knowledge of it, is the subject of analysis.' But what is to fill the role of 'analysis' here? In the case of Ricoeur and Freud it is a question of the alternative interpretation of 'symbols' derived from the unconscious (although the images in question can hardly be 'symbols' until they are in some way interpreted), and these alternative readings are not dissimilar to the alternative interpretations two critics might give of a text. Freud, of course, in the effort to give his work a scientific footing, has claimed, surely falsely, the certainty of a mode of interpretation when the symbols once properly understood bear a clear one-to-one relationship with their significance in psychic life. The model of literary criticism may be set against this, where alternative interpretations can be illuminating without totally excluding each other, and where criteria are elusive to state, but involve the close weighing and testing of the particular case without an ultimate and single determining rule of correctness. Here criticism may come close for all of its devious follies to touching upon the exploration of the ambiguities of the psyche and its products.

The implications may seem too appallingly permissive as they do to some critical theorists like E. D. Hirsch. But it is a particular and consequent possibility that one may state an interpretation without allowing for a discussion of its epistemological status that bothers Warnock. However, in this particular case it would seem that the epistemological status of the two conflicting interpretations would be exactly the same, and what is at stake is rather the 'status' of interpretation itself. Here one might wish to point to certain features of interpretation, that are a 'making intelligible' without necessarily explaining, because they are not directed, *pace* Freud, to a conceptual and abstract statement consonant with other kinds of scientific statement, but to the human continuum of experience and feeling, where one asks instead 'Was it like that?' and the answer comes back 'Both yes and no.'

This problem is seen by Warnock to lead into a larger one: 'For the point at issue between the continental and the Anglo-Saxon schools of philosophy could be put in this way: What is the place to be allowed in philosophy for the imagination?' This means in at least one of its aspects, how seriously are we to take any kind of claim put in terms of experience and feeling? The case suggested is that of Sartrean viscosity; 'Are we to absorb his feeling as we absorb the feeling of a film-maker or

[16] Mary Warnock, review of *Freud and Philosophy: An Essay in Interpretation* by Paul Ricoeur, *New Society* 16 (1970), no. 412.

a novelist?' Surely the answer 'yes' can be given without thereby downgrading the experience described to a passing mood, or psychological aberration. For it is not the unique experience of one man in one moment—nor the feeling of all men at some moment (surely false)—that Sartre is trying to describe, but one aspect of all men's relation with their environment, whether actually felt or not. And what we might hope for to validate it (or otherwise) is partly the sense of recognition, the ability to say, 'Yes, living in a world of objects and places and people is in some important aspect, like that.' The word 'absorb' itself suggests the problem. We shall return to viscosity.

But how is the authenticity of the experience determined? And is the authenticity as experience related to 'epistemological status'? This is not unrelated to certain fears of the artist that the intensity of realisation in a literary work may conceal a falsification. For it is tempting to say that some sort of epistemological status is attained through the very degree to which the novelist or whoever wields the imaginative power manages to convince us that 'the thing is real'. And we certainly also evaluate the works of imaginative philosophers in this way, saying of *Zarathustra* that it rings false with its portentous rhetoric while other things of Nietzsche, often in bits and pieces, such as the fragments from *The Will to Power*, ring true. Not, of course, that as sequences of propositions they are either true or false, but that we feel the falsification of something in one work while of another we say 'It goes to the bone', it somehow touches on life in a way which I recognise as profound and important, which becomes coherent and whole in terms of experience, if not as a series of logical propositions. This 'recognition' may itself seem in a loose sense empirical knowledge although not subject to the tests to which empirical knowledge is put. It is perhaps connected with other terms that imply seeing in depth or in special ways such as 'insight' or even 'understanding', in which the imagination also has its role.

One word which was used of the 'imaginative' sort of philosopher was the 'attraction' which was felt for such an alternative philosophical tradition, for something involved in and referring to the human situation in a way that Anglo-Saxon empirical and linguistic philosophy has failed to do. The desire felt and expressed for some viable role in philosophy for the imagination echoes in its essential motives the search for appropriate forms for the imagination, for a sense of something to give the appearance of respectability to its operations.

This handling of the problem seems to me to beg some important questions which I shall raise at a later point. Here I am most concerned with the habit of mind which sees feelings and attitudes, framed necessarily in some imaginative sort of way, as separate in kind from the world of evidence and argument. I shall wish to argue that this separation is not only unnecessary, but is in fact a misrepresentation of the way in which philosophy is done, and that the modes of argument and imagination are interdependent. There will be a minimal sense of this interdependence where argument is contained in the imaginative forms that 'act it out'. And there is a more extended claim to examine: to what extent is it possible for an imaginative work to do a 'philosophical' job? This will involve us directly with *Nausea*, but it is first worth saying something about the minimal interdependence.

This is of course something which is so obvious that it is perhaps easy to overlook its implications. But I mean the simple fact that all reasoning about human affairs is dependent on some picture of actions, events, relationships, with which argument may be concerned. Human actions and their consequences, the working out of situations, the wish to become clear about problems in the philosophy of morals or society, depend upon a sequence where 'arguing' and 'imagining' are insepar-able. There must be someone to borrow books, and someone to whom promises are made. There must be varying circumstances in which in-tentions, moral or otherwise, choices and decisions, have one or another kind of sense. And it is by altering the picture, by setting different terms or conditions, or telling a different kind of 'story' that arguments become relevant or irrelevant, have force, look foolish—and even, persuade or fail to persuade. This lowest level may contain several kinds of pictures of states of affairs, or of narrative which may or may not be extended. And our pleasure or excitement in what we think to be an argument of consequence is often in the ingenuity with which some such picture is altered, or the perfection or finesse with which the case is reinvented, the telling example found. Perhaps I am suggesting that even at the minimum level the imaginative demand is connected with some kind of aesthetic of argument.

More extended imaginings, where the narrative or descriptive element takes on a life of its own, create a more serious awkwardness. With Plato there are usually clearly marked passages in the dialogue when a certain phase of argument comes to an end, and the 'myth' is introduced, something that suggests a necessary complement to what the argument has done, and the recognition that the mode of discourse must now be different, that a new means must be employed. Yet the example of the Cave, so often called a 'myth' is odd. Is this extended picture less of an 'argument' than the Divided Line? The complex visual demonstration is in some way related to the diagrammatic, yet has, perhaps because of its very elaborateness a 'life of its own'. Do we then regard the sense of the argument as something we can abstract from it, somehow leaving the 'picture' behind? And can we, having done so, turn on the picture in a dismissive way, as something pretty and illustrative, but as such entirely a 'means'?

On the other hand compare Plato's Cave with Pascal's prison[17] which seems to stand on its own as a simple irreducible image, introduced by the expression 'Qu'on s'imagine . . .' and ending with 'C'est l'image. . . .' The men in chains suggest a picture which is not visually developed. Nor is it part of a complex demonstration or argument, but simply poses in itself the whole of man's condition and dilemma. You may draw your conclusions, and there is no doubt from the wider context what sort of conclusions Pascal wishes us to draw. Yet in itself the picture simply confronts us with a kind of directness and simplicity, an ostensive feel to it, like the 'nausea' itself—or for that matter, Moore's hand. Is it this shift from Plato's Cave to Pascal's prison that would mark for Pole the shift from philosopher to prophet? Or is the cave itself already in some ambiguous middle ground? And compare again the simple force of the prison image with the elaboration of it in Malraux's *La Condition Humaine*. In Malraux it is given a context, characters and their destinies fill it out, purposes and ideologies surround it. How different is the sense of any conclusion to be drawn, where the individual fate is set in a Marxist and materialist world? Certainly the drama of Malraux may involve us in the figures he has created—it is a 'story' and not an image. But the image and the story may implicitly involve, in so far as they have a philosophical point, the same question.

I have emphasised this pictorial quality, this imaging and embodying because I think it has interest of a kind quite different from one, at least, of the normal ways in which philosophical and imaginative enterprises have been distinguished: the contrast between logical form and implication and the rhetoric of persuasion. The study of the linguistic means through which such a rhetoric works has a venerable history and its own intrinsic interest. This to a large extent lies in the detailed study of the language through which it might be presumed to work. However, the very interest in language points away from the directness of confrontation with which one is concerned in *Nausea*, where the language is by its own terms subordinate to the kind of experience for which language may be the necessary medium, yet where the whole point of it all lies somewhere beyond language, where the tactile and taste sensations are I think deliberately chosen for their very inaccessability to language, and for their immediacy to our own feeling of physical identity.

In trying to come to some sense of the claims of the nausea itself, or of the viscosity that puzzles Mary Warnock I shall not be much con-

[17] *Pensées* 341. (Chevalier).

cerned with *Nausea* as a novel, or at least not with an overall reading of it. Nor is there any particular interest in working through the usual notions belonging to the Sartrean philosophical apparatus in which the book has its curious place. Because there is a sense in which the experience has greater authenticity if the conceptual frame is not quite in the foreground. The gradual encroachment, compared with a disease, the sense of *dérèglement*, in some way strains against the feeling that the whole thing is rigged. *Nausea* seems a fusion of certain preconceptions and something that is vividly lived. In so far as it is working out of specific philosophical intentions, concerning contingency and freedom, consciousness and the world of objects, all that concerns me here is that these intentions do exist, have been fully worked out, and the imagined experience is inevitably conditioned by reference to them.

It is also perhaps worth mentioning that *Nausea* is connected with a genre which explores what one might call the 'aesthetics of disgust'. Certainly the influence of Céline, recognised in the epigraph, is of importance to it, in locating the sources of revolt in the tactile and physical, and in using this moment of revolt as a psychological pivot. The nauseous, the disgusting, the unacceptable physical face of life is shared, although in Céline they are perhaps less internalised and are viewed with a more clinical detachment. A characteristic pattern in Céline is nausea, revolt, flight—flavoured by a tone of ironical deprecation. With *Nausea* the nausea is diffuse yet pervasive and inescapable; the objects of the world lack the particular dramatic presence of those of Céline, or if they do attain it do so through the very face of being commonplace. The characteristic nightmare works through banality rather than the extreme. The nausea is with us and around us, we're in it up to the nose, simply as an ordinary condition of life.

How necessary is it in any serious assessment of *Nausea* to be convinced that this is an authentic version of the relation of self to the external world? One thing that we need not believe is that its authenticity depends upon its being the only acceptable version of this relation. Suppose we invent a world which is the antithesis of the Sartrean one, where instead of clinging to us, invading us, sticking remorselessly to our surface, objects instead flee from us or elude us. Suppose rather than the sludgy viscous, glutinous objects of Sartre we find the external world composed of objects that are bright, hard, cleanly delineated and separate, with the sort of surfaces that turn the slightest contact into pain. In either case the imaginative impact may be equally intense. And if we are required to point to the truer case, do we turn and argue or give evidence which points to the predominance of any such description in our view of the world around us? Or do we say that the claims of novelists are not of this sort, that alternative visions of the world may easily co-exist and that the whole point of such imaginative enterprises lies within such inverted commas as deprive it of any form of universalisability? The first way surely madness lies, and the latter suggests that form of liberal equanimity in which all literary works may slot in or out of our psychic economy with equal weight or lack of it. Of course, Pole is correct, all prophets disagree, and certainly without all but one of them being wrong, and the visions of particular literary works differ without exactly excluding each other.

One can argue perhaps that the feel, the experience, the impact of nausea may have implications which seem consequential without supporting any particular range of conclusions, or that the notions of contingency and freedom might have a number of alternative forms of presentation without invalidating the imaginative claims of this one. Are we to focus on the link between representation of experience and imaginative hold, or admit that somehow this escapes the possibility of further explanation? Does taking this seriously at all lead us to Pole's dictum that 'about the things that really matter we can't communicate at all . . .'? This depends, I think, on what we mean by 'communicate' and at what level we feel communication to be successful. What I think Sartre has done is provide us with a model of the kind of intensification of a moment of life which perhaps has validity at several different levels of response. 'It's rubbish, I've never felt like that nor could feel that way, yet I know what he means.' 'I could conceive of life in these terms, alien as they are.' The picture somehow 'makes sense', or is in its way 'absurd' in such a fashion that we feel it relevant to a world that 'makes sense' in other terms.

But when we think of making sense, we don't think easily of what Pole has called 'tone', and the suggestion that the prophet both convinces us through tone, yet falsifies himself if he tries to articulate that tone too fully, raises a matter of the greatest importance which is not at all well understood. That raising of the voice, that moment of excess insistence, may have no appropriate and ready description and yet separate an Isaiah from a clown. Yet the deflationary urge is one with which we all sympathise, and I feel there is an unresolved dilemma in Pole's preference for the comedy of the satirical passages in *Nausea* to the excessive articulation of that damned portentous root. One sympathises, but uneasily, because the satire on bourgeois society is the part of the novel which fits into a conventional and non-prophetic notion of what novels do. In the stock responses to bourgeois life the comedy is good. But however ingenious and bitter, however concentrated (and perhaps un-English) in the consistency of its malice, it joins company with a wide literature, and poses no unfamiliar problems. In

Nausea however the very presence of this comedy perhaps contains the implicit suggestion that absurdity as metaphysical anguish and absurdity as comic disproportion are in a closer relation than we might usually allow. Is the latter aspect lying in wait to swallow the former, just as the comic contingency of a *Nightmare Abbey* may mock the intensity and consequentiality of the Sartrean sense of the contingent? It has a more accommodating mood, and the 'tone' itself is more welcome. Beyond the nightmare illogic of the unexpected, Peacock returns us to the calm daylight of the socially well-ordered world. Yet the order implicit in the comic balance is precisely that destroyed in *Nausea*; the consequence of the nightmare is that its terms are utterly open—the randomness is absolute.

If the 'prophecy' is there it is in the intransigence of the root, of the nausea itself. For by its very nature the nausea states a refusal to assimilate to a sensible, rationalised, relatively routine world. It need not be that of the *salauds* but simply any in which systematic explanations are given, relationships established, beginnings, middles and ends so well fitted as to be taken for granted. Prophets require not only a certain tone, but their due sense of the extreme, and stubbornness. It is this refusal, the series of negative gestures by which consciousness is isolated, as the nausea invades and absorbs it through the world of which it is aware that creates a challenge to our own capacity to encompass exactly what we cannot 'fit' to appropriate categories or see as part of a structure which admits of the familiar. It is not that it is important that the objects for which the usual names exist become objects of another sort, turn into centipedes or sea monsters. Nor is it necessary to see all such usual and convenient forms of speech as nothing but the bourgeois lie, the containing and paralysing fictions of the *salauds*. But merely that we are capable of admitting of something that comes between ourselves and this habitual order, and that what does so may be represented by a simple physical fact or sensation, a concrete realisation of which the implications must be worked out. The success or failure of *Nausea* may to some extent be judged in terms of whether or not such a sensation does lodge itself in one's consciousness in such a way, or whether it is simply an aberration or colossal bore. But the imaginative demand is reciprocal and seen in terms of response as well as means. Earlier I mentioned the dependence of the slightest fragment of argument upon the imaginative framing of its context. The nausea presents us with the pure, naked and unassimilable, which paradoxically creates through its very presence the basis of an argument which it is its own purpose to reject.

How does this help us with Mary Warnock's problem about the place of imagination, or perhaps the 'imagined' in our philosophical scheme? We've hardly begun. But it might be worth noting that the sense in which nausea rejects the rationalising and explanatory applies equally to philosophies of the Anglo-Saxon or the continental type. Neither is prima facie more acceptable to the brutely unaccommodating, nor more obviously designed to suit the imaginative intruder. If a philosophical criticism which admits the intrusion is to be evolved, it is back to back with its starting point.

III. *Literature and Prophecy: A Reply to Righter*

William Righter's approach, it seems to me, is rather exploratory than apodeictic. I would feel happier in seeking to answer him if I could more confidently credit myself with a sure grasp, a clear broad perspective on the movement of his thought. I must hope that the attempt at least will prove useful.

To dispose of one other point first. My indiscriminate use of the term 'prophet' has provoked criticism from various quarters. Nietzsche and Carlyle may be called prophets, at least in the popular sense; but if Johnsonian moralising and the fantasies and gleeful *jeu d'esprit* of Peacock are admitted too, the category becomes altogether too capacious. But in fact what I need is a capacious category. I ought, however, to have defined it merely negatively. My interest is in persuasive writing of all sorts, or all that are expressive of conviction and genuinely aiming at truth—which excludes Plato's rhetoricians and TV commercials—using methods other than those of logico-analytic philosophy (itself of course only an ideal type). Some quite neutral word, 'persuasion' itself possibly, would have done better.

To return to Righter: A philosophical novel for him, or the sort he is interested in, confronts us imaginatively with some 'experience' or 'aspect of life' so as to give it ' "philosophical" implications'. Well, yes; one would expect it to do that. But to give any stuffing to the last phrase, I must take it as something revalatory not only of particular things—Sir Plume's well-groomed fatuity, for instance—but some deeper wholly general reality. We are to see the whole world, to take the example we have been concerned with, *sub specie disgustus*; which is to see it truly and profoundly. But the consequences are awkward, I think; for it seems now that we shall have to take sides. The comfortably tolerant relativism—a sort of have-it-both-ways relativism, I suspect—in whose amplitude Righter relaxes, is something we must now turn our backs on. It is madness, he tells us, to commit oneself to any one viewpoint at the expense of excluding all the rest; and yet hopelessly permissive to let in everything. The same goes for the interpretation of art and literature as for the 'philosophical' interpretation of the world. For them one might as sensibly ask students to study the contents of the wastepaper basket as Shakespeare and Michelangelo. The preferred solution, rather than to fall between two stools, seems to be to hop from one foot to the other; (though a third possibility might be to display the wastepaper basket at the Tate Gallery). But I have written elsewhere of the self-indulgent licentiousness of interpretation, and shall not repeat myself.[18]

Righter must commit himself; or at least, as we all have to do, recognise the existence of large alternatives which cannot merely peacefully co-exist; of divergent views that serious people take equally seriously. So that, even in firmly committing ourselves, we may yet treat other views with respect; or alternatively honestly suspend judgment. He will also need procedures more rigorous than broad appeals to what 'rings true' or 'somehow touches on life in a way which I recognise as profound and important'.

Sartre, according to Righter, seeks to bring home to us 'one aspect of all men's relation with their environment'. One might query that 'all'; but let us waive that. So much is certainly true: moods of all sorts occasionally affect us. One may be capable of feeling disgust pretty generally, or indignation, resignation, what you will. That is hardly a philosophical revelation. But existence itself as disgust, as contingency which makes it disgusting—it is, so to speak, embodied disgust—that, I think, sounds rather more like Sartre; less, I myself feel, like sense. To speak even of reality as a whole: at different times, of course, different aspects are apt to strike us. No logical problem arises here. Nor does it where we live with uncertainties, as wise men, I hinted, are bound to—though it is of course, logically speaking, a kind of admission of defeat. Now *Nausea* never offers what it offers as one possible view among others; if it did, the imaginative result would be catastrophic. But even with that tolerant reading I am left with a view I find strange. The equation of 'real existence' with contingency—one might better say predication by the latter of the former—has been widely accepted since Hume, whether rightly or wrongly. But that I do not exist necessarily, as there exists a natural number greater than any given number: this nowadays tolerably familiar fact seems to me the oddest of objects for disgust. For that matter I am tolerably resigned to not being a jazz tune or concerto, or any other work of art—whatever else about my condition I may be unresigned to.

[18] 'Presentational objects and their interpretation' in *Philosophy and the Arts*, ed. G. N. A. Vesey (London, 1973), pp. 147–64. In this article I criticised Professor Wollheim for advocating such licentiousness. However, he has told me that I misunderstood him. He never advocated what I call licentious liberty. Those psychoanalytic examples, for instance, pointed to meanings that were present and active all along both for Shakespeare and his audience. Only the conceptual means of articulating them was lacking.

But Righter, it would seem, means rather more. We hear near the start of his paper of that 'aspect of all men's relation with their environment'—something, I suppose, rationally recognisable. But what we arrive at before the end is rather different, something 'pure, naked and unassimilable'; and the force of the phrase in the whole sentence is something I do not perfectly follow. But I think that this unassimilable something is meant to defy reason itself. Now I grant that the world we live in is a messy one; and that rationalists' overenthusiastic attempts to tidy it up, inevitably falsifying it in the process, can produce a legitimate reaction. That reaction as we find it in *War and Peace* is intelligible enough, and impressive, too; if possibly a bit overdone. But what is one to make of 'unassimilable'? Clearly, no verbal utterance, logical, literary or what you will, can literally assimilate its object; and no one, I hope, supposes otherwise. We can describe, of course, partially describe, leaving open alternative descriptions. They reflect different interests and points of view. What (though perhaps unjustly) I suspect Righter of, is the wish for a realised paradox; a verbal statement that remains a verbal statement, yet *is* also the thing that it states. That would be an unhappily 'metaphysical' extension of the familiar truth that good imaginative writing brings its objects impressively home to us.

14

Disgust and Other Forms of Aversion

To the pure intellect all things are pure. I shall not ask whether disgust is itself a disgusting topic to any wholesome mind; as in poetry sometimes love is hailed as a lovely thing or hate is called hateful. Approaching it in that spirit of theory, with more chaste, more clinical ideals; looking closer and using our eyes and if necessary holding our noses, we may at least find it a perplexing one. But if the thing itself is perplexing, still more so is its general neglect—common even to thinkers credited with the coolest scrutiny of objects that others prefer to overlook. In the *oeuvre* of Freud, who writes at length of infantile sexuality, incest, aggression and so forth, I recall only brief and no very searching discussion of disgust. Nor does the notoriously tough-minded Hobbes find a place for it, though he undertakes a systematic setting-forth of 'the interior beginnings of voluntary motions, commonly called the passions'.[1] His account none the less makes a convenient starting point. Hobbes, the unacknowledged parent of all our behavioural and experimental psychology, based his work on the following dichotomy:

> Endeavour, when it is towards something which causes it, is called appetite or desire; the latter, being the general name; the other often-times restrained to signify desire of food, namely hunger and thirst. And when endeavour is fromward something, it is generally called aversion. These words *appetite* and *aversion* we have from the Latins; and they both of them signify motions, one of approaching, the other of retiring.[2]

With one stroke of the pen, with a single distinction, to reduce to order the whole heterogeneous mob of human attitudes—that surely required a touch of genius. Yet some of its consequences look strange. Love and hatred, or at least aggressive hatred, will fall together on one side of the boundary, and fear and disgust on the other. We retreat both from things that frighten and that disgust us; but anger, like love, seeks its object, though each seeks it with different ends in view. 'The lover's

[1] *Leviathan*, ch. 6.
[2] Ibid.

nip and the grip of the torturer's tongs are all . . .' I quote Auden, 'variants of one common type.'[3] Both of them, unlike disgust, are naturally called 'hot', or if you like, both are passions. And in fact it was natural enough in a way that in drawing up a list of the passions Hobbes found no place for disgust. But it can hardly be proper to find no place for it in psychology at all.

Change the phrase, speak, not of 'disgust' but of 'hot indignation'; it strikes the ear naturally enough. In fact one way of handling disgust, itself an unmanageable feeling, is precisely to turn it to anger; thus transformed it can also be got rid of. But the feeling itself is what I just called it, unmanageable; it is paralytic. With disgusting things, what can one do? All we want, or would want, were it possible, is not to have known of their existence; whereas anger, by contrast, has outlets. It involves motion towards, not away from; seeks its objects, and seeks to destroy them. Among the ancient Germans, according to Tacitus, the following distinction was maintained; they hanged traitors and renegades on trees but cowards and infamous persons were put to death by suffocation in slime: 'The idea being', he helpfully adds, 'that crimes be made a visible example of, but abominations be buried from sight.'[4] Surely, too, there was some savage satisfaction in it; otherwise, I think, the ritual must have failed. Thought is not something physically buriable but remains, pervading the atmosphere; it also seeps through the thickest material paste. Before Oscar Wilde or—to hark back some eighteen years—Stephen Ward could be finally buried from sight disgust had first to be changed to anger. That anger could issue in action, and so at last disgust was got rid of.

Disgust, too, can be made to subserve anger, can be used, as it were, in its interest. And some writers, for instance, positively exhibit disgust, thrust disgusting things under our noses; which is plainly a partly aggressive performance. But of course that possibility would give us no better reason than the possible metamorphosis I spoke of, that changes disgust into anger, for confusing or identifying the two things.

Nor does fear—not at least at first sight—seem to throw much more light on it, although this much is true: fear resembles disgust, and differs from hatred, aggressive hatred, in expressing itself in avoidance, not advance. But the roots of that difference are hardly obscure; fear and hatred are evidently cognate. Their natural objects are things that cause one pain. Certainly there remain broad differences; I hate things, typically, for harm they have done me, I fear what they threaten to do. But the difference that concerns us at present, between movements towards objects and away from them, rests normally on

---

[3] Cf. Auden, *The Sea and the Mirror*, in *For the Time Being* (London, 1945), p. 45.
[4] *Germania* 12.

nothing more recondite than my relative estimate of their size and strength and my own. What I avoid, generally speaking, are hurtful things that look bigger than me; though a sort of desperate fear exists, too; fear heroically transformed, or madly transformed, that goes forward regardless of consequences. But, it seems, neither our eminently rational avoidance of things likely to harm us, nor the attempt, where they look destructible, to destroy them, will serve greatly to illuminate disgust. Disgusting things, apart from this mere fact of their disgustingness, would often appear to be wholly harmless.

A further difference: before leaving this part of the subject, let us notice that fear, and even hatred, are not thought incompatible with respect. 'Let them hate me so long as they fear me,' is a saying ascribed to a tyrant, and as such intelligible. Disgust is, I suppose, of all feelings the one we would least wish to arouse. One might add its connection with dirt—not that the latter notion is much more perspicuous. I mean not only that dirt itself, but that the concept is murky, too. Yet anger, one is tempted to say, is a clean feeling. Disgust, being, so to speak, contagious, contaminates its subject as well. I suggested that the condition of feeling disgust always brings with it a certain helplessness; but, as I say, far more desperate is that of inspiring it. You can often, being frightened, hope to find safety elsewhere; being angry, you can face danger and fight. Even pain touches pity at times and hence need not be hidden from view; you can show it to other people in hope of help. But disgusting things are what they move away from; or at least, being decent, avert their gaze.

Pain, fear and anger, it seems the feelings and appropriate behaviour—whatever further points remain obscure—form a set that is intelligibly related. Disgust is different and seems to stand apart. Let us note one other feeling, however. What we call horror is nearer to it, a much more promising springboard, I think, for our present project; while 'abhorrence', its verbal cognate, is often almost a synonym for 'disgust'. Further, horror is helpless, like disgust; being horrified, there is nothing one can do. Milton, in Book ix of *Paradise Lost*, describes how, on hearing Eve's story, when she returns bringing apples, eager and gay,

> Astonish'd stood and blank, while horror chill,
> Ran through his limbs, and all his joints relax'd;
> From his slack hand the garland wreath'd for Eve
> Down dropp'd, and all the faded roses shed.

Let possible action once suggest itself, action with appropriate calculations and tensing, with attentiveness and resolve: mere horror has given place to something else. Freaks and monsters are disgusting and abhorrent, goats with human heads as portrayed by Piero di Cosimo, pigs with six legs, and the like. Yet it is true that tragedy that involves no disgust, outrageous things, the brutalities of chance that seem to violate natural teleology, may also appropriately, or at least normally, horrify us. (As to abhorrent-disgusting things, one might, as it were, drown disgust in anger, in the way I spoke of earlier; and thus relieve it in violence, in destroying and possibly dismembering them. But it falls short of what one would call a clean fight; even a born fighter, I think, would choose for preference a different sort of opponent.)

To return to our problem: attitudes and the like prima facie can be characterised in two different ways, both behaviourally, in terms of the actions they issue in, and also in terms of their objects; and further, of course, the two things must be intelligibly related. I have mentioned the proper objects of hate and fear; broadly speaking they are things that cause pain—appropriately dealt with, either by aggressive action rendering them harmless or alternatively by putting oneself out of reach. (Vengeance may raise further problems, but those I must leave undiscussed.) My own present problem is simply this, to name the proper objects of disgust; (I mean 'object' grammatically, of course, as a predicate clause, not necessarily mentioning a real thing.)[5] But we need objects in this sense, that serve not only to make intelligible the occurrence of such a feeling but also the action, or inactivity, in which it issues. Sartre, who might well claim the title of grand master of the theme, holds semi-liquid and viscous things to be generally disgusting; which he sees as threatening us with loss of self-identity. They tend to be disgusting, he might more truly have said. I find no evidence, to take his own example, that honey, anyway honey in its right place, on bread and butter or in a jar, is normally viewed with disgust. Surprisingly, he says nothing of odours, that might in fact have suited his book rather well. More promising candidates, perhaps, are inedible or at least distasteful things—as, indeed, etymology suggests. But there are things of others sorts to be fitted in, too. We must also find a place, logical accommodation, for monsters and freaks and for cosmic or existential disgust, typified, perhaps, by Sartre himself; for the notoriously easy transformation—though perhaps less familiar in our permissive society—of erotic desire to disgust, especially, as Shakespeare says, of lust on obtaining its object; and lastly for the fact that the actual taste of things that are eminently disgusting, for instance of creatures like slugs—their taste itself, anything else left out of view—may, for all one knows, be quite agreeable. It is because they

[5] See G. E. M. Anscombe, 'The intentionality of sensation: a grammatical feature', in R. J. Butler (ed.), *Analytical Philosophy, Second Series*, Oxford, 1965.

are disgusting that they are thought distasteful, not conversely.

In default of a general characterisation, one might resort to drawing up an inventory or list. But, like other feelings, disgust is partly educable; different people find different things disgusting, the individual's taste often reflecting that of the group. Nearly all men would perhaps be disgusted by things that carnivorous animals do instinctively, by eating living prey, for example, or only killing it in the process itself. Some vegetarians going further express a doubtless quite genuine disgust at the mere thought of meat-eating. Any list, we may be told, will be arbitrary. Yet modes of feelings only admit of social training, which means modification, in so far as they arise spontaneously in the first place; and in any case there is no need to look for a kind of object that never disgusts or never fails to disgust us. It will suffice to find tendencies; to find the process of training will sometimes be easier, sometimes harder. Sartre calls all sticky things disgusting; and of honey spread on one's face, hands or shirtfront, it seems plausible to say so. But imagine a different sort of object, for instance, a neat silver box, approximately the size of a lump of sugar; it would, I believe, need a pretty intensive course of training to make one vomit or turn sick at the mere sight of it.

To descend, then, to particulars—assuming the enterprise to be a feasible one. It would seem that slugs, lice and the like are naturally disgusting to most people; so is excrement and dirt generally—whatever we mean by 'dirt'; and, not uncommonly at least, sexual intercourse in unorthodox forms—here, however, with much cultural variation. And indeed even the orthodox act would appear secretly, sometimes overtly, to disgust a sizeable sect. Certain smells, perhaps connected with tastes; monsters, deformities and mutilation; entrails, especially human entrails; vegetable and still more animal decay, are commonly regarded with disgust. The most disgusting sight I can myself recall was a bin full of rotten apples turned wholesale to maggots; a yellow sea that rose and fell heaving, like Macbeth's, multitudinously (there were multitudes of maggots), and gave evidence of astonishing vitality.

At least we have before us a pretty collection of specimens, though on the face of it a pretty various collection too. Before I renew the attack and attempt some generalisation, I wish first to return to my starting point; which was Hobbes's dichotomy of human attitudes. After all, I believe, Hobbes was right; pursuit and avoidance are fundamental, and their first correlates are pleasure and pain. Disgust, and the avoidance of disgusting things, as opposed to the avoidance of pain, is more complex and calls for special explanation. Disgust is a form of aversion; aversion itself being, in the appropriate sense, prior to it. In default of some general correlation between inner experience and behaviour; between what we like and what we seek, what we dislike and seek to avoid; these concepts would lose their application. The point is familiar, after all. To tell me of a species of being the whole course of whose behaviour runs opposite to ours; who normally, not only in special cases, seeks for and clings to whatever hurts it, and shuns everything it expects to enjoy; is to give me a description I cannot use. Allow, as is normally allowed, that our chief test of liking and aversion can only be found on behaviour which even overrides verbal testimony. Now, for argument's sake, let us speak of a man who in fact enjoys being flayed or burnt alive; and detests food and wine, sex and friendship. Suppose, further, that he himself testifies to these odd preferences; yet so long as his behaviour remains normal, so long as he systematically seeks and avoids the same sorts of objects as other people, clearly his mere words will carry little weight.

If disgust were a simple sensation and produced in some sense-organ, say, our tongue or our skin, by contact with things of a particular sort, it would raise no special problem—though we might further find that we in fact liked or disliked the things in question. But disgust is already dislike, a form of dislike; in Hobbes's phrase, of aversion. That is something essential to its nature. One might argue, on roughly Wittgensteinian lines, that outward criteria must be found at least to make public sense of the notion, to give it a place in a public language.[6] Minimally at all events we want some intelligible connection between feeling and the behaviour that expresses it.

I suggested that the first object of aversion, its basic object and simple, in a sense, is merely pain; but disgust is derivative and needs accounting for. We need, I said, a general account; let me now confess that—perhaps unsurprisingly—I have no one simply unified account to offer. At best I find a number of fairly closely connected generalisations rather more like a structure of analogies. Disgust first, broadly speaking, is of two sorts, either physical or mental; and other differences follow accordingly. The former is connected with food; but not simply with inedible things, let us note, where the latter are also unappetising. Wood and paper arouse no disgust though neither of them is appetising or edible (in fact pencils and bus tickets are often chewed). To eat anything is to incorporate it with myself, to make it a part of my own body; but, at an imaginative level, the two notions run together. Objects of physical disgust, then, are things either actually or prospectively part of myself; where further, that prospect or accomplished fact—I repeat the crucial term, which I shall need to say more of—is

[6] L. Wittgenstein, *Philosophical Investigations,* tr. G. E. M. Anscombe et al., Oxford, 1953, part i, s. 580.

also horrifying. They are things at first sought, it seems, but simultaneously, for whatever reason, we find them hateful or fearful in the event. In other words, disgust involves ambivalence, or something, so to speak, beyond ambivalence: beyond ambivalence is the effort or desire to extrude what is already half part of me. At which point we find the only positive action closely connected with disgust; that of retching or vomiting. As to mental disgust, so far as any practical posture accompanies it, any general way of dealing with objects, it would seem to be merely this negative one; let me call it the posture of dissociation, which announces their unconnectedness with me.

But that announcement, I shall argue, is always false; for otherwise they would never disgust me. Disgusting things, in order to be physically disgusting, must either be also seen as simultaneously appetising, desirable, or worse still, already be part of me. Much the same holds of mental disgust; here, too, there stirs some sort of desire or anyway interest. Curiosity stirs at least; curiosity being (as Hobbes also observes) the appetite of the mind—whose reward, he says, 'exceedeth the short vehemence of any carnal pleasure'—and bringing with it further specific desires, for instance, to investigate its objects, probe, get closer to or handle them. Or alternatively I find in disgusting things some bond that identifies them with myself. This desire, then, like hateful stuff mistakenly consumed, is something I wish to be rid of. Yet in striking it I also strike myself. Self-disgust perhaps is partly involved in all disgust; which if so, alone would be sufficient to puzzle the will. (Shame, too, is another related feeling and often not far from self-disgust; it differs in the absence of appetite; which may be present but is obviously not an essential part of it. Yet think of a horror of shame combined with appetite; that would perhaps amount to self-disgust.) Certainly this latter term, we keep returning to, horror, still requires more explicit attention; but one thing that is certainly horrifying is oneself or one's own body seen as hateful. Again, other creatures, different but like me, or, say, the sight of human bodies mutilated or deformed, arouse horror—amidst a mixture of feelings, pity, curiosity and fear. Roughly, the upshot is this, then; their mutual inhibition is disgust.

That deformity is fearful to us, the sight of it apt to be horrifying, is perhaps unsurprising. So far, however, we have looked only at one type among all the variety of disgusting things. My first rough general account, if it is right, requires the co-presence of two factors; on the one hand they are desirable or interesting, exciting us in various ways, yet somehow fearful or horrifying too. Now slugs, excrement, dirt generally and sexual perverts, threaten us with no obvious harm; their harmfulness, to people whom they disgust, consists precisely in this fact of their disgusting them. Say that dirt, or at least—given our thesis—interesting dirt, is normally seen as disgusting; what in any case remains to be explained is the basis of our antipathy to dirt. For the connection between health and rules of hygiene must surely be a relatively late and sophisticated discovery.

But happily this part of the problem has not escaped attention; there is other work to draw on. Mary Douglas, in her study of pollution among African tribes, quotes a happy definition of dirt, ascribed to Lord Chesterfield, as 'matter out of place'.[7] That indeed belongs to her earlier views—views that since have been radically modified. But that is a point I shall return to. She was struck then by certain ritual prohibitions in the Old Testament forbidding the use of certain food-stuffs—apparently of living things hard to classify. That linked with other objects of interest for her; her interest in things to be avoided, things that pollute. It was, broadly speaking, in those misfits that, so to speak, violate our scheme of things; that general classificatory scheme into which, half-consciously or unconsciously, we seek to fit every new thing we meet. The same description applies admirably to cross-breeds, freaks, monsters and the like.

These things appear as anomalies; whatever scheme we bring to materials we meet with recalcitrant specimens that break down any boundaries we had relied on. But attitudes to anomalies vary widely; they vary from culture to culture—and even indeed within our own. A multitude of factors, themselves variable, determine the way in which we see them. But it was the anthropological evidence, naturally enough, that chiefly impressed Douglas; the anomalous, specifically anomalous animals, appear sometimes as abominable or sometimes as sacred; sometimes again they form a focus of a complex of ambivalent attitudes. What is striking, however, is this, that they always seem to matter, to fix attention. It would be outside my present concern, to say nothing of competence, to pursue Douglas's account—itself a general anthropological theory, despite her professed hostility to generalising—of the basis of these variations. Nor shall I pursue the epistemological views, though I confess to being far from happy with them, that she connects it with. As to disgust, I recognised variations here, too; it would suffice, I suggested, to find tendencies. Besides, need one be an anthropologist to say this?—that merely to think is to classify; not solely to classify no doubt, yet essentially; and that all action, all manipulation of objects or movement among them, pre-supposes and relies on the same process—the most basic of cognitive processes.

[7] Mary Douglas, *Implicit Meanings* (London, 1975), p. 50.

But for the variousness of the objects of disgust: suppose in other cultures they proved different again, then of course empirical inquiry might throw light on these putative differences—given only some initial theory to work with. Even within our own culture, our reactions to anomalous things, are, I said, strikingly various. Where we feel safe they may intrigue us, while elsewhere they might worry or alarm us. Again, where we ourselves not only feel safe—enough so at least to look tolerably coolly at things that might otherwise discomfort us—but where, secondly, anomaly in one way combines in another with startingly congruence, we react not with fear but with laughter. Yet potentially, I suspect, fear or something like it remains active; our laughter negotiates fear.

I am not speaking here of explicitly rational views; rather of certain rooted tendencies that grow in us as part of rationality. There are, to repeat, certain presumptions or demands that the anomalies I spoke of offend against; specifically, they violate a classificatory scheme. Now in the abstract certainly that indictment may not sound a very grave one; the offence we accuse them of, it might seem, is nothing outrageously offensive. But look closer, make it concrete, and the impression we get begins to change. We move among objects, I said; we live and move safely among them by this and this only, that in general we know what to expect of them; we go forward feeling the ground underfoot and take hold of predictably solid things. Overall we know what to expect, dealing confidently according to its nature either with solid earth, slippery water or impalable air. Now if in general, as I have suggested, all odd things disturb or at least tend to disturb us, yet nothing is more radically disturbing than basic categories that get out of hand—not merely in the clinical, controlled space of a seminar where we toss to and fro in the late Gilbert Ryle's surrealist 'absurdities', examples like 'Saturday equals the square root of five'; but in things moving about or beneath us in the world. Nothing is more fearfully disturbing than experiences that seem to call in doubt the whole scheme of known distinctions by which we live.

Yet disturbance—if 'disturbance' is the word for it—even horror, dismay or the like, are still not identical with disgust. One thing is still lacking, it seems; but I have already spoken of it. What is lacking is some element of self-identification, some active appetite or interest, or the like, that makes the horrifying thing also a part of me. Last, for we can now be explicit, horror is indeed a form of fear. It is fear in face of things before which I am helpless, moreover radically helpless. How to think of them, not only how to handle them practically, baffles me, leaving me at a loss. And the same holds in less extreme form of unlooked-for and cruel disasters, where natural events approximate to what we tend to think of and describe as unnatural.

Yet the potential roots of horror are very various, and different fears may reinforce the same effect. Sticky things, despite Sartre, need not be disgusting; but disgusting things, being also sticky, are yet more so. Things, conversely, that are hard, solid and compact, which, significantly, we describe as 'clean-edged', lend themselves least readily to these attitudes, are least apt to give rise to disgust. Imagine a hostile critic of modern architecture or, more specifically, of Mies van der Rohe: he might, I think, not wholly implausibly condemn the Seagram building as 'chilly' or 'inhuman', but hardly as 'revolting' or 'disgusting'—adjectives freely thrown by contemporaries at Whistler and the impressionists. (Mumford, with his eye on the Modern Movement, generally calls the interior of the Grosvenor Square American Embassy 'hospital cold'.) The root feeling, I suggest, is still fear; stickiness aggravates it, however.

Stickiness or mess of any sort in objects we no longer wholly love or even no longer feel sure of loving always are viewed with a certain alarm. Distinctively, they cling. True, one may love things that one loves to cling close to one, and promise to stay with one for ever; yet, as we know all too well, even our own feelings are not incapable of changing. At least we shall need to feel tolerably sure. And short of that total commitment, things that we can definitely handle, can pick up as we please and put down again, are safer, and likelier to be acceptable. Otherwise, with adhesive, clinging things, the mere speculation that one might some time cease to like them, even come to feel positive antipathy to them, may shift and quite unsettle the balance of feeling.

Glutinousness, in fact, raises twofold uncertainties; only touch it and it may permanently adhere—without being permanently agreeable. But worse, its very limits are uncertain; if I do in fact succeed in clearing myself of it, it is still hard to be confident, to give myself a clear certificate and go free. To that extent Sartre may be right that they threaten us with loss of self-identity; but that fear does not act in isolation.

As to objects of horrified curiosity, they might in a way be called messy; they defy or mess up existing categories. But they surely need not, as Sartre would have them, be sticky or viscous. A possible answer would be that mere abnormalities and enormities are less disgusting than disturbing; at worst they are dismaying or horrifying. But generally they are interesting too, and interesting precisely because they are anomalous; we stare at them curiously and palely, and thus they become objects of disgust as well. The same general pattern reappears. We find that horror, a form of fear, to repeat—fear, more specifically, of what we can neither fly from nor fight—mated with desire, begets disgust. But in all this what initially disturbs us is most often merely the jumbling of kinds; many cultures give forcible evidence of being disgusted by sexual intercourse between people of the same sex or using organs otherwise than for their biological functions; those most disgusted, one can hardly help but suspect—glib as it may sound—combining with their dismay at the anomalous, some livelier element of interest or even desire. But, no doubt, in this common reaction other factors also enter.

I have spoken of fear of anomalies, of stickiness—itself, neither solid nor liquid, a kind of anomaly—and of different sorts of interest and curiosity, identification and desire. Different factors combine in different ways; much disgust must be overdetermined further, predictably enough, they reinforce each other. Why are slugs, to take our previous example, so eminently disgusting? There is no single answer, of course. Partly, no doubt, by reason of their association with sewers and dirt, that is to say, with other independently disgusting things; again, they are not only jelloid, but also are slimy and alive. As such they are curious and interest and further, in view of their size, in a certain sense obviously edible. (Hedgehogs, I am told, feed on slugs.) I own that for myself I should not wish to eat dead slugs either, least of all if I thought that they came from the sort of place in which slugs are most often found. But the force of association is strong, and ordinary meat served at table is sometimes repellant rather than appetising if its form too strongly suggests the living animal. Let some sea creature in other ways like a slug, be dug out of its shell and nicely served it might even, I think, be viewed with relish.

Jelly is a popular food; it melts in the mouth, people say. But that jelloid yet animate body, with its slime and indeterminate whitish colour, its peculiar mode of locomotion, alternating contraction and distention, that further reinforces our strange sense of its inward homogeneity and shapelessness—all these have part in the strong effect. A bright yellow slug, for example, would be at least one degree less disgusting, yellow being a colour that stands out; while pallor is connected with sickness. But what, perhaps, we are chiefly disturbed by is the strangeness of that glutinous semi-substance, not solid nor liquid, not properly insect or animal, lacking distinct parts and articulate members, lacking even boundaries one can be sure of, and always leaving behind it a slimy trace; yet somehow, in spite of all this, a unitary organism and alive. Different factors contribute, as I said; on the one hand edibility and curiosity, on the other, not only stickiness but monstrosity of various sorts. Disgust is no ultimate datum of experience, like the sweet taste of sugar, for instance; it is a complex phenomenon requiring to be made intelligible.

A further large topic I shall briefly touch on is what I called cosmic disgust; an attitude recurrently to be found in Jacobean drama but still more typically in the literature of our contemporaries. It largely arises, I suggest, from a violent reaction, like sickness, against a world one has loved; a world, exciting equally to mind and sense, of things to touch, taste and get close to; yet further, for thinkers of certain periods, the world of their predecessors' hopes; which seemed to promise—say, to Leonardo or even Leibniz—a perfect and beautiful order to satisfy the intellect as well; but which often, on better acquaintance turns out to be infinitely cruel, largely joyless and, humanly speaking, arbitrary or blind. For the rest, lack of space compels me to leave unconsidered sexual disgust, and disgust with the body in general; a strange, interesting phenomenon prominent in European thought from Plato onwards and visible enough in Sartre himself.[8]

One further main point remains, and one main objection to be made. For of course frightening or partly frightening things, where they are thrilling too, can sometimes be more thrilling than frightening; I mean things we approach with excitement, virgin-like, on the edge of an irrevocable step. Hesitation still presumably expresses fear. Yet happily fear—though it is said that 'perfect love casteth out fear'—the mere presence of fear in some measure, need not taint desire or turn it to disgust. I must shortly return to the issue. Let me first briefly review the main argument.

It was indeed with fear that I started; but that as it stood looked unpromising. I turned to one form of it, horror. Horror seemed nearer the mark. But it in turn stood in need of analysis. Things both fearful and deeply disturbing are, broadly speaking, what horrify us; objects of obscure implications, only certainly far-reaching and bad; objects such that in face of them no help appears possible, and no possible view or way of handling of them safe. In a sense, to enlarge on the point, digressing for a moment, I, too, the agent, am implicated in the presence of horror. For I cannot easily separate myself from all that objects of this sort call in doubt; from such ways of thinking and proceeding, that arise in me more like instincts than acts of intellect; from which my whole outlook takes its shape. The point may be pursued further still. To find myself implicated here, in things that I hate and am afraid of, and so implicated that I scarcely dare trust myself—dare no longer trust my own thoughts or feelings or spontaneous promptings to action—is of all discoveries the most disabling, and hence horrifying.

[8] But cf. Mary Douglas on 'external boundaries' in *Purity and Danger* (London, 1966), and Yeats's observation that

> love has pitched his mansion
> in the place of excrement.

The ground, I may say, shifts beneath me; not only that. My very centre shifts—I myself, my focus of vision, being withdrawn, as it were, from itself. As to past acts, wrong or foolish acts, I may be ashamed of them, and resolve to act differently in future. I feel horror on discovering in myself hateful things whose presence I never dreamt of, that leave my own will and deliberate purpose irrelevant or null. It is a horrifying thing, too, to be confronted with the worthlessness or non-existence of things one has reverenced or clung to, or something one has loved.

Now here we might seek nuances of usage, grasping at vapours. I shall not pursue them or ask at what point a feeling such as this, roughly horror at oneself, becomes self-disgust, or whether one can rigorously distinguish between them. Evidently the two are pretty close; it seems that horror such as I have described hardly differs from disgust in what one might call its more abstract or mental forms. And any physical admixture, any stirring of appetite or desire leaves it in no doubt; it suffices to make the latter feeling explicit.

Horror has such roots as we have seen. And horrified desire is disgust, or horrified self-identification with strange or anomalous things. But even now more needs to be added. Recall the objection I spoke of. The situation might be entirely as I have described it except in one respect only, but that a crucial one: the balance of feelings remains pleasurable, which would turn my whole account of it inside out. We need only recall another feeling, one of which I have said nothing so far, the feeling we call 'fascination'.

Horror and fascination may have common features; both express themselves in fixity, in mere gazing, and doubtless they readily combine. 'Horrible fascination' is a frequent phrase; and here it, too, becomes part of disgust. But plainly the two things are also separable. Fascination, where horror is absent, may be all pleasure and purely exciting. Even uncertainty points either way. The half-fear of indefinite possibilities, that partly frighten us without our understanding them, where none the less hope still predominates over fear; where those dim expectations, disturbing us (as Wordsworth says) disturb us with joy; is the feeling of exaltation and wonder. Conversely, all that becomes failure, a breakdown of orientation. Now where panic is in question, I suppose, no sensible person will look for patterns of action belonging to it, or think of their absence as puzzling.

Appendices

I. The Social Vocation of Art

For an old bitch gone in the teeth,
For a botched civilisation.

Charm, smiling at the good mouth,
Quick eyes gone under earth's lid.

For two gross of broken statues,
For a few thousand battered books.

POUND

Clive Barker asks in *Views* (Spring 1964, p. 43 b), for 'a tough appraisal of the place of the arts in our society'. That would be a sizeable undertaking; I do not mean to attempt it here. But it will do no harm to recall, if not re-appraise, a few basic and rather obvious questions—not, I hope, to be tough for toughness' sake, but because there is something to be said for giving the Devil's Advocate an occasional hearing. It is good advice, almost platitudinously—but I do not mean advice often followed—to scrutinise with special impartial thoroughness those opinions that all our instincts prompt us to reject.

I assume that we care about the arts and instinctively feel that they matter. The trouble is to justify the feeling—to ourselves or to others. For not everyone cares. And such questions are notoriously embarrassing, like the question St Augustine put himself, 'What is time?' ('When I do not ask myself, I know.') Or again, if the justification of the arts presents difficulties, what about science?—for science presumably matters too. Science, it is easy to answer, is practical and useful, it yields results; its theories, systematic theories, are verified by experience. Now it is doubtful whether most scientists chiefly value science for its usefulness; but that apart—seeing we were speaking of embarrassing questions—it would be possible to ask why one should accept what is systematic and verified by observation rather, say, than alchemy and astrology. 'Oh, well it's obvious; you just should.'

Doubtless. And art just matters. But the embarrassment is not wholly dispelled.

Other things serve to heighten it; it is, I think, felt especially acutely by those who care deeply, not only about the arts, but also about the state of society. One curiously obstinate bent of human nature is to treat two different things both of which deeply concern us—perhaps rightly, though for quite different reasons—as therefore related in themselves. A man stands at the crossroads, at the crisis of his fate, weighing his choice, and at that moment, perhaps, a storm breaks with bursts of thunder: I think the most sophisticated and rationalistic of us would still half-feel it as a comment on his case. But, further, the question is most troublesome of all to those whose instincts or training, while they care about art, make them despise the luxury goods cf bourgeois society. For unless art can be shown to be 'socially relevant' to what other division of things can its produce belong?

We spoke of science, and it might seem strange that these same advocates, the socially committed, never seem to raise similar questions about the value of pure science or of pure mathematics, luxury goods too; or to demand 'a tough appraisal' of their place in our society. Neither does the good taxpayer, who so largely supports these activities, and in all probability never dreams that for most scientists and mathematicians they are, what art has more often been thought to be, simply beautiful and wonderful things to be valued for themselves. All the same we can silence the taxpayer, if he should sometimes think of asking questions: for (we shall explain) you can never know in advance whether a calculus developed for its own sake may not turn out to be applicable and useful; we may even use it in making bombs or electronic brains. So pure mathematics is safe, but what of pure art? And, apart from the taxpayer—there may be some other formula to silence him in this region too—what of the restless social conscience?

People notoriously talk more nonsense about art than about almost anything else. Not for nothing, of course; bad proofs of the existence of God play a similar role. One whose conscience needs quieting will buy almost anything. In the same issue of *Views* Arnold Wesker, answering questions put to him, talks plenty of sense, so it seems to me; but he prefaces his answer by a sort of declaration of faith which I am less happy with. (Artists and dramatists are generally better on particular concrete questions than on 'The Nature of Art'.) Wesker writes (p. 45 a) 'I believe that art is the key to man's understanding of man, and therefore that until it plays a dominant part in his existence he will continue to be unaware of the nature of that existence and in this way a prey to all kinds of exploitation, i.e., gullible.' Though he introduces that as his 'view of art', Wesker, perhaps, hardly writes as a theorist, and to come down on it heavily might seem inept; we all need an occasional rhetorical gesture—'man's understanding of man' for instance—to keep us going. Still, clarity and self-knowledge are always values, and the gesture is significant, I think, because it seems designed to allay a certain sort of anxiety—'exploitation', somewhat unexpectedly, comes in too. And the anxiety is not peculiarly his.

Suppose, then, we take him literally, naïvely if necessary, and see what follows. A modern Londoner or New Yorker, being 'unaware of the nature of his existence'—his social existence, I suppose—may search for a key to understanding. Imagine the following: I meet a friend, let him be a New Yorker, who tells me with excitement that he has found some sort of key. Now he had intended, as I happen to know, to do two different things today, to read a book he had not read before, Riesman's *The Lonely Crowd*, and to stop and look at the Seagram Building in Park Avenue. The former is, by common consent, a notable piece of sociology, the latter a great work of art. But which of the two can have given him what he spoke of; his new awareness of his society and himself? I am assuming an ordinary speaker who uses words like 'awareness' and 'understanding' in their ordinary sense: so it won't be hard to guess. You may say perhaps that the business of art is to deepen our understanding—as the deity is said to have human attributes—*in sensu eminentiore*; and we need not quarrel with extended, even paradoxical uses of words. One would, however, like them explained. Or perhaps it is unfair to take an example from architecture; Wesker probably had his eye on the theatre—or the theatre, the cinema and literary art generally—a context in which this sort of talk is not, at least, patently absurd. Now it seems to me unwise to generalise about art while ignoring half the data; but let us by all means take a literary example.

I suppose the books we care about can belong to the fourteenth century, for instance, as well as the twentieth: let us take Chaucer. . . . Surely, an advocate of the 'socialist' view (so to call it, with apologies to the many socialists who would sensibly reject it) may say there is much social insight in Chaucer, much understanding to be got from him. Yes, certainly—chiefly of fourteenth-century England. (As to individual psychology, if we are to be honest, Freud and the modern novel have outdistanced him by miles.) Social history is a fascinating study, at least to those who care about the past; but that is not my chief reason for reading Chaucer. I read him, rather unoriginally perhaps, for his poetry. Besides Wesker was speaking of ourselves. Satire on the worldliness and corruption of the monastic orders in the reign of Richard II does not seem the shortest cut to understanding how I am 'prey to all kinds of exploitation'.

I said I should have to be naïve; but it is excusable to insist that grass is green where influential people—deservedly influential—keep telling us in earnest voices that it is deep scarlet. Some small part of what has traditionally been called art can be partly justified in terms of its social relevance; the bulk of it cannot. One might, of course, bluntly conclude that the bulk of 'what has traditionally been called art' is worthless and ought to be scrapped; but that conclusion is in fact rarely drawn. It is perhaps worth asking why not. Partly, I suspect, because the advocates of social relevance do really, in spite of themselves, care about art; partly from intellectual confusion. It might seem at first glance eminently natural to equate the conditions under which art is produced with—something really different—those in which it is generally appreciated. Now the fact is, to repeat, that they are different; one need only look. As to creation, we can agree that works of art generally reflect a good deal of the society that produced them; the Seagram Building is plainly the product of one sort of society and Salisbury Cathedral, for instance, and again the Louvre, of others. So each work in some sense—a pretty obscure one at present—reflects or embodies different 'values'. We can admire them without belonging to the society or sharing its values. (The artist or architect could not have produced them without belonging to it.) Or, if you like, we share them in a very general way, but they have little relevance for us—except so far as fine discipline and purity of purpose (say, the Seagram Building), fervent spiritual aspiration (Salisbury) or high poise and conscious courtly pride (Perrault's facade of the Louvre) are always relevant. The Louvre, grand as it is, matters least—to me anyway—of these three; I suppose because it embodies values less sympathetic to me—though one should add that each of these three masterpieces is purely formally a masterpiece too. And this dishing-out of appropriate adjectives may be a bit crude; but it will serve. For even allowing that the society which it is relevant for me to understand is not my own, but the aristocratic, courtly society of Louis XIV, it is one thing to say that works of art bear the mark of the age that produced them, quite another to claim them as the key to understanding it. Trivially, of course, you must understand something of its art to understand the values of an aristocratic culture, one of the things it set a value on being art itself. For the rest, perhaps, you might do pretty well without ever looking at the Louvre—without seeking that strange and unique thing, their quasi sensible expression in art. 'But,' you say, 'such understanding would be merely intellectual; it requires to be deepened and made concrete.' By looking at the Louvre? I think a better course would be to look more closely at the life of the society itself.

Confine yourself to literature, and Wesker's formula is plausible enough; it is so because of the part-truth contained in it. Art yields awareness, he writes, understanding of man. Surely it does, literature especially: insight into people and issues—war and what it does to men, the machinery of powers and politics and so forth, heightened awareness of individual things, we should add, rather than new knowledge of general truths; but certainly one must acknowledge all the rest. So what's the fuss about, I may be asked; have I said anything Wesker need deny?

Well, I have attributed to him (wrongly I hope, but there seem to be signs) a certain sort of anxiety; in fact the converse of the old petty bourgeois or Victorian anxiety, the anxiety to make art respectable—with all those chaste nudes and academies. The new problem is to make it respectable, or acceptable at least, to the politically committed and the Left; to find for it a social role, give convincing statement of function, so that the broken statues in museums and battered books aren't just connoisseurs' luxury goods after all. Unless some such anxiety exists, why this talk of gullibility and exploitation which art, 'the key to man's understanding of man', is to help save us from? But if it exists you cannot hope to treat it, save superficially, by pointing to one special aspect of one branch of art, roughly literature: which hope grows still fainter as we find, even here, that what we have got hold of is not a social role for art in our own society, but insight, largely historical insight into a very different one. We noticed, incidentally, that pure mathematics has no obvious social role either, except to be appreciated for what it is; which does not mean that it has no value or significance.

We see, however, that some forms of art do sometimes play such a role; and that, though it is not what makes them art, is important too. It also further complicates the issue; hence the special need for clear thinking. Because of this fact, and because art, though it has no essential social function, decidedly has social roots, it is fatally easy to blur all the distinctions, ease our social consciences and make everything look all right after all.

Oscar Wilde said, and has never been forgiven for saying, that all art is quite useless—wrongly in fact, since many works are useful adventitiously. In essence, however, he was right; which does not, of course, mean that art is valueless. And lastly, the point is worth making a fuss over for no better cause than intellectual clarity and honesty.

The appreciation of art, it has often been said, requires a certain reconciliation of detachment and involvement; and, if the art of a society reflects its values, this attitude must sometimes be hard. Barker, in the article I have already quoted from, confesses that he always feels uncomfortable in a theatre—not in a cinema. He writes of the old days when 'the theatres and concert halls belonged to "Them" and if we went we went either as humble servants or proud rebels. . .' The English Theatre has a pervading air of 'having fallen on hard times socially, rather like the Palace of the Czars in Leningrad'. The trappings, certainly, belong to a vanished or vanishing age; but then, so does a great part of the art. Someone uncomfortable with the one might be expected to be uncomfortable with the other. Barker is, I think, a bit uncomfortable about the status and function of the arts generally—though as to their present state in the West, we shall shortly meet his answer. I am led to reflect, too, that I used to feel mildly uncomfortable in Roman Catholic churches in Italy, where I went to admire the masterpieces of the Baroque—the art of the triumphant Counter-Reformation. I dare say I should still feel uncomfortable in a mosque. Discomfort is, perhaps, a natural part of cultural education. Part of the value of culture, I believe—of culture generally, I do not say of art qua art—is that it makes us enter remote worlds, see things in new and strange ways and entertain views deeply alien to us.

But the Counter-Reformation is a long way off; its very remoteness helps. What Barker reacts against is uncomfortably close. It seems that every group, every culture, living by its own code, its standards and values, carries on a ceaseless campaign to perpetuate them; every culture is partly its own cheer-group—which is probably a condition of survival. We see how under pressure or in danger, in young states or besieged states, the cheering grows in volume. Moral language, the language of obligation and 'right' and 'wrong', shares partly the same function; it bolsters the values of the existing order. So far Marx was right—and Plato's Thrasymachus long before Marx. (I say, partly: for subtleties apart, one can use moral language precisely to question those values, to ask, for instance, 'Is what our society calls right really so?') The art of a culture, generally speaking, does the same—though with many complexities and exceptions; our own is too much perplexed and divided, perhaps too self-conscious, to play its traditional role.

And, of course, no society is really static or homogeneous. Let me take up Barker's story, and attempt some summary social history, in phases and broad sweeps. Within an earlier aristocratic culture there grew up a new commercial one, which gradually transformed and was absorbed by it. Plenty of bourgeois gentlemen, we know, were made to feel uncomfortable; they none the less determinedly set out, like Hoggart's 'earnest minority' of working people, to acquire the culture of their social betters—who seem often to have been their persecutors too. And, even culturally, they won in the end, or rather, the two currents merged; they made the old culture their own, and imperceptibly modified it in the process. The next phase, to talk in 'phases', is the emergence of an industrial society, and finally an industrial proletariat, absorbing and transforming the aristocratic-commercial one. True, the nineteenth-century industrialists, brasher than their predecessors, perhaps, seem to have absorbed what they inherited less deeply, and transformed it less happily; the collapse of a tradition is what we chiefly see in Victorian visual art—despite, here and there, an unknown masterpiece, like St Augustine's Kilburn. Then comes the art of the mass media, pop art, and lastly real working-class writing, the vigorous burst of the last decade. Yet all art hitherto, all major art, if you like to generalize, belongs to the aristocratic-bourgeois tradition, or at least bears traces of it visible enough to anyone alerted to react against them; which has fairly obvious social consequences. The present position is an uncomfortable one for anyone disposed, first, to see in anything bourgeois—still more anything aristocratic—the mark of his natural social enemy, who, secondly, cares much about art. The thing to insist on, even so, is the complexity and interpenetration of social forces.

Barker, whose problem is different from Wesker's, though related, also has a formula to help him out. He contrasts the 'fresh and energis-ing' writing of forward-looking people with 'the introvert, self-exploratory, masochistic work of the decaying bourgeois tradition'. That is a large contrast, no doubt; there is hardly space here for a general appraisal of the significance of, for instance, Brecht, Bergman, Golding, Osborne and so on, even if I were competent to attempt it. But a few things seem worth saying; one being that the whole picture is extremely complex. And all this work, one may bear in mind too, is still even now minority art; the true old middle-class taste being represented by Harrods and the Board of Works; by Sir Anthony Eden, Mr Kruschev and the Pope. (Soviet Russia seems to be the sole remaining bastion of bourgeois architecture; and even there Kruschev has had to denounce the morbid and introvert (bourgeois) tendencies of the younger generation of Soviet writers. His sentiments have been echoed very closely, though in a slightly different context, by the Pope.) Another consequence of Barker's distinction, which I find strange, is that, for instance, *Look Back In Anger* is a typical product of middle-class culture—or should I say 'bourgeois', not 'middle-class'; or do the two words really mean slightly different things? The whole picture, I said, is a complex one.

The social roots of art—at least of literary art, the cinema and the like, which are likeliest to reflect social issues—let us look at them again. It is no discovery that people generally write best about what affects them most deeply; and that where they shirk such things they tend to write badly—it leads to certain kinds of badness. Great social movements appear, mirrored in the minds of individuals, for instance, in feelings of discomfort; the problem might be to live with complexity, at once assimilating an alien tradition yet retaining one's own social identity. And presumably the best imaginative writing comes from those who, feeling such things more keenly than other people, explore and portray them more honestly. Barker's 'self-exploratory' is a good word, I think; exploring the microcosm of oneself, one might partly explore one's society as well. The great philosophical voice of the Victorian establishment, F. H. Bradley, declared that 'The will of the public world wills itself through me.' In other times the tensions of the public world may fight their tug of war within me.

I said before, however, and repeat, that we must distinguish between the conditions in which serious art is produced from those in which it may be appreciated. Each group and each individual artist, differently placed, writes out of his own local problems (some, but certainly not all, finding themselves at special foci of social pressure); happily, appreciation is not so limited. Let me return to the previous example: why, for instance, should Chaucer's problems concern me? The relations of knights and tavern keepers, the state of the monastic orders six hundred years ago, do indeed interest me; yet that interest is not urgently personal. Human nature, if you like, always matters, is always relevant; and Chaucer, it is worth noting, for all his good humour and gusto, still suffers and holds on to complexity—he still believes in the Church that he satirises. (But at this point we seem to be moving from 'the socialist view of art', as I called it, to a quite different social approach, namely the Cambridge approach, which it is too late to start examining now. Perhaps one's moral organisation is deepened—or, to put it badly, bad people are made good, or good people better—by the study of works such as Chaucer's. I should like to think so, but I know of little evidence.)

I have tried to hint, with suggestions and examples, at—what I do not pretend to analyse or define—the kinds of ways in which art is a social thing; and in the process, not certainly to belittle, but to set in some kind of perspective, social tensions of the sort that Barker bears witness to. Further, actualities of cultural history, even crudely sketched, may at least serve a corrective purpose; may leave us less apt to find comfort in a ready-made formula. Say that we talk in terms of 'classes'—a vague enough notion. Then social classes in successive waves rise, break, fuse and overlap; are what they are in some measure by virtue of thinking themselves so, are heirs to their predecessors and rebels at the same time; and art partly reflects, partly reverses, those currents and struggles; and individuals here and there, who are artists, strive among such forces, and gather or focus them. These are the things to bear in mind while we affix labels, even reflective, careful or specific labels, like 'Victorian commercialism' or 'mid-twentieth-century working-class art'. But all this, once again, is to grope for the social origins or roots of art, to try to understand it better, but not to assign it a function. Its function is to be art, to be appreciated—by anyone of any culture who can.

One reads Chaucer, then, not for his 'relevance', not because one shares his social problems or expects help from him. Why then, after all? I read him, I think, chiefly because his voice makes me listen—his many voices. Partly for the vivid portrayal of people and happenings, the heightened sense of individual things. One can value that too. The voice also makes me regard with respect the things it expresses, even strange views and notions I can hardly share; at this point, indeed, talk of complexity, or the mind that holds on to complexity, may really be relevant. Yet the voice itself—all this matters here only so far as we hear it, as it were, audibly in the poetry, in the voice; the presence and force of mere expression which, like Rheims or Salisbury, makes (I said before) a quasi-sensible quality out of such intangible things.

Not to value that quality is not to value art; and then your cry should be, not 'socially relevant art', but the abolition of art in favour of something else. If so, we need not prejudge the issue; but the desirability of abolishing art would be a theme for another discussion.

II. *Aesthetic Involvement and Detachment*

The aesthetic attitude, in contrast to ordinary practical attitudes, is generally characterised as detached; but contrast it to what I shall call the scientific attitude, and you will find it involved or *engagé*. For we view things here, not analytically, but holistically; not as neutrals, concerned only to describe and explain, but interestedly—for or against. And this mode of vision peoples the world or paints the face of things with qualities, so-called tertiary or physiognomic qualities, which traditional scientific thinking knows nothing of—or knows only as illusions or the like. Let me illustrate, and I shall use Shakespeare for the purpose. King Lear, returning from hunting and finding Kent, disguised as a poor man, waiting in his hall, asks him who he is and what he wants. He is a man, Kent answers (characteristically), and wants service. The dialogue proceeds, 'Who wouldst thou serve?'—'You.'—'Dost thou know me, fellow?'—'No, sir; but you have that in your countenance which I would fain call master.'—'What's that?'—'Authority.'

Now the authority in Lear's countenance is in the strictest sense a physiognomic quality. By all means let us call it a quality (as Sibley and Beardsley do); but let us recognise, if so, that it is a quality in a very different sense from qualities like colour and shape. It is a quality inherently connected with action; Kent sees Lear as a man to be obeyed. At its core, therefore, there is a kind of appraisal or judgment—an intuitive or telescopic judgment. For to call a man fit to command—that is obviously to judge and appraise. Hence I called this attitude involved or *engagé*, not simply detached.

Yet, perhaps not precisely 'this attitude'. I suppose that the authority visible in a man's face is an aesthetic quality; much like, say, the giant grandeur of Michelangelo's dome, or the quieter dignity, serenity of St Paul's. Kent's attitude, however (or that of the poor man he is impersonating), is not aesthetic but practical; he sees, and at once acts accordingly—certainly not pausing to contemplate that aesthetic quality for its own sake. Yet, such contemplation will be one development, a natural and inevitable one in appropriate circumstances, of that primary practical stance, our normal stance amidst those 'currents of action' (Eliot's phrase) which are bound to constitute the main business of most people's lives. An alternative development exists as well, in another, almost opposite direction. 'Intuitive' judgments are notoriously fallible; appearances are deceptive. Kent, we saw, has no time for aesthetic contemplation; neither does he pause, suspending judgment as a scientist would, till he can analyse and rationalise, and make explicit all those various slight signs that the first immediate response was probably based on. To do that, as I have hinted, would be to move in the direction of science. It is characteristically the scientific attitude that requires us to suspend judgment and wait for evidence; to suppress natural promptings and put aside moral views, for or against. Science sets out to be 'ethically neutral'—or, more widely, evaluatively neutral (a goal which, of course, it can never reach; but it can, so to speak, postpone the issue, push overt evaluation towards the horizon of its concerns).

'Scientific' detachment, no doubt, is often practically necessary too; to judge soundly of practical things, of people and policies, we shall need precisely that capacity to attend coolly and impartially to evidence and argument. That is certainly one side of it; yet, strange as it seems, what might be thought just the opposite bent or tendency is no less essential to it. A quick and strong sense of those physiognomic qualities of things—what elsewhere we should call aesthetic qualities—a gift for making immediate judgments, like Kent's judgment of Lear—all this is at the core of practical sense and ability. We need both, then; but here, in this sphere, we cannot fully indulge either. The practical attitude has its own concerns always pressing on it. It cannot pause over aesthetic qualities just to contemplate them, to see or feel them to the full. Nor can it stop to pursue merely intellectual interests, to analyse given material and explain it solely to satisfy curiosity, to satisfy the desire to understand. But let that practical pressure be once removed; leave us free to indulge those divergent tendencies, each for its own sake, and you have a development pointing, one way, towards pure science; and in the other towards pure art. Neither pure art nor pure science is immediately useful or practical; one has traditionally been said to pursue truth and the other beauty; yet each in its origins is bound up with the practical, and grows naturally out of it. Those tendencies conflict at first; within the practical sphere we are bound partly to inhibit each in the interest of the other. Hence each, in a sense, demands its liberty, and that demand grows out of the practical attitude itself.

There is a permanent tug of war, it seems—we recurrently hear of it—between the scientific and humanistic outlook; between the approach of analytic minds and that of intuitive-holistic ones; between *l'esprit de géométrie* and *l'esprit de finesse*. That opposition, I think, is real and inevitable. These things are not merely external to each other, however. And I hope, at least, that the relations between them may be worth drawing attention to as a possibly rewarding field for investigation.

III. Kant's Aesthetic Theory

Donald Crawford's excellent commentary on Kant's third critique,[1] the first half of it, rather, perhaps deserves a reviewer more sympathetic to the original. His book will certainly do much for readers perplexed or baffled by Kant's tortuous text; little to convince those sceptical as to his doctrine.

To retrace step by step Crawford's careful argument, itself a retracing of Kant's, would serve little purpose. But one may note that he restates it, very plausibly, as a sequence of five major stages; and indicates by the way, and clears up where he can, minor—only minor—incoherences or ambiguities. The sublime, indeed, gets skimpier treatment; which is a pity. For Kant here, and I think only here, writes convincingly from first-hand experience. Elsewhere doubts trouble the reader, which Crawford notices but hardly allays, as to the limitations both of his taste and connoisseurship. And deeper problems will engage us directly.

He begins with the inevitable complaint, namely the general neglect of the third critique—given the mountains of commentary piling up on the second and first, that threaten to make Ossa like a wart. But, one

---

[1] *Kant's Aesthetic Theory* (Madison, 1974).

may think, that only reflects the respective attention generally given to aesthetic issues as against ethical and epistemological ones. A good commentary, however, is no less welcome. Kant's best insight, I think, is his first, that judgments of taste are 'aesthetic'—in his own technical sense. We cannot be argued into an aesthetic response however convincing the argument. Kant, even so, sharing the general contemporary neglect of reflective argument, something involved in all discourse, makes the difference look sharper than it is.

As to disinterestedness, that most influential of Kantian doctrines: Crawford having dismissed one 'poor argument' of Kant's, relies on a second; one which proceeds by elimination. Aesthetic concern or its objects—to avoid the word 'interest'—appeal neither directly to morality nor yet to *de facto* desires. It is what it is and not another thing—for that is all the argument amounts to. And, one may remark, of any interest whatever the same is true. A disinterested judge in a law court no less than a judge in a picture gallery will confine himself to relevant factors, and not give weight, say, to the witness's pretty eyes. The pleasure of a pleasant sensation has as good a right to be called 'pure', at least in any sense Kant is entitled to—that is, if we suppose that nothing extraneous contributes to it—as an object of aesthetic contemplation. And likewise one may dwell on it for its own sake. (I leave undiscussed Kant's awkward manoeuvres with the problematic notion of existence.)

Disinterestedness helps Kant to universality; for *de facto* interests are bound to differ. The next step, that wonderful product of misused ingenuity, is 'formal purposiveness' in objects, inducing in us, in our minds, a harmonious state felt as pleasant; hence subjective yet available to everyone. For what it harmonises are imagination and understanding—rational faculties, presumed the same everywhere. The harmony, however, is free harmony; for the object (or 'representation') is adapted to what Kant calls—constantly repeating the phrase—'cognition in general'. It is a doctrine I do not pretend to understand. Part of the point must be the old one: we have here no arguments, no fixed concepts. But what are we to make of 'free harmony'? We have to do with a sort of mental mechanism that runs freely, like an engine disconnected—which must be connected none the less. For the two faculties are said to interact, to do so harmoniously in fact. I am, you may say, forcing on Kant a model extraneous to his thought; yet some intelligible reading must be given it. These faculties, be their ontology what it will, are presumably in the nature of particulars. They act, therefore, in specifiable ways. How should any mechanism engage, yet engage non-specifically; its parts interact, but only 'in general'? It seems you have either mere words, an indefinite blur, or else—make the thing explicit—a contradiction.

Next comes a full discussion of Kant's formalism. Crawford acknowledges his wide vacillation; for he moves between two extreme views: one that allows us, by way of aesthetic satisfaction, little but the pleasure of sea-shells and free linear ornament; the other, all but opposite, the theory of 'aesthetic ideas'. Here poetry—especially poetry, the highest art—points to what it cannot delineate, such notions as majesty and blessedness; and, surprisingly, envy and evil. Neither, surely, has much to recommend it. The former would do little but bear witness to Kant's failure to grasp or accommodate the major phenomena of art. For the latter, Crawford himself writes, 'Kant's rhetorical concepts are not sophisticated enough to allow him to give a very complete or convincing description of what he has in mind.'[2] He was groping perhaps towards some theory of expression or expressiveness—a theory, suppose it worked out, that might have enabled him to dispense with half the elaborate machinery of the Analytic. His own view is different, of course. That such ideas are vague, though one presumes vivid, too, suffices for Kant to refer them to 'the free play of our cognitive faculties'.

Crawford stresses, and rightly, the unclarity of Kant's form-matter dichotomy; but notes, too, that he might plausibly have got what he wants from all sorts of more complex relationship, which are still 'formal' relationships, though their *relata* are material. (Kant also toyed with the notion that responses to colours and sounds, based though non-consciously on various frequencies of vibration, might also be counted as formal.) As to formal purposiveness in general, this much, I think, can be saved: in a work of art, as in an instrument, each part is as it is, and not arbitrarily. There are reasons why it is so and not otherwise, though they point to no function it subserves—nor, indeed, according to Kant, admit of being explicated at all.

Most students in examinations, I have noticed, get no further than the argument of the Analytic; and, I imagine, few readers, suppose it had appeared by itself, would have taken it to be radically incomplete. Kant thought very differently, and Crawford is certainly right to put a heavy emphasis on what follows, the supposed connection of beauty with morality. Rightness of aesthetic response is somehow required of other people; in a passage Crawford repeatedly quotes we are said to impute it to them 'as a duty'. So Kant says; that we do so in fact is far from clear. Rather, as in philosophy itself, we postulate attainable agreement as a sort of ideal by which we work. Kant's own view is explicit, however. The beautiful is the symbol of the moral qua object of disinterested value. But we need further premises, Crawford tells us: first a duty to cultivate sensibility to what forms 'the basis of morality';

[2] Ibid., p. 122.

secondly, and harder to establish, an interest in whatever serves to symbolise it.

Professor Crawford writes lucidly and carefully. It may be as ill apropos to complain of a philosopher's prose style, as of a politician's oratorical clichés; they go with the trade. Yet a work on aesthetics at least might suggest an awareness of such things. Minimally that ugly stock phrase, 'Kant claims that . . .' (or whoever is in question) need not quite so monotonously recur. It brings no hint of a metaphor, no suggestion of 'rival claims', 'staking claims' or the like—and often blurs significant differences, at least stylistically significant, between, say, 'Kant argues that . . .' and 'Kant holds' (or 'maintains') 'that . . .'

My numerous objections, let me stress, are objections rather to Kant than to Crawford; or to him only in so far as his criticisms, excellent in detail, never touch radical difficulties—itself, I appreciate, decidedly a controversial issue. They will not, I hope, be seen as detracting from the proper merit of a workmanlike and valuable commentary.

IV. Disgust and Other Forms of Aversion: Abstract

Disgust seems to stand apart from other sorts of feeling, emotion, etc. It is, as it were, paralytic and leaves us helpless; there is no action in which it naturally issues (except in so far as we seek, vainly, to dissociate ourselves from whatever gave rise to it). It seems to be connected with fear and hatred; but those emotions have each their 'proper objects', namely things seen as dangerous or hurtful, and accordingly to be avoided or destroyed. Disgusting things need not be noxious— apart from the mere fact of our finding them disgusting.

To understand the objects of our feelings is also to make intelligible the actions they issue in. It is hard to name the 'proper objects' of disgust (just as there seems to be no characteristic pattern of action in which it expresses itself).

We can try listing particular objects; but they seem, on the face of it, to be pretty various. And, of course, they may differ in some degree from group to group or culture to culture. That need not discourage us; feelings can admit of being modified by training or conditioning without being wholly arbitrary. They seem to arise spontaneously in the first place; and sometimes the training will be easier, sometimes harder.

In fact I can find no one common thread throughout; though there is, I think, a tolerably close pattern of analogies. We can usefully distinguish physical and mental disgust. There is, we find, a connection, as etymology suggests, between taste and disgust, and more specifically eating (though it is easy to put it in the wrong place). And the one physical action at all closely tied to disgust is that of retching or vomiting.

These all-but-simultaneous and contrary actions may give part of the clue to disgust; it involves ambivalence. On the one hand we have some sort of desire, appetite or curiosity (which Hobbes calls the appetite of the mind) which brings with it, in turn, the desire to take to bits, peer into or get closer to. On the other there is fear, or more specially horror; a variant of fear that we need to look at.

Fear, generally, is of dangerous things, which we can flee from. Horror, broadly, belongs to objects in face of which we are helpless; or, more accurately, which bewilder us and leave us baffled. We lack, not only particular steps we might take, but any way of coming to terms with or grasping them. (One might face certain death, which there is no escaping; and still properly be described as frightened, rather than horrified.) It would seem too abstract to connect disgust and horror with a breakdown of a system of classification (though people are in fact often disgusted with cross-breeds, freaks and monsters). Of course, Rylean category-mistakes, academic absurdities, are more often amusing than disgusting; (and in fact there seem to be connections between laughter and disgust) these, being harmless, cannot be horrifying; though even they may be potentially 'disturbing'. But after the setting and the picture changes. There are, first, things that we simply fear or grieve over; they may, next, be such that we cannot face them or scarcely know how to face them. In themselves or in their implications they unsettle us, our frame of reference seems in danger; we no longer know, or feel sure that we know, how to orient ourselves in the world. This is to feel horror. But where horror is combined with some tolerably strong element of desire or curiosity, we feel disgust.

Like panic, then, horror and disgust represent a kind of breakdown in face of unmanageable situations; hence the lack of patterns of action that they might issue in. (And obviously a breakdown of effective responses cannot serve any biological purpose.)

There remains one further qualification. We spoke of ambivalent feelings of fear and attraction, and of uncertainties that disturb and excite us. In that uncertainty and excitement, however, pleasure and hope—good feelings—can still predominate; in which case we have fascination, not disgust. Disgust is the combination of horror with excited interest or desire, where bad or unpleasant feelings predominate over good.

Index of Names